Treasures of the Taylorian:
Reformation Pamphlets
Volume 6

Martin Luther

'Mönchkalb' and 'Ursache und Antwort'

Two Anti-Monastic Pamphlets from 1523

Edited by Florian Gieseler, Henrike Lähnemann, and Timothy Powell

Taylor Institution Library, Oxford, 2023

TAYLOR INSTITUTION LIBRARY
St Giles, Oxford, OX1 3NA

http://editions.mml.ox.ac.uk

Digital downloads for this edition are available at https://editions.mml.ox.ac.uk/reformation.shtml. They include audio recording, facsimiles, and a pdf ebook of the text.

The facsimiles are of:

Deuttung der grewlichen figur des Munchkalbs tzu Freyberg in Meyssen gfunden.
[Erfurt: Wolfgang Stürmer 1523]
Taylor Institution Library, ARCH.8°.G.1523(8)

Vrsach. vnd anttwortt. das iungkfrawen. kloster. gotlich. verlassen mugen.
Wittenberg: [Lukas Cranach und Christian Döring] 1523
Taylor Institution Library, ARCH.8°.G.1523(34)

The cover image is from the titlepage of ARCH.8°.G.1523(8), showing the eponymous monk-calf.
Typesetting by Henrike Lähnemann
Cover design by Emma Huber

ISBN 978-1-8384641-6-5

Printed in the United Kingdom and United States
by Lightning Source for Taylor Institution Library

Table of Contents

Preface

This has been a collective editing process, starting simultaneously with a historical linguistics seminar led by Timo Bülters and Simone Schultz-Balluff in Halle, and with History of the Book projects supervised by Emma Huber and Henrike Lähnemann in Oxford. 'Ursache und Antwort', Martin Luther's justification of nuns leaving the convent, was prepared by Florian Gieseler, who did the bulk of the research for the introduction and the discussion of Martin Luther's treatises on marriage, and Timothy Powell, who was mainly responsible for the translation. The three versions of the other 1523 pamphlet, 'Mönchkalb', about the monstrous monk-calf, were transcribed and encoded by Master students Katarina Ristic (German), Ksenia Dugæva (French), and Elena Trowsdale (English). Katarina Ristic also provided the modern English translation of the pamphlet which was revised by Howard Jones. Anja Peters and Elena Trowsdale curated the 'Early Modern Monsters' exhibition in the Taylorian which brought the pamphlets to a wider audience.

Additional encoding and editing was done by Kira Kohlgrüber and Karen Wenzel during an internship with Henrike Lähnemann who compiled the bibliographic descriptions of copies held in Oxford and was responsible for the final shape of the linguistic and historical commentaries.

A large number of colleagues in Oxford and beyond helped with critical feedback on this multilingual endeavour: Raphaële Garrod and Raymond Carlson organized a workshop on the Grotesque which provided a platform for discussing the monk-calf in context, Jim Harris opened the print-room of the Ashmolean for inspecting more monsters, Sebastian Dows-Miller, Howard Jones, Philomen Probert, Lena Vosding, Edmund Wareham, and Wes Williams provided linguistic, literary, and historic expertise.

We are grateful to numerous libraries who helped with images; beyond the Taylorian and the Bodleian Library, also the librarians of

Balliol College, Jesus College, Magdalen College, New College, The Queen's College and Worcester College helped to source pictures for an image matching exercise with Giles Bergel; Sven Limbeck contributed a copy from the Herzog August Bibliothek.

As for the previous volumes of the Taylor Editions and especially the Reformation Pamphlet series, Emma Huber's expertise and help both as German Subject librarian and as Digital Humanities lead have been crucial in turning the initial transcriptions, translations, and ideas into a finished volume.

Oxford, 31 October 2023
Florian Gieseler, Henrike Lähnemann, Timothy Powell

Ill. 1: Printouts of the monk-calf woodcut from editions of Luther's works from libraries in Oxford (full list with shelfmarks in the survey of copies under 2.1.2)

Introduction

1523 was a crucial year for the German Reformation. Following the success of Martin Luther's writings of the early 1520s, particularly his 1520 treatise 'Von der Freiheit eines Christenmenschen' (On Christian Freedom) and the 1522 translation of the New Testament, the practical consequences of his teaching were made manifest, not least in the growing numbers of monks and nuns leaving behind the monastic life. Our Taylor Editions series, which has traced this development in the previous five volumes, follows this focus by exploring two-lesser known short pamphlets which illustrate the local as well as global influence of Reformation printing. The first is the 'Deutung der greulichen Figur des Mönchkalbs' (Interpretation of the gruesome figure of the monk-calf),[1] a polemical interpretation of the monstrous birth of calf with a cowl-like neck in Saxony, published in January 1523, which entered into circulation across Europe via Latin into French and from there into English (Introduction 1.2.8.). The second, 'Ursache und Antwort, dass Jungfrauen Klöster göttlich verlassen mögen' (Reason and justification why it pleases God that nuns may leave their convents), provides a justification for the decision of Katharina von Bora and other former nuns to leave their convent in April 1523 (Introduction 1.2.9.).

The historical introduction shows how Martin Luther's anti-monastic stance evolved in the run-up to these publications, followed by a survey of his pamphlets and sermons promoting marriage from 1519

[1] Pamphlet titles are given in the normalized bibliographical 'Werktitel' in the form of the 'Verzeichnis der im deutschen Sprachbereich erschienenen Drucke des 16. Jahrhunderts' (VD16), followed by an English translation; later references are given with the German short title, here 'Mönchkalb'. The original spelling is used whenever a specific edition or copy is referenced, for example for the Erfurt edition by Wolfgang Stürmer, Taylor Inst. Library, ARCH.8°.G.1523(8), VD 16 L 4424 *Deuttung der grewlichen figur des Munchkalbs tzu Freyberg in Meyssen gfunden.* Full bibliographic references for all discussed pamphlets in chronological order are given in the 'Bibliography' under 'Primary Works'. Quotations are from the WA, additionally referenced by folio numbers of the first editions.

onwards and an exploration of the afterlife of the debate on monastic vows and marriage. The chapter on printing history provides catalogue entries for the Oxford copies of the pamphlets edited in this volume – Oxford being probably the only institution which holds copies of the 'Mönchkalb' in German (Taylor Institution Library), French (New College Library), and English (Bodleian Library). The last chapter gives advice on how to read the Early New High German texts.

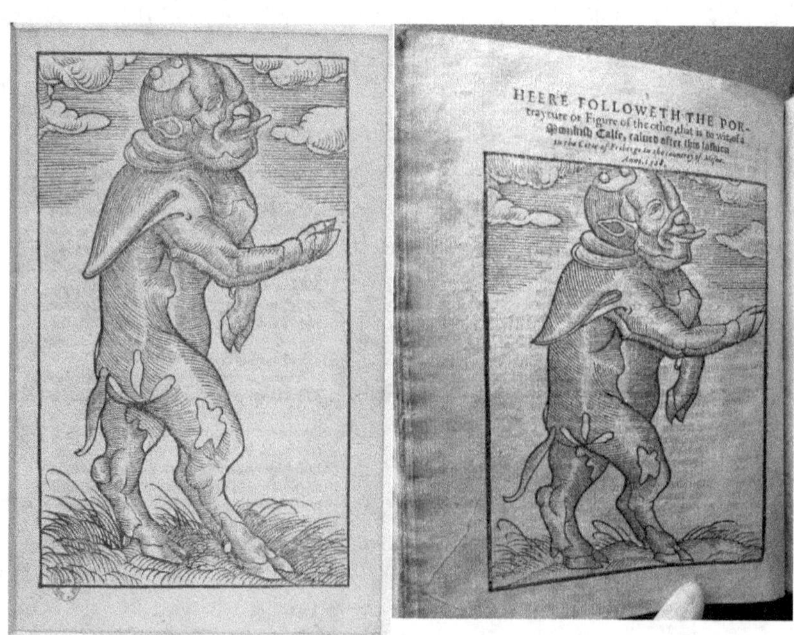

Ill. 2: The French and the English editions of the 'Mönchkalb'
Left: New College Library BT1.17.6(1), p. 29
Right: Bodleian Library, Douce B subt. 268, fol. d3v

1. The Historical Context

In December 1522, a woodcut began to circulate, showing a deformed calf with a flap-like neck fold, a bald patch and two small bumps on its head which was reported to have been born in a village near Freiberg in Saxony.[2] It soon became a talking point for a wider audience interested in monstrous births and other miraculous signs, so much so that at Prague the court astrologer issued a forecast based on the image, interpreting the neck-fold as a monk's cowl and declaring it to be God's sign of displeasure with Luther as a runaway monk. The interpretation soon reached Luther and he responded in the way he had grown accustomed to: by issuing a pamphlet.

Whilst most of Luther's previous texts had been conceived in Latin, even if the German version ended up being published earlier,[3] this pamphlet, as far as we know, was planned from the start to be published exclusively in German; the Latin version for the 'Mönchkalb' in the collected works of Martin Luther was probably produced by somebody else.[4] Luther plays with the popular genre of sensational broadsides in this pamphlet. The text accompanying the image of the monk-calf fits a single printed sheet, as the Erfurt edition which forms the basis of our publication shows, and sold for little more than the price of a meal.

To underline his point that monstrous births were anti-establishment signs, Luther encouraged Philipp Melanchthon (1497–1560), a fellow Reformation theologian, to recast an earlier publication of his – the interpretation of a donkey signifying the pope, in the 'Figur des antichristlichen Papsts und seiner Synagoge' (figure of the anti-

[2] There is a wealth on literature on monstrous creatures in the Reformation period; for a recent overview cf. the chapter 'The Monk Calf and the Papal Ass' in Spinks (2009: 62–79), with further literature given on p. 165, fn. 25.

[3] See the discussion of the order of composition for 'Von der Freiheit eines Christenmenschen' (1520) and the 'Passional Christi und Antichristi' (1521) in the previous volumes of the Taylor Editions, listed in the Bibliography.

[4] On the later date of the Latin version, see Introduction 2.1.2. below.

Christian Pope and his synagogue) which worked perfectly as a companion-piece for the deformed calf. This prodigious creature, reportedly washed up on the banks of the Tiber in Rome in 1495, had been doing the rounds in anti-papal circles in Germany. Luther had previously mentioned the "gruesome animal which the Tiber in Rome threw out which signifies the papacy" in a sermon on the Last Judgement held on the Second Sunday of Advent in 1522.[5]

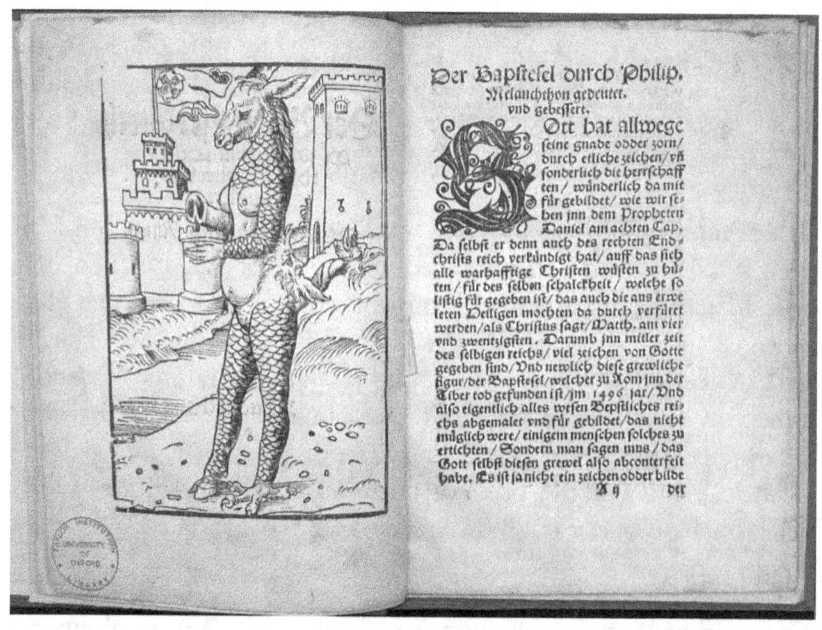

Der Bapſteſel durch Philip.
Melanchthon gedeutet.
vnd gebeſſert.

GOtt hat allwege ſeine gnade odder zorn/ durch etliche zeichen/ vñ ſonderlich die herrſchafften/ wůnderlich da mit für gebildet/ wie wir ſehen jnn dem Propheten Daniel am achten Cap. Da ſelbſt er denn auch des rechten Endchriſts reich verkündigt hat/ auff das ſich alle warhafftige Chriſten wůſten zu hůten/ für des ſelben ſchalckheit/ welche ſo liſtig für gegeben iſt/ das auch die aus erweleten Heiligen mochten da durch verfüret werden/ als Chriſtus ſagt/ Matth. am vier vnd zwentzigſten. Darumb jnn mitler zeit des ſelbigen reichs/ viel zeichen von Gotte gegeben ſind/ Vnd newlich dieſe grewliche figur/ der Bapſteſel/ welcher zu Rom jnn der Tiber tod gefunden iſt/ jm 1496 jar/ Vnd alſo eigentlich alles weſen Bepſtliches reichs abgemalet vnd für gebildet/ das nicht můglich were/ einigem menſchen ſolches zu ertichten/ Sondern man ſagen mus/ das Gott ſelbſt dieſen grewel alſo abconterfeit habe. Es iſt ja nicht ein zeichen odder bilde

A ij der

Ill. 3: Philipp Melanchthon's 'Bapstesel' in the expanded edition of 1535
Taylor Inst. Library, ARCH.8°.G.1535(9), fol. a1v

For the 'Deutung der zwo greulichen Figuren Papstesels zu Rom und Mönchkalbs zu Freiberg in Meißen gefunden' (Interpretation of the two gruesome figures of the Pope-Donkey found in Rome and the

[5] WA 10, 105: *Szo wirt auch keyn sternkundiger thuren sagen, das des hymels laufft hab vorkundiget das schrecklich thier, das die Tyber zu Rom tod außwarff fur kurtzen iaren. Wilchs hatte eyn esells kopff, eyn frawen brust und bauch, eyn Elephant fuß an der rechten hand, unnd fischschuepen an den beynen, unnd eyn trachenkopff am hyndersten &c., darynn das Bapstum bedeuttet ist, der grosse gottis tzorn und straffe.*

Monk-Calf found in Freiberg in Meissen), Luther persuaded Melanchthon to write in a more popular style, replacing learned Latin phrases with vernacular proverbs, and encouraged him to exhaustively interpret the beast's features. Melanchthon turns his interpretation into a numbered list, going through the body-parts as if they were a mnemonic device of the 'ars memorandi' such as Ill. 3 where the devil next to the number '4' pointing to the stones at the tail of the bull helps to remember that chapter four in Luke (for whom the symbol is the bull) talks about temptation.

Ill. 3: The bull as symbol for Luke with numbered body-parts Petrus de Rosenheim, *Rationarium evangelistarum*, Pforzheim: Georg Simpler 1522 Bodleian Library, Douce S 255, fol. c2r

The woodcut of the donkey by Wenzel von Olmütz had established the iconography of the monstrous creature with ten distinct body parts. The beast is reported to have had four differently formed extremities (an elephant hoof-shaped right hand, a human left hand, the right foot of an ox and the left of a griffin), female breast and belly, fish scales, and double hindquarters with the head of an old man 'issuing out of his buttockes' and a 'Dragon comming foorth of the Asses arse' as the English translator puts it.[6] Only the head remained recognisably donkey-like. Luther then mirrors this approach in his interpretation of the calf, discussing all its attributes, from the prominent cowl-like neck-flap to its posture with its right hand outstretched and its left hand pointing to its belly.

However, the most innovative aspect of the double-bill was the names that Luther coined for the creatures: *Bapstesel* (pope-donkey) and *Munchkalb* (monk-calf). Whilst the identification of the pope with the donkey-headed creature had certainly been implied before, Luther's compound made it eminently more memorable and marketable. Furthermore, the 'monk-calf' played on the established compound *Mondkalb* (moon-calf), a deformed creature born under the malign influence of the moon,[7] a usage also attested in other European languages and a wordplay clearly picked up by the English translator when spelling the name of the beast as *Moonkish Calfe*. Luther published their joint effort with new woodcuts from the workshop of Lucas Cranach, showing the two beasts as a diptych on a1v / a2r.[8] It was probably published in early March 1523, since Hieronymus Emser (1478–1527) refers to Luther's 'Shrovetide booklet' (*faß-nacht buchlin*) in his rebuttal of the anti-papal interpretation of the calf.[9]

[6] 'Of two wonderful popish monsters', c3r, see below 2.1.4. for full bibliographical details and an online version of the English translation by John Brooke from 1579.
[7] DWB 6 (1885), col. 2504, s.v.
[8] On the visual aspects, later editions and the development of the woodcuts, see Introduction 2.1., discussing the different versions of the pamphlet in Oxford libraries.
[9] On the reaction to the publication see below Introduction 1.2.8.

Whilst both Melanchthon and Luther had foregrounded the apocalyptic aspect of their earlier discussions of the donkey-creature in line with the tradition of the 'Fifteen Signs before the Last Judgement', the juxtaposition of this creature with the monstrous calf shifts the new publication's focus to criticism of the Church. Luther and Melanchthon argue that the stubborn monk-calves following the monstrous pope in their preaching indict all of monasticism and enclosed religious communities. This turns a theoretical discussion into one with very practical consequences. As Luther writes (4v): 'Take heed, monks and nuns, this really and truly applies to you, and do not treat God's admonition as a joke. Become different monks and nuns, or leave monastic houses and habits behind, and become Christians again before time catches up with you: you could not possibly do so later even if you wanted to, you who do not do so now when you actually can.' It is against the backdrop of this explicit encouragement to leave monastic life behind that the events unfolded which led to the publication of the second pamphlet edited in this volume, 'Ursache und Antwort'.

1. Nuns on the Run or: Leaving the Convent

"Grace and peace! Those nine apostate nuns, a sorry lot, have come to me".[10] On 10 April 1523, Martin Luther informed Georg Spalatin (1484–1545), a fellow Reformer, of the arrival of the women which he discusses in his open letter and pamphlet 'Ursache und Antwort'. Luther had planned the nuns' escape on 5 April in advance in co-operation with Leonhard Koppe (d. 1552) and two further "honourable citizens" to avoid "unjust suspicion", as mentioned in the letter to Spalatin quoted above.[11]

---

[10] WA.B 3, no. 600: *Gratia & pax! Ad me venerunt nouem istę Apostatę Moniales, vulgus miserabile.*

[11] WA.B 3, no. 600: *per honestos ciues Torgauienses aduectę, nempe per Leonhardum Koppe & fratruelem suum, & Volffium Tomitsch, vt nihil ibi sit suspicionis inique.*

Leonhard Koppe or Köppe was a prosperous merchant, brewer, innkeeper and farmer in Torgau, who supplied the Cistercian convent Marienthron at Nimbschen, near Leipzig, with fish for consumption on fast days, and was well-connected with Frederick the Wise (Prince-Elector of Saxony from 1486 to 1525). Torgau was situated half-way on the 100km route from Nimbschen north to Wittenberg which made Koppe the ideal go-between, as did his social status. He sat on the town council of Torgau between 1504 and 1509 before serving as town tax collector from 1510 to 1519. Martin Luther's address as *fürsichtig und weise* (a1v)[12] reflects that although Koppe did not hold a high office at the time of writing, he came from a patrician family which had held various municipal offices, emphasizes Koppe's status as a respected pillar of the community in Torgau and preempts any aspersions that Luther anticipates might be cast on the personal honour of Koppe and his associates by those opposed to his actions. He was a married man, another fact which Luther stresses by adding regards to "dear Audi", Koppe's wife, at the end of the pamphlet. This is part of the traditional end for a letter but in this context also emphasizes the status of Koppe as respectable citizen – and the advantages of marriage.

The nine women had been prominent members of the convent and belonged to very well connected families which turned this into something of a celebrity case. The order in which they are mentioned in the pamphlet (on b2r) seems to reflect both their status in the convent and that of their families.

Magdalena Staupitz (d. 1548), nun in Nimbschen between 1501 and 1523, had served as *cantrix* and organist. She was the sister (according to Luther) or cousin (by some other accounts) of Johann von Staupitz

---

['brought by honourable citizens, namely by Leonhard Koppe and his cousin and Wolf Dommitzsch, so there may be no unjust suspicion.'].

[12] See Bubenheimer (2022: xvi) for further information about the Nuremberg *Titelbüchlein* and forms of address in the German-speaking world of the early sixteenth century.

(d. 1524), Professor and Dean of the Faculty of Theology in Wittenberg 1502–12, Vicar-General of the Augustinian Order in Germany 1503-20, Cathedral Chaplain in Salzburg 1520–22 and Abbot of the Benedictine Arch-Abbey of St Peter in Salzburg 1522–24. Johann von Staupitz had known Luther since the former's visitation of the Augustinian abbey at Erfurt in 1506, appointed Luther to succeed him as Professor in Wittenberg in 1512, and later served as his confessor. They remained friends until von Staupitz' death in 1524.[13] Magdalena served as mistress of the girls' school in Grimma from 1529 to 1548. Luther later wrote to the Elector of Saxony on her behalf on 3 July 1531, urging him to prevent her from being evicted from a cottage she had been granted in the grounds of the former Augustinian priory there;[14] the Elector replied in a letter of 14 July 1531 that she should be allowed to remain there.[15] Originally intended to be married to the historian and Protestant reformer Georg Spalatin, she later married Tiburtius Geuder, a patrician of Grimma.[16]

Elisabeth Canitz (d. aft. 1537) returned to live with her family in the village of Thallwitz near Wurzen in modern-day Saxony. Luther offered her a position as a girls' governess in Wittenberg in a letter of 22 August 1527. She later moved to Grimma, where she was recorded as living in 1537, but is not known to have married after leaving the convent.[17]

The sisters Veronica and Margaretha Zeschau both entered the convent at Nimbschen in 1505. They were nieces of Wolfgang von Zeschau, a former Augustinian prior in Grimma and friend of Luther, who had himself left religious orders the year before his nieces left their convent. Initially, they came to Wittenberg, to which they had family connections. Nothing is known for certain of their lives

[13] See Wriedt (2013: 95–96).
[14] WA.B 6, 147f.
[15] WA.B 6, 152f.
[16] WA.B 3, 56f.
[17] WA.T 4, 236 and WA.T 3, 57.

after this except that Margaretha was still living on 1 July 1537, when she was granted 40 guilders by the Elector of Saxony. They may either eventually have returned to live on their family's estates or else may have become nurses in the hospital in Grimma of which their uncle had become director after leaving his priory.[18]

Laneta von Golis (d. aft. 1527) married Heinrich Kind, pastor of Leisnig (Saxony) and former monk from the nearby Cistercian abbey at Buch, on 24 August 1523.[19] On 24 January 1523, the town council of Leisnig had written to Luther requesting his advice on and support for their intentions to institute a parish chest, to nominate their own parish priest (who had previously been nominated by the Abbot of Buch), and to ensure that they complied with new regulations devised by the council.[20] Luther enthusiastically expressed his support,[21] turning this into a general point by writing one pamphlet 'Dass eine christliche Versammlung oder Gemeine Recht und Macht habe, alle Lehre zu urteilen' about reasons from Scripture of the right of a Christian assembly to judge on all teaching, and one 'Von Ordnung Gottesdienst in der Gemeinde'.

Ave Gross (d. aft. 1540) had lived in the convent at Nimbschen since childhood. She initially returned to her family home in Trebsen (in modern Saxony) after leaving the convent, and later married a man called Hans Marx from the village of Schweinitz.[22] Katharina von Bora (1499–1552) joined the convent in Nimbschen in 1509, taking religious vows as a nun in 1515. She is believed to have been a niece of Margaretha von Haubitz, the last Abbess of Nimbschen from 1509 to 1536. She married Martin Luther in 1525 and spent her married life managing the family household in the former Augustinian priory in Wittenberg.

---

[18] WA.B 1, 127; WA.B 3, 57; WA.B 3, 57. See Kröker (1906: 98).

[19] WA.B 3, 22 and 57, dated 29 January 1523.

[20] WA.B 3, 21-23.

[21] WA.B 3, 23f.

[22] WA.B 3, 56.

The second pairs of sisters among the nuns were Ave and Margaretha von Schönfeldt. They initially remained in Wittenberg because it was too dangerous for them to return to their family home in the Catholic (Albertine) Duchy of Saxony. Ave von Schönfeldt (d. 1541) had been a nun of Nimbschen since 1515. Martin Luther reportedly first intended to marry her but she married the physician Basilius Axt (d. 1558) in 1524 whom Luther supported in the early years of his medical career.[23] Margaretha von Schönfeldt married a von Garsebüttel who lived in the Duchy of Brunswick.[24]

Three further nuns escaped with these nine from the convent, but are not mentioned by Luther since they were able to return immediately to their families. Such a return was only possible because their families were based outside the realm of Duke Georg of Saxony, known for his anti-Reformation attitude. Duke Georg reportedly had Heinrich Kellner, a citizen of Mittweida in central Saxony, decapitated for his part in the escape of nine nuns from another convent in 1525 and claimed that he followed the law of the Holy Roman

---

[23] In 1525, Luther wrote a letters of recommendation for Axt as town physician to his fellow reformer Nikolaus Hausmann for Zwickau (WA.B 3, 587f) and to the town council of Torgau (WA.B 3, 596) which worked out. On 3 January 1526, Luther wrote to the Elector of Saxony since Axt's proposal to lecture on surgery at the University of Wittenberg had encountered strong resistance from the Faculty of Medicine because anatomy was not widely studied and it was felt that lectures delivered in German would not be taken seriously. Luther asked the Elector to give Axt a paid position for a year or two, stressing that Axt did not dare to leave the Electorate of Saxony to find a position in another state because he had married a former nun (WA.B 3, 7 notes that Luther believed Axt was overworked and underpaid in his role as town physician in Torgau). Axt later served as personal physician to the Duke of Brandenburg-Ansbach from 1531. Luther wrote to the Elector of Saxony on 15 August 1531 requesting twenty guilders to cover Axt's expenses for his journey to Prussia (WA.B 6, 160), and sent two letters of recommendation ahead of him, one to Duke Albrecht of Prussia and the other to a pastor in Königsberg, both dated 24 August 1531 (WA.B 6, 166-69). See WA.B 3, 56, and WA.T 4, 503 for further information on the couple.

[24] WA.B 3, 56.

Empire of the German Nation.[25] In fact, it was possible to leave a convent if the Curia acknowledged that a vow had been taken because of coercion.[26]

Leonhard Koppe smuggled these nuns out of the convent on the eve of Easter Day 1523. It is likely that they made use of a covered wagon for the escape usually transporting fish, which gave rise to the popular version of the story that the women were hidden in herring barrels when escaping, as an entry in a 17th century chronicle of Torgau reports.[27] The following month, he helped five other Cistercian nuns to escape from the Cistercian convent Marienpforte at Sitzenroda. Luther invited Leonhard Koppe to his wedding in 1525 and to supply a barrel of beer for the reception afterwards. Luther also stayed at his inn in Torgau on a visit to the town in 1529. Two of Luther's letters to him (dated 17 and 21 June 1525) have survived.[28] This action was staged as an example enacting Reformation theology with an autobiographical link to Luther's own time as an Augustinian. Luther briefly addresses the subject matter to Spalatin, but his main concern at the time is to provide for the newly arrived women with modest means in his simple household (which ironically enough was located in the former Augustinian Priory):

> I pity them strongly, especially those who perish in great numbers through damnable and impure chastity. This sex is by far too weak, and joined to man by nature or rather by God, it will perish if separated by so great a cruelty. Oh, you tyrants, oh, you cruel parents and relatives in Germany! But even more oh, you pope, and oh, you bishops, who can rightly condemn you? Who can sufficiently curse your blindness and the madness which teaches and demands such a thing? But this is not the right place for that. You wonder what I am going to do with them? First, I will inform

---

[25] See Treu (1999: 17f).

[26] Schlotheuber (2010: 165–176) and Makowski (2019: 25–77).

[27] *Chronik von Torgau bis zum Jahre 1627* – Mscr.Dresd.d.1, fol. 233r.

[28] See WA.B 3, 56 for further biographical detail and WA.B 3, 534 and 538f. for Luther's further letters to Koppe of 1525.

> the relatives so that they can take them back. If they refuse, I shall arrange for others to accommodate them, for I have received promises from some others. I will also arrange marriages for some, where I can. They are truly in need of mercy; Christ is served in them. They have miraculously escaped. I beseech you to perform your work of charity, and to beg some money from your rich courtiers for me, with which I can provide for them for a week or a fortnight until I can comfortably hand them over to their own relatives or those who have given me their promise.[29]

Luther's specific plea for the nine women exemplifies his criticism of the state of the convents, arguing that most men and women who entered religious houses based their decision, although with the best intentions, on false grounds, or worse, had this decision made for them by others on equally false grounds.[30]

Luther's marriage to Katharina von Bora in 1525 set an example for this theology, but Luther was by no means the first former member of a religious order to marry. In fact, the marriage of the Swiss Reformer Huldrych Zwingli (1484–1531) preceded Luther's by a year, and there were other instances of Protestant clergymen marrying before that, such as Bartholomäus Bernhardi (1487–1551), Professor of Physics and 1518/19 Rector of the University in Wittenberg when he defended Luther in the debate about the '95 Theses'. "Marriage

---

[29] WA.B 3, no. 600: *Miseret me illarum valde, maxime autem & aliarum, quę vbique tanto numero per[d]unt maledicta & incęsta illa castitate. Sexus iste per sese longe infirmissimus & ad virum natura, imo diuinitus coniunctus, tanta crudelitate separatus perditur. O tyrannos, o crudeles parentes & cognatos in Germania! Sed te, papa, & vos, Episcopi, quis digne maledicat? quis vestram ęecitatem & furorem talia docentem & exigentem satis execretur? Sed hic non est locus. Quęris, quid cum illis agam? Primum cognatis significabo, vt eas suspicant, Qui si nolint, curabo eas alibi suscipi. Nam est mihi promissio facta ab aliquibus. Aliquas etiam matrimonio iungam, vbi potero. Tales sunt, quibus opus est misericordia vere, in quibus Christo seruitur. Satis autem mirabiliter euaserunt. Te autem oro, vt & tu opus Charitatis facias, & pro me mendices apud aulicos tuos diuites aliquid pecunę, qua eas ad octiduum vel quindenam aliquas alam, donec eas comode suis cognatis aut meis promissoribus tradam.*

[30] See below the discussion in Introduction 1.2.6. 'De votis monasticis'.

emerged as one of the most provocative steps taken by evangelical-leaning clergy during the early Reformation."[31]

Not all former nuns were as fortunate as those involved in the Nimbschen episode, or as Elisabeth von Meseritz (1500–1535). After leaving the convent in 1522, she married the Protestant theologian Caspar Cruciger (1504–1548) in 1524, and belonged to the Wittenberg circle of proponents of the Reformation. She contributed the highly influential hymn 'Herr Christ, der einig Gottssohn' to the first Protestant hymn-book.[32] In it, she merges the bridal mysticism of the convents with the Protestant doctrine of salvation by faith alone.

The contemporary phenomenon of monks and nuns leaving their convents posed a challenge for the implementation of Protestant theology in society. Luther's criticism of unwilling service in convents encouraged male family members to have their female relatives abandon this service regardless of their own will, even though Luther had conceded that "those who are spiritually sage and know how to make good use of life in the convent, and are willing to be there, let them remain there in the name of God".[33] These over-eager critics of monastic live failed to consider that at least some of the nuns might have wished to remain in the convents and were then forced out despite their willingness to stay – almost ironically turning the former compulsion to enter a convent into one to leave. Some of them were certainly genuinely devoted to their service as nuns, while others may have been just as content to be cared for in the convent as a place of safety.[34]

---

[31] See in particular Plummer (2012: 52–60). Plummer also lists 211 weddings of Protestant ministers between 1521 and 1525, including secret weddings in regions and cities in Switzerland and southern and central Germany, table 3.1, p. 115.

[32] Reich (2001: 48).

[33] WA 11, 400: *Wilche aber geyst verstendig sind / vnd klosterey nutzlich wissen zu brauchen / vnd gerne drynnen sind / die lassz man bleyben ym namen Gottis* (b2r).

[34] See Gößner (1999: 108f).

In the 1520s and 1530s, convents such as those in Augsburg and Nuremberg came under great pressure, not only from within, but especially from outside, from the general population and legal guardians, who thought they were saving their daughters, sisters, and nieces from damnation. However, there was strong resistance from within, with the most prominent case being Caritas Pirckheimer (1467–1532), sister of the Humanist Willibald Pirckheimer (1470–1530) and Abbess of the Convent of St Clara in Nuremberg. Her 'Denkwürdigkeiten',[35] a journal kept during the upheaval, provides a vivid insight into the eloquent case for regarding vows as indissoluble since they are given to God. She managed to convince Philipp Melanchthon to lobby the Nuremberg city council to leave the community in peace, and they were allowed to stay in their convent.

Many other monastic communities energetically and strongly resisted the call to leave, particularly if it appeared to be motivated by princes interested as much in the property and assets as in the Protestant cause. The case of the Lüne convents shows how a well-organized and flourishing community of women could successfully argue in favour of continuing their cloistered life as a religiously motivated choice.[36] There was also actually an appreciation of marriage within the church, reflected in the fact that it had been one of the seven sacraments since the twelfth century. The Lüne nuns regularly highlight that marriage was instituted by God in paradise when writing congratulatory letters on the occasion of weddings, praising "the highly worthy state" which a brother about to be married should receive, "namely the state of marriage which the almighty God Himself has blessed and instituted in the first beginning with our first parents which makes us keenly aware that marriage pleases God".[37]

---

[35] The journal is edited by Pfanner (1962) and translated by MacKenzie (2006). See also Machilek (1998).

[36] Lähnemann (2016) and the introduction to *Netzwerke der Nonnen* (2023).

[37] *Netzwerke der Nonnen* (2023), e.g. Letter 269 (quire 19, fol. 17v): [...] *hoghen werdighen states, den du nu scholt entfanghen alze den stad des hilgen echtes, den de*

2. Sermons – Pamphlets – Treatises

Luther's criticism of monastic vows was expressed in numerous pamphlets, in which he criticized the Church and sought to establish a new value for marriage and chastity based on Scripture, arguing with increasing polemic that vows can endanger salvation. The texts followed a contemporary cause-and-effect logic of publication and counter-publication as can be seen in the case of the 'Mönchkalb'. Practical help for the nuns to leave their convent on 5 April 1523 was the public confirmation of the previously published view that no-one should remain enclosed against their natural disposition. Having a group of women prepared to leave the convent thus offered the opportunity to put the theory publicly into practice, and making other people "more courageous and daring" (*mutiger vnd thurstiger*; 'Ursache und Antwort' a2v).

Luther mentions to have commented on the topic "in other pamphlets" (*ynn andern buchlin*; a2v). Sixteen texts from 1519 to 1530 discuss monasticism and matrimony, other sources include Luther's table talks and letters. Luther is reacting to events that are going on around him – the marriages of early Wittenberg reformers such as Bartholomäus Bernhardi and Andreas Karlstadt (1486–1541) who weighed in on the Protestant side with pamphlets "against the papist laws forbidding marriage" and "why priests should marry".[38]

This bibliographic survey charts the publication trajectory of Luther's pamphlet production and as such by its nature presents a partisan Protestant view of the contested question of marriage and monasticism. Some of the counter-arguments are presented in the third section, but it would be the scope of another book to fully embed

---

almechtige God sulven heft ghebenedyet unde anghesettet an dem ersten anbegynne myd unsen ersten olderen, dar wy enkede uth merket, dat he Gode wol behaghet heft.

[38] 'Contra papisticas leges sacerdotibus prohibentes matrimonium' (Against the papist laws forbidding the marriage of priests) and 'Dass die Priester Eheweiber nehmen mögen und sollen' (Why priests should marry).

this debate also within the different fractions of Protestantism and those monks and nuns who negotiated their way in the ever-changing landscape of religious controversy.

1. 'Ein Sermon von dem ehelichen Stand' (1519)

A sermon held on 16 January 1519 is one of the first known instances where Luther deals with marriage. Wolfgang Stöckel immediately published a hastily arranged unauthorized transcript in Leipzig. Luther criticized the edition and published a revised version with a note where he insists that only authorized written versions should circulate: 'Ein Sermon von dem ehelichen Stand, verändert und korrigiert durch D. Martinum Luther, Augustiner zu Wittenberg' (A sermon on marriage, revised and amended by Doctor Martin Luther, Augustinian in Wittenberg). Both versions became very popular. There have been 14 editions of the revised version and even one translation into Danish. It establishes what may not seem particularly controversial but is closely linked to the leaving of convents. This sermon is Luther's first attempt to describe and praise matrimony as a state that pleases God as well as chastity.

The key point of this sermon, although not yet as explicitly polemical as later, is to re-evaluate chastity and matrimony. Marriage is not necessarily inferior to a life of chastity in a religious house, but chastity is a rare gift given by God and cannot be kept without His grace. It was this new assessment that, in interaction with the overall critique of papal laws and decrees, increasingly gave more weight to matrimony than the Church had acknowledged for centuries.

The tone of the sermon is of a relatively conciliatory nature and contains arguments for and against both marriage and monasticism. Luther lists the characteristics of a Christian marriage and already assigns matrimony a well-founded place in God's order which does not necessarily require celibacy as a necessity. Luther's first text on marriage already contains important and enduring elements of his doctrine of marriage which later he articulated with different emphases.[39]

With reference to Genesis 2:18–24, Luther argues that men and women are brought together solely by God, just as only God could give Eve to Adam. Matrimony, according to this reasoning, is part of the divine order of creation. It can be open to the temptation of selfish pleasure-seeking since not everyone can live in chastity because it is a special and rare gift from God, but, as Luther points out, God does not require chastity. Commitment and faithfulness are the essence of matrimonial purity. The only rules to follow are not to get married in secret without parental consent and blessing, and to disdain 'false love' (*falsche liebe*), as Luther puts it, that seeks pleasure outside marriage. Before concluding, Luther praises and warns: "O truly, what a noble, grand, blissful state matrimony is if kept properly! O truly, what a miserable, frightening, dangerous state matrimony is if kept improperly!"[40] Finally, Luther stresses the importance of a Christian upbringing for children which compensates for the sin of the flesh.

2. 'An den christlichen Adel' (1520)

Luther addressed an indisputably wider audience in his three treatises from 1520 (a year which marks a peak in his publishing output), in which he argues for a reformation of the ecclesiastic order to be implemented in particular by secular authorities.[41]

---

[39] Beyer (1999: 62).

[40] WA 2, 170. *Eyn Sermon von dem Elichen standt …*, a4r. *O warlich eyn edler, groszer, seliger standt der ehelich standt, szo er recht gehalten wirt. O warlich eynn elender, erschrecklicher, ferlicher standt der ehlich stand, szo er nit recht gehaltenn wyrt.*

[41] See Clemens (2020: xix–xxv) and Kaufmann (2022: 125).

An den Cri
stlichen Adel deüt
scher Nation: von
des Christlichen
stands besserūg
D. Martinus
Luther.

Vuittenberg:

Ill. 4: Titlepage of 'An den christlichen Adel' with a garden of Paradise
Taylor Institution Library, Arch.8°.G.1520(5)

In 'An den christlichen Adel deutscher Nation von des christlichen Standes Besserung' (To the Christian nobility of the German nation concerning the improvement of the Christian Estate), Luther chastises the clergy for not fulfilling their educational obligations and links this attitude to the necessity of reforming convents, or rather: to have them returning to their original state:

> In my opinion, it would be a necessary regulation, especially in our perilous times, to re-establish religious houses and monastic

institutions in the manner in which they were originally organized in the times of the Apostles and for a long time thereafter: when they were all open for everyone to choose to stay there for as long as they desired; for what else were religious houses but Christian schools where Scripture and Christian discipline were taught and people trained to govern and to preach? We read for example that St Agnes went to such a school, and we still see this in a number of convents, such as Quedlinburg and other similar convents. Indeed, all religious houses should allow just as much freedom to serve God willingly and not by compulsion.

But later they introduced vows, turning them into an eternal prison by elevating them higher than even the baptismal vows. What kind of fruit this bears, we can see, hear, read and learn more and more every day. I realize that my advice will be considered most foolish, but this does not matter to me for now. I give advice according to what seems good to me; let it be rejected by whoever wants to; I see very well how vows are being kept, especially of chastity, which are becoming so common because of such convents, and yet were not ordained by Christ, but only given to very few, as He Himself and St Paul say.[42] I would like to see everyone helped and no Christian soul ensnared by man-made ways and laws.[43]

---

[42] See Matthew 19:10–12 and 1 Corinthians 7:6–7.

[43] WA 6, 439–440: *Es were meynis bedenckens ein nottige ordnung / beszondern zu unsern ferlichen zeytten / das stifft vnnd kloster widderumb wurden auff die weysze verordenet / wie sie waren ym anfang / bey denn Aposteln vnnd ein lang zeit hernach / da sie alle frey waren / einem yderman drynnen zubleyben szo lang es yhm gelustet. Dan was sein stifft vnd kloster anders geweszen / den Christliche schulenn / darynnen man leret / schrifft vnnd zucht nach Christlicher weysze / vnnd leut auff ertzog / zu regieren vnnd predigen. wie wir leszen / das sanct Agnes in die schule gieng vnd noch sehen / in etlichenn frawen klostern / als zu Quedlingborg vnnd der gleychen / furwar es sollten alle stifft vnd kloster auch szo frey sein / das sie got mit freyem willen / und nit getzwungen dienten. Aber darnach hat man es gefasset mit gelubdenn / vnd ein ewig gefencknisz drausz gemacht / das auch die selbenn mehr / dann die tauff gelubd wirt angesehenn / was aber fur frucht drausz ist kummen / sehen / horen / leszen und erfaren wir teglich mehr und mehr. Ich acht wol solcher mein radschlag sey auffs allertorlichst angesehen / da frag ich itzt nit nach. Ich radt was mich gut dunckt / vorwerff wer es wil / ich sieh wol / wie die gelubd werden gehaltenn / szonderlich der keuscheit / die szo gemeyn durch solch kloster wirt / vnd doch von Christo*

In his argument for the reform and restoration of Church and convents, Luther also focuses on the clergy, whose authority is granted by God, unlike that of the Pope, bishops, convents, and monks. With reference to 1 Timothy 4:1–4, which predicts that "in latter times some will depart from the faith, giving heed to deceiving spirits and doctrines of demons, speaking lies in hypocrisy, having their own conscience seared with a hot iron, forbidding to marry", Luther describes the doctrine of clergy refraining from marriage as demanded by the devil (*das hat yhn der teuffel geheyssen*, fol. g4v), leading only to more harm: "which sadly has brought about so much misery which cannot be fully told" (*dadurch leyder szoviel iamers erstanden / das nit zurtzelen ist*; fol. g4v). He argues that clergy should therefore be free to choose whether or not to get married according to their will and disposition without any disadvantage. He stresses that no bishop has the authority to require anybody to take a vow of chastity:

> Furthermore, I advise those who henceforth intend to receive Holy Orders in no way to pledge celibacy to the bishop, and to reply that he has no authority whatsoever to demand such a vow, and that it is devilish tyranny to require it. If, however, as many people do, they are obliged or wish to say 'as far as human weakness allows it', everyone should freely interpret the same words openly in the negative sense, i.e. 'I do not pledge chastity', for it is not human weakness that enables people to live a chaste life, but only angelic fortitude and heavenly virtue, meaning that one may maintain a clear conscience without any vows.[44]

---

nit gepoten / sondern fast wenigen geben wirt. wie er selb vnnd sanct Paul sagt / Ich wolt gerne yderman geholffen sein / vnd nit fangen lassen Christliche seelen durch menschliche eygene erfunden weysze vnd gesetz. (g3v–g4r).

[44] *Weytter rad ich / wer sich hynfurt weyhen lessit zur pfarr odder auch sonst / das er dem Bischoff / in keinem weg gerede / keuscheit zuhalten / vnd halt yhm entgegen / das er solch gelubd zufoddern / gar kein gewalt hat / vnd ist ein teuffelisch tyranney solchs zufoddern. Musz man aber odder wil sagen, wie etlich thun, Quantum fragilitas humana permittit. szo deutte ein yglicher die selben wort frey negatiue, id est, non promitto castitatem / den fragilitas humana non permittit caste vivere / sondern allein / angelica fortitudo et celestis virtus / auff das er ein frey gewissen / on alle gelubd behalte.* Fol. g5r.

3. 'De captivitate Babylonica' (1520)

Luther's second major treatise, 'De captivitate Babylonica ecclesiae' (On the Babylonian Captivity of the Church)[45], was published on 6 October 1520. According to Luther, the Church takes itself captive with its teachings. He borrows the expression of Babylonian captivity from the exile of the Jews after the siege of Jerusalem by Nebuchadnezzar II.[46] Luther's tone becomes very radical, and he questions the number of Sacraments recognized by the Church: Baptism, Eucharist, Confirmation, Reconciliation, Anointing of the Sick, Marriage, and Holy Orders. Luther writes that the idea of Penance and Reconciliation as a sacrament, with which he disagrees, devalues the promise of baptism. Baptism means a lifelong promise, with penance as an integral part of it. Hence, the grace of baptism is neither enhanced nor replaced by any monastic vows of chastity or obedience, rather abolishes the self-imposed sanctity of monastic life.[47] He blames a misunderstanding of Jerome for this:

> A dangerous saying of St Jerome, whether wrongly placed or wrongly understood, gave rise to these opinions, in which he calls penance the 'second plank after shipwreck', as if baptism were not penance. That is why, once they have fallen into sin, despairing of the first plank or ship as lost, they begin to only trust and rely upon the second, that is, penance. This gave rise to those countless burdens of vows, religious orders, works, satisfaction, pilgrimages, indulgences and sects, and of these floods of books, questions, opinions and man-made traditions, which the whole world can no longer contain, so that these tyrannies afflict the church of God incomparably worse than any synagogue or other nation under

---

[45] A contemporary translation of the treatise was provided by Thomas Murner (1475–1537) in the same year to expose the public to Luther's bolder tone aimed at the clergy.

[46] See 2 Kings 24:10–16.

[47] Mühlen (1983: 18–20).

> heaven ever has.[48]

The significance of baptism as a promise is stressed with reference to Mark 16:16: "Who believes and is baptized will be saved; but who does not believe will be condemned" (KJV). Luther insists that this divine promise of deliverance in the face of baptism and faith is the only assurance required: "This promise is infinitely preferable to all the pompous displays of works, vows, monastic orders and whatever else has been introduced by human means; for our whole salvation depends upon it".[49]

Luther states that the Sacraments, on their own, have no power. He writes that their indispensable requirement is faith, but claims that true faith is consistently withheld from the people. Instead, he argues that they are imperilled by the Church's teaching that taking vows and keeping them is sacrosanct in and of itself, thus equating the vows with faith:

> Here I add one thing, of which I wish I could convince everybody, that is, that all vows should be abolished or avoided entirely, whether they be of monasticism or pilgrimages or any other works, and that we should remain in the most religious and efficacious freedom of baptism. It cannot be stated how greatly this widely held belief in vows detracts from baptism and obscures the knowledge of Christian freedom, not to mention the unspeakable

---

[48] WA 6, 527: *prebuit his opinionibus occasionem verbum illud periculosum divi Hieronymi, sive male positum sive male intellectum, quo poenitentiam appellat secundam post naufragium tabulam, quasi baptismus non sit poenitentia. Hinc enim, ubi in peccatum lapsi fuerint, de prima tabula seu nave desperantes velut amissa, secundae tantum incipiunt niti et fidere tabulae, id est, poenitentiae. Hinc nata sunt votorum, religionum, operum, satisfactionum, peregrinationum, indulgentiarum, sectarum infinita illa onera et de iis maria illa librorum, quaestionum, opinionum, traditionum humanarum, quas totus mundus iam non capit, ut incomparabiliter peius habet Ecclesiam dei ea tyrannis, quam unquam habuit synagogam aut ullam nationem sub coelo* (e2v).

[49] WA 6, 527: *Quae promissio praeferenda est incomparabiliter universis pompis operum, votorum, religionum et quicquid humanitus est introductum. Nam in hac pendet universa salus nostra* (e3r).

> and boundless dangers to the soul which this craving for vows and its imprudent audacity daily increase.[50]

Luther continues to criticize the belief that works carried out as a result of vows are better than others carried out independently of vows. He identifies in this a clear lack of faith like that found among the Pharisees, who believe that they will be made holier through their works. He claims that, to God, there is no difference in the works to be measured, only a difference in faith. The splendour and renown which such Pharisees ascribe to themselves lure ordinary uneducated people into believing in the outward appearance and the sanctifying effect of these works. He argues that such a multitude of vows and works, not ordained by God, necessarily leads to a lack of faith and, eventually, loss of faith. Hence, he writes that the promise of baptism is taken captive, and that entering a monastic order is proclaimed to be a second baptism: "Thus, these people who take vows have exclusively ascribed righteousness, salvation, and glory to themselves; they have left nothing at all to the baptized people with whom they can be compared."[51] Luther writes that the hypocrisy engendered by this practice has even led to competitive efforts among monks and nuns to be divided into strict and lax brothers or sisters, who only seek renown in their works, "which cannot be magnified without harm" (g2v).

As in his previous treatise, Luther strongly states that the way of life in convents should be abolished, and both men and women to abstain from lifelong commitments arising from vows in order to escape from the captivity of the Church and its self-righteous attitude. True

---

[50] WA 6, 538. *Unum hic addo, quod utinam cunctis queam persuadere, id est, ut vota prorsus omnia tollerentur aut vitarentur, sive sint religionum sive peregrinationum sive quoruncunque operum, maneremusque in libertate religiosissima et operosissima baptismi. Dici non potest, quantum detrahat baptismo et obscuret scientiam libertatis Christianae opinio illa votorum plus nimio celebris, ut interim taceam infanda etiam eaque infinita pericula animarum, quae vovendi ista libido inconsultaque temeritas quotidie auget* (g1r).

[51] WA 6, 539: *ita votarii isti sibi solis iustitiam, salutem, gloriam tribuerunt, baptisatis prorsus nihil reliquerunt, quo possint eis conferri* (g1v).

faith, Luther claims, is difficult to find amongst the clergy, who he suggests deem themselves to be above ordinary married people. "In the meantime, this is enough about baptism and its freedom. When the time comes, vows will perhaps be discussed more thoroughly, because it is indeed highly necessary to consider them."[52] This announcement is developed in 1521 in 'Themata de votis' (On the Topic of Vows) and, on a more personal note, 'De votis monasticis Martini Lutheri Iudicium', both discussed below (5./6.). Before that, however, he returns to the subject in the conclusion of his third treatise of 1520.

4. 'Von der Freiheit eines Christenmenschen' (1520)

The bestselling pamphlet of the 15th century was Luther's treatise 'Von der Freiheit'.[53] The main hypothesis is that the true Christian is a perfectly free person and submits to God's will because of this freedom. This obedience flows from the heart and is not restricted to fulfilling demands and obeying laws. Luther claims that the essence of salvation does not lie in works, whether good or evil, but in faith alone; a good work does not make a good person, and an evil work does not make an evil person, because only faith is good and only faithlessness evil. Faith alone delivers Christians from evil and sin, which pose no danger to the faithful.[54]

With a particularly powerful emphasis on faith, Luther once more formulates his criticism of the practice of compliance with religious laws and vows which are not founded upon faith. He concedes that good works can be helpful for others because they can set a good example, but people should "always take care not to resolve through becoming pious and holy to do that which lies only within the power

---

[52] WA 6, 543. *Verum haec interim de Baptismo et libertate eius satis. Suo forte venient tempore vota latius tractanda, ut sunt revera tractatu vehementer necessaria.*(g3v).
[53] WA 7, 12–38. For the success of the print distribution see Krümpelmann (2020). By 1563, there were eighteen editions, including pirated ones.
[54] For a more detailed account of Luther's concept of freedom, see Clemens (2020).

of faith".[55] Luther concludes that it is not against God's will for Christians to do good works, but that it is wrong for the Church to require good works for the sake of salvation.

> This is why I fear that few collegiate churches, abbeys, altars, masses, or legacies are Christian, nor the fasts and prayers offered for many particular saints. For I fear that in all these, everybody only seeks their own advantage, thinking that, by this, they may atone for their sin and attain salvation. All this comes from ignorance of faith and Christian freedom. And many blind prelates urge people on in this, and praise such activity, adorning them with indulgences, and no longer preaching the faith.[56]

5. 'Themata de votis' (1521)

In 1521, Luther returned specifically to the value of monastic vows. Following the academic conventions of his time, he started with a list of 280 theses to be discussed: 'Themata de votis'. The title of the contemporary German translation, although not by Luther, calls it a 'Kurze Schlussrede von den Gelübden und geistlichen Leben der Klöster' (Short Summary concerning vows and religious life in convents). The German translation has 139 theses with an additional summary.

The theses are divided into two sets, the first of which draws on Scripture, especially the Letters of St Paul, as the foundation for the following theses. They begin with the statement that everything done without faith is sinful. This is also true of any works done with

---

[55] WA 7, 36–37: *altzeit fursehen, das nit da durch frum vnd selig werdenn furgenommen werd, Wilchs allein des glaubens vormůgen ist* (c3v).

[56] WA 7, 37. *Daher kumpts das ich sorg / wenig stifft kirchen / clőster / altar / mesz / testament / Christlich seinn / Datzu auch die fasten vnd gepett / etlichen heiligen sonderlich gethan. Denn ich furcht das ynn den allen sampt ein yglicher nur das seyne sucht / vormendend damit sein sund tzu bůssen / vnd seligk werden. Wilchs allis kumpt ausz vnwissenheit des glaubens / vnd Christlicher freyheit. nnd etlich blind prelaten die leuth da hynn treybenn / vnd solch wesen preyssen / mit ablas schmucken / vnd den glauben nymmer mer leren* (c4r).

good intentions but without faith, leading to the fallacious opinion that a good work must in itself be pleasing to God: "A good work is sometimes done with the idea of seeking righteousness and salvation through it", but this "opinion constitutes nothing but impiety, infidelity and idolatry".[57] Luther claims that idolatrous man-made laws provide the appearance of faith, but are not ordained by God:

> 29) Vows of the clergy and any others are, in their entirety, a law which, by its nature, holds the conscience captive.
>
> 30) And the clerical or devotional life is by its nature nothing but the works of the law.
>
> 31) Consequently, whatever Paul thinks of the laws and works must also be thought of the vows and the clergy.
>
> 32) It is therefore lacking in faith to vow virginity, celibacy, religion, or anything else.
>
> 33) Any such sacrilegious, impious and idolatrous vow is vowed to demons.[58]

Luther stresses that this critique only applies if vows are taken without faith. Instead, he writes that he intends to give instructions on taking vows properly, i.e. without the false presumption of gaining salvation by taking a vow in order to achieve righteousness.

> 71) We do not wish to condemn all religious vows or ways of religious life by this.
>
> 72) But, as Paul teaches the right use of the law, so do we teach the

---

[57] Theses 1.13 and 1.14: *Opus bonum fit aliquando opinione iustitiae et salutis querendae per ipsum. Haec opinio universa impietas, infidelitas et idolatria est.*

[58] Theses 1.29–1.33: *Votum religionum aut quodcunque omnino quaedam lex est conscientiam natura captivans. Et vita religiosa aut devotaria non nisi opera legis natura sunt. Quaecunque ergo de lege et operibus Paulus sentit, de votis et religiosis sentienda sunt. Est itaque vovere virginitatem, coelibatum, religionem et quodlibet sine fide. Tale votum sacrilegum, impium, idolatricum demonibus vovetur.*

> vows.
>
> 73) For the New Testament is the kingdom of freedom and faith.[59]

Luther argues that free and faithful vows show the correct use of vows in monastic or religious life, because they are not made in the spirit of religious legalism, i.e. the belief that a person can attain salvation by doing good works:

> 81) Thus, the one who lives by faith in them both makes vows and lives in religious orders,
>
> 82) and does not trust that through them one becomes righteous, holy, and saved.[60]

Luther concludes in this first set of theses that life in the convent often deceives a person's conscience if they put all their trust in this way of life. Luther returns to this in his second set of theses by examining whether it is actually permissible to take a perpetual vow.

He states that the freedom granted by God as a right and gift also makes vows free. He suggests that this means that monastic vows should neither be encouraged nor ordained, since, as Luther argues Scripture reveals that the gift of celibacy is particularly rare. He proposes that all vows can be dissolved when the person who made them feels unable to live by them. There seems to be no clear conclusion, since Luther concedes: "To conclude: vows are free, not condemned, and can be kept either temporarily or permanently."[61]

---

[59] Theses 1.71–1.73: *Non per haec omnium religiosorum vota aut vitam damnasse volumus, Sed sicut Paulus legis usum legitimum, ita nos votorum docemus. Novum enim testamentum regnum est libertatis et fidei.*

[60] Theses 1.81–1.82: *Sic tute et vovet et vivit in religionibus, qui fide in illis vivit, Et non per eam vitam iustus, sanctus et salvus fieri confidit.*

[61] Thesis 2.141: *Summa: Vota libera sunt, non damnata, tum temporaliter, tum perpetuo servabilia.*

6. 'De votis monasticis' (1521/2)

The question of celibacy had been a hotly debated for centuries, in theory obligatory for all clergy but with monks and nuns in the spotlight, especially with a stricter understanding of enclosure in the reform movements. When in the early years of the German Reformation, more and more monastics left the convents, the arguments had to justify this step not just as a pragmatic arrangement but explain on a fundamental level "why they should leave the convent and even more so why they should marry".[62]

The treatise 'De votis monasticis' (1521/1522)[63] provides a justification of the theses previously published in 'Themata de votis'. One of Luther's intentions behind this treatise was to offer comfort to those nuns and monks who were willing to renounce their monastic vows. It allowed him to come to terms with the vows that he himself had taken when becoming an Augustinian in July 1505. This becomes apparent in the dedication to his father:

> It was my intention, dearest father, to dedicate this book to you, not so that I might bear your name out into the world and boast of it in the flesh against Paul's teachings, but so that I might seize the opportunity that presented itself between you and me, to explain briefly in a prologue the cause, argument, and example set by this little book to pious readers.[64]

Luther is referring to a conflict which arose from his decision to become an Augustinian; his father had opposed it, arguing against it on the grounds of the commandment to honour parents. This precedes Luther's most elaborate treatise on monastic vows and marriage, in

---

[62] Plummer (2012), 165.

[63] Luther wrote the text in late 1521, but it only seems to have been published in 1522. Two German translations followed in 1522 and 1523.

[64] WA 8, 573. *Hunc librum tibi, parens carissime, nuncupare consilium fuit, non ut nomen tuum ferrem in orbem et in carne gloriaremur adversus doctrinam Pauli, sed ut occasionem apprehenderem, quae sese inter te et me opportune obtulit, brevi prologo et causam et argumentum et exemplum huius libelli piis lectoribus enarrandi* (a2r).

which he harmonizes all the key arguments of his previous writings on the subject into a relentless condemnation of monastic vows. His discussion of this topic begins with an examination of what a true vow is:

> Not to debate whether a vow can be kept, but which vows are truly vows.
>
> No-one can deny that divine law has instituted the obligation to fulfil a vow, as Scripture says: 'Make vows and keep them' [Ps. 76:11], so it is not permissible to dispute whether a vow should be kept. We are not debating whether a vow should be kept. Instead, we are aiming to distinguish between vows and to understand which ones are pious, good, and pleasing to God. These are the only vows that should be considered to be mentioned and required in the Scriptures.[65]

Luther suggests that honest vows taken in faith and piety are hard to find because vows are frequently little more than promises that only imitate holiness. Luther does not hesitate to put them on the same level with ungodly vows, for example, as if somebody had vowed to be adulterous (*adulteram fuisse*). He argues that monastic vows, in particular, are not mentioned anywhere in Scripture and, therefore not founded on the word of God, which is what makes them so dangerous. He voices this concern in the first chapter of the treatise and expands on it in several sub-chapters that anticipate potential counter-arguments, such as people's reasons for taking religious vows and their concept of the value of virginity. The following chapters echo the arguments of 'Von der Freiheit' and the treatise concludes with an explanation of Paul's advice to widows (1 Timothy 5).

---

[65] WA 8, 577. *NON DISPVTARI, SITNE PRESTANDVM VOTVM, SED QVAE VOTA VERE VOTA SINT. Nemo potest negare divinitus esse institutum ius reddendi voti, dicente [Ps. 76, 12.] scriptura 'Vovete et reddite', ut prorsus nulli fas sit disputare, an votum sit reddendum. Neque nos disputamus, an reddendum sit votum, sed hoc agimus, ut inter vota discernamus et cognoscamus, quae sint pia, bona et placita deo, quae et sola sunt censenda vota in scripturis nominari et exigi* (b1r).

Luther elaborates on what he sees as misconceptions derived from the earliest teachings and good examples of pious Christians whose beliefs were rooted in Scripture. Here, Luther identifies what he considers to be a consistent discrepancy in the history of the Church: over the centuries, he claims, there have been good Christians who were deeply familiar with the word of God and could thus serve as examples for other Christians. However, this, according to Luther, is the crux of the matter. He writes that the Church began to glorify these praiseworthy Christians, leading to the sanctification of human beings, whereas this glory should be given to God alone. He suggests that these pious men and women who lived according to God's rule served as holy examples for others to follow, but that the Church allowed believers to model their lives on the saints rather than on Christ and to study the lives of the saints more diligently than Scripture. This idolatry, he concludes, led to the captivity of vows and of the Church.

> St Antony, the very father of monks and the initiator of monastic life, most wisely and in a most Christian manner believed and taught that nothing should be attempted which did not have the authority of Scripture. And he himself did not know this kind of monks who where bound by vows and ceremonies at all. Instead, he dwelt in the desert and lived freely without marrying, in accordance with the Gospel. Those who came after him turned his endeavour into bondage and servitude; they followed only a pretence and a deceptive imitation of Antony's rule, which is the rule of Christ, being merely human in their wisdom.[66]

Luther goes on to expose what he perceives to be this error with a series of biblical references which state that everyone must follow

---

[66] WA 8, 578. *Sanctus Antonius, ipsissimus monachorum pater et monasticae vitae princeps, sapientissime et Christianissime censuit et docuit, nihil prorsus esse tentandum, quod autoritatem scripturae non haberet. Et ipse devotarium hoc et cerimoniale monachorum genus prorsus ignoravit,sed libere incoluit Eremum et libere coelebs vixit, iuxta formam Euangelii. Posteri eius votum, necessitatem et servitutem ex illius instituto fecerunt, nihil nisi speciem et fallacem aemulationem Antonianae regulae, quae Christi regula est, secuti, humana tantum sapientes* (b1v–b2r).

Christ just as Paul followed Christ, for salvation can only be attained through Him.[67] "These and similar oracles of Scripture, being clearer than light and entirely faithful, certainly compel us to condemn any rules, statutes, orders and sects that either fall short of or deviate from or go beyond Christ […]."[68] Luther argues that it is therefore baseless and blasphemous to take monastic vows, since those who are praised for their devotion in doing so do not pledge themselves to the service of Christ, because this practice was, in fact, not required by Him, but by saints and founders of monastic orders, such as Francis of Assisi:

> But St Francis, an admirable and most spiritually fervent man, very wisely stated that his rule was the Gospel of Jesus Christ. The Gospel, however, considers celibacy to be free and nothing like what these Franciscans now hypocritically observe. Clearly, when Francis wished that his followers should live according to the Gospel, he wanted them to be free from both vows and all other human traditions, so that the Franciscan Friars would also have the power through their own vows and rules to choose whether or not to lead celibate lives and to remain in their convents subject to all their statutes as long as they wished; for those who vowed [to live according] to the Gospel neither did nor could vow anything else.[69]

Luther argues that the Gospel is already vowed in Baptism, which would render the practice of monastic vows superfluous, but notes

---

[67] "I am the light of the world. He who follows Me shall not walk in darkness, but have the light of life." (John 8:12); "I am the way, the truth, and the life. No one comes to the Father except through Me." (John 14:6)

[68] WA 8, 579. *Haec et similia oracula scripturae, cum sint luce clariora et fidelissima, certe cogunt damnare, quicquid est regularum, statutorum, ordinum, sectarum, quod vel citra vel praeter vel ultra Christum incedit […]* (b2r).

[69] WA 8, 579. *Sed et S. Franciscus, vir admirabilis et spiritu ferventissimus, sapientissime dixit, Regulam suam esse Euangelium Ihesu Christi. At Euangelium castitatem liberam habet, nec aliquid eorum, quae nunc isti Minores incredibili hypocrisi servant. Plane Franciscus, cum voluit suos ad Euangelium vivere, liberrimos esse voluit tam a votis, quam ab omnibus humanis traditionibus, ut fratres Minores etiam iure sui voti et regulae potestatem habeant, celibes et non celibes vivendi et manendi in Coenobiis et omnibus suis statutis, quam diu voluerint, aliud enim neque voverunt neque vovere potuerunt, qui Euangelium voverunt* (b2v).

that the Church has introduced new requirements which it considers conducive to Christian perfection. He argues that the Church has transformed counsels on how to lead a good life into laws of celibacy and virginity, which he immediately challenges with reference to Christ stating (Matthew 19:11–12) that not all can accept this saying, but only those to whom it has been given. Luther concludes that celibacy, according to Christ's words, is a special gift, and that it is a matter of personal choice whether or not to keep it.

Monastic vows do not merely consist of chastity. They also include obedience and humility, but Luther notes that these vows can be contrary to Christian doctrine, since he claims that they give the Church ultimate authority above that of Scripture.

> I implore you: what kind of obedience is it to be exempt from everything and to be subject to only one – but that again only in part? Is such a vow of obedience not a subtle deception?[70]

The question of obedience, on another level, plays a vital role for every Christian, since it is their duty to obey their parents and to do good to others: "For after faith in God, there is nothing greater than obedience to parents".[71] Luther argues that monastic life prevents people from caring for family and friends, thus alluding to the conflict with his father mentioned in the preface. Luther was eager to help monks and nuns to decide to leave their religious communities with a clear conscience.

> And to put an end to the falsehoods and fabrications: Of all the monastic vows, none is less important than the vow of obedience, and none more irrefutably demonstrates that the monastic system is a mere primary instruction for young Christians, to be temporarily observed according to the ancient custom of the

---

[70] WA 8, 586. *Obsecro, quae et qualis est ista obedientia, ex omnibus eximi et uni, nec huic nisi partim subdi? Nonne pulchra illusio est talis obedientiae votum?* (c3r).

[71] WA 8, 623. *Nam post fidem in deum nihil maius est parentum obedientia* (i1v).

> Fathers, to enable them to learn the faith.[72]

Despite all the additional polemical remarks with which Luther occasionally colours his criticism, he ends on a conciliatory note, addressed directly to the nuns and monks who were planning to leave their convents or had already done so as a result of his arguments:

> Therefore, for the sake of Christ, I also beseech all those who wish to make use of this advice of mine to leave the convents and return to freedom to examine their consciences first of all, lest they be tempted by the novelty of the matter or by mere contempt and hatred of humanity.[73]

This sophisticated treatise marks the culmination of Luther's arguments for renouncing monastic vows. Most of his writings from the following years focus on marriage and echo his verdict in 'De votis monasticis'.

7. 'Vom ehelichen Leben' (1522)

In a series of sermons in 1522, Luther addressed the general discipline of the people so as not to be misunderstood with his Reformation ideas. One of the sermons, probably an amended version for printing, addresses the topic of marriage, and appears to be based on the same principles as Luther's earlier 'Ein Sermon von dem ehelichen Stand verändert und korrigiert durch D. Martinum Luther Augustiner zu Wittenberg' (Sermon on Marriage) of 1519.

---

[72] WA 8, 648. *Et ut mendacia et figmenta finiam: Inter omnia vota monastica nullum est minus substantiale quam obedientiae votum, nullumque irrefragabilius convincit esse monasticum institutum merum rudimentum iuventutis Christianae ad priscum patrum morem temporaliter observandum, pro discenda fide et disciplina Euangelica* (n1v).

[73] WA 8, 669. *Unde et ego per Christum oro omnes, qui meo voluerint hoc consilio uti et deserta monastice libertati sese reddere, ut ante omnia suam conscientiam probent, ne forte hoc tentent novitate rei allecti, aut solo hominum contemptu vel odio* (p3v).

Vom Eelichen
Leben.
Martinus Luther.
Wittemberg.
M.D.xxij.

Ill. 5: Titlepage of 'Vom ehelichen Leben' with Amor as honey-thief[74]
Taylor Institution Library, Arch.8°.G.1522(19)

The new 'Vom ehelichen Leben' (Sermon on Married Life)[75] makes it clear that men and women are not only encouraged to marry, but are commanded to do so to multiply (see Genesis 1:28 and 9:7). Indeed, he writes that doing so is "naturally implanted" (*eyngepflantzte*

---

[74] On the border which the publisher had already used in 1520 for 'Von der Freiheit' see Krümpelmann (1520: xlvi.

[75] WA 10.2, 267–304. See especially 267–268 for a discussion of the authenticity of the text as a sermon.

natur) in God's creation. This nature cannot be suppressed by human beings, but only by God. Luther claims that when human beings try to oppose this nature without God's gift, it leads to deadly sins such as fornication and adultery.

At this point, Luther addresses the impossibility of changing this nature by taking vows. He claims that, no matter how frequently and vehemently one vows to remain unmarried, no-one can ultimately vow not to be a man or woman, whose nature leads to marriage: "I advise you thus: If you want to make a prudent vow, then make a vow not to bite off your nose, for that you can keep."[76] In other words, Luther argues that nothing can be promised that cannot be kept. This assessment leads Luther into a lengthy discussion of marital relations and the right to divorce. He writes that a forced marriage is not pleasing to God, and it puts the spouses at risk of seeking that which they cannot find in marriage elsewhere. Furthermore, he states that adultery is sinful enough to justify divorce, meaning that the righteous spouse can remarry, because otherwise, they cannot live in a marriage that is pleasing to God.

The conclusion of the sermon encourages people to enter into marriage freely and without complaint. Luther also urges them to refrain from un-Christian books and works that demonize women and portray marriage as a captivity of husband and wife which only breeds resentment. Instead, they should rejoice to be united in a state ordained by God – which is more than he can say for monks and nuns.

---

[76] WA 10.2, 284. *Hie radt ich: wenn du weyszlich geloben wilt / szo gelobe / die naszen dyr selb nicht ab beyssen / das kanstu halten* (b2v).

8. 'Papstesel und Mönchkalb' (1523)

Luther's most polemical writing on monasticism is, as discussed in the first paragraphs of this introduction, his collaboration with Melanchthon on the double-bill allegorizing the "gruesome figures" of 'Papstesel und Mönchkalb'. The polemical interpretation of the monsters proved popular; Melanchthon expanded his part for an updated version in 1535, with Luther providing an addendum; it circulated throughout Europe via Latin (1545), French (1557), and English (1579) translations, as detailed in the Publications part of the Introduction and explained in the footnotes to the edition of the 'Mönchkalb' part of the double-bill below.

Ill. 6: First double-spread of the first edition of 'Papstesel und Mönchkalb' in the collection of Lutheran Tracts, Bodleian Library, Tr.Luth.95(15), fols a1v/a2r

9. 'Ursache und Antwort' (1523)

The second pamphlet edited here promises in its programmatic title to give a reason and justify *why it pleases God that nuns may leave their convents.*[77] Luther uses the popular form of an open letter to immediately publicize the collective defection of the nine nuns from their convent in order to avoid any allegations of secrecy, "because whatever we do, we do in God, and we are not ashamed of it in the light" (a2r).

His other reasons for announcing it include stressing the honesty of all those involved in the escape, preserving the honour of the (former) nuns and their families, and encouraging others, especially the nobility, to follow suit. Luther emphasizes that the escape was orderly and dignified, leaving intact the honour of all involved, in order to refute any accusations and retorts from "slanderous mouths" (*lester meulern*) who "wipe their tongues with these pious children" (*yhr lugenhafftige tzungen mit frumen kindern tzu wasschen*, a2v).

The pamphlet goes on to give a succinct summary of Luther's criticism of monastic vows, semi-explicitly referring to earlier texts on the subject: "even though I have already often done so in other pamphlets" (*wie wol ichs sonst ynn andern buchlin reichlich gethan habe*, a2v). The novelty of this text is its very specific focus on nuns, whose (legal) opportunities before and after leaving their convents were particularly limited. For this reason, Luther urges their male relatives, as their legal guardians, to withdraw them from the convents.

Furthermore, in this pamphlet, Luther claims that the nuns in question, with convincing arguments, asked their family and friends to allow them to be taken out of the convents because they did not consider themselves fit for such a life. Luther argues that, when this was refused, it was only right that the nuns should be helped by Christians, whose unending duty of charity was to support them. Nuns

[77] WA 11, 395. The following quotations are taken from our new edition.

are therefore permitted to flee their convents by any means necessary for the sake of their salvation if their pleas and entreaties to be allowed to leave their convents are refused by their families. Luther was disturbed to see mere children, especially women "pushed" into convents (a3r), even though unwilling service is not pleasing to God, for He only loves a cheerful giver (2 Corinthians 9:7).

Luther concludes that the inability to lead a monastic life and the lack of God's word being heard and practised in convents do not merely justify, but actively call for monks and nuns to escape or be rescued even if they had sworn a thousand "oaths or vows" (*eyd vnd gelubd*, a3v). Luther goes even further to claim that there are hardly any nuns who are able to devotedly perform their service since the word of God is not served and thus they earn a place in hell rather than heaven (a4r).

Luther, referencing God's command to "be fruitful and multiply" (Genesis 1:28), thus urges those people who do not consider themselves fit for such a life to get married, as God intended. He continues to argue that what God said to Eve is true for every other woman, that is, that they should bear children, unless they are exempted from it by God. Luther also objects to the counter-argument that people can preserve their celibacy through prayer because it would be tempting God to pray for a different state of living to the one that He has ordained for them. He stresses that people should not strive to make themselves better than God intended.

The pamphlet concludes with a list of the nuns who escaped from the convent and Luther's expression of certainty that God will approve of this action, even if others who know no better may be furious about it.

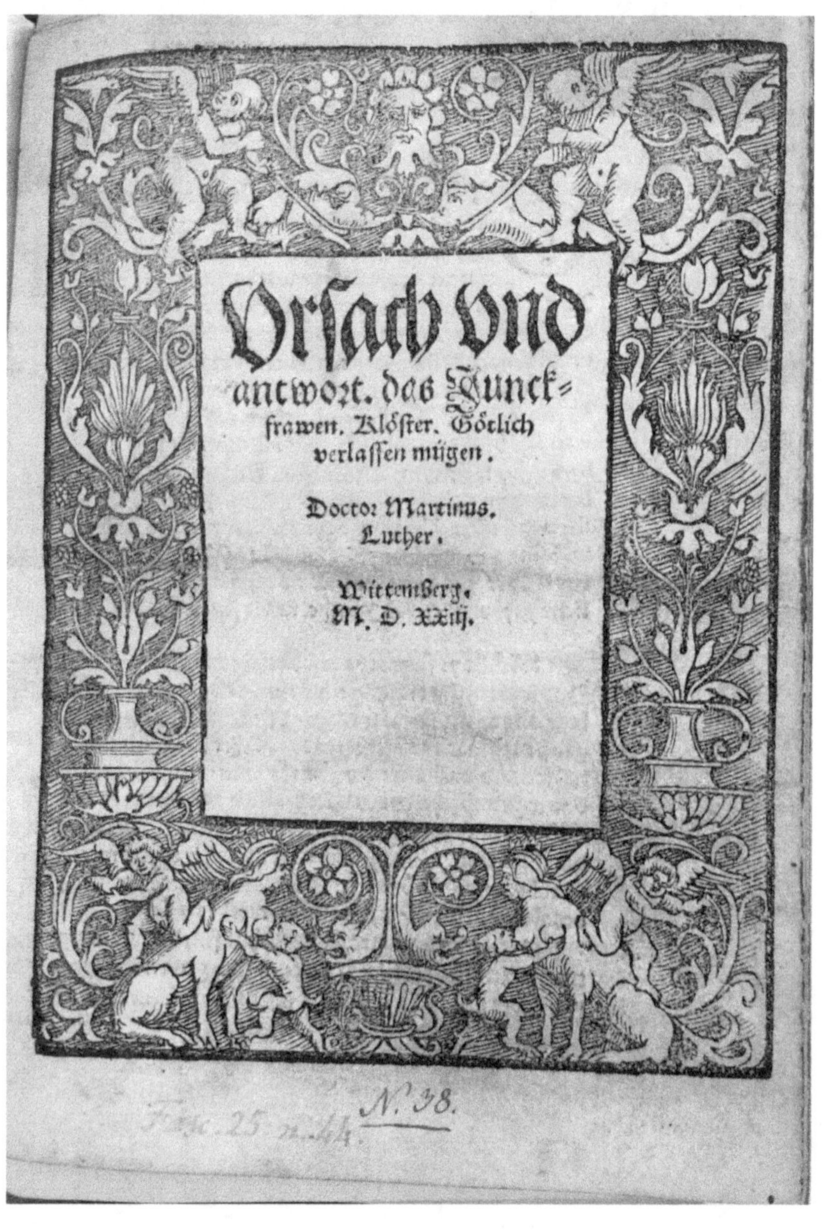

Vrsach vnd
antwort. das Junck=
frawen. Klöster. Götlich
verlassen mügen.

Doctor Martinus.
Luther.

Wittemberg.
M. D. XXiij.

Ill. 7: Titlepage of the Augsburg reprint of 'Ursache und Antwort'
Bodleian Library, Tr. Luth. 94 (9)

10. 'Das siebte Kapitel St. Pauli' (1523)

Paul's teachings on the principles of marriage form the basis of a treatise which seeks to challenge the ecclesiastical interpretation of these teachings. 'Das siebte Kapitel St. Pauli zu den Korinthern' (The Seventh Chapter of St Paul to the Corinthians) undermines his opponents' strongest arguments in favour of virginity being superior to matrimony.

Since the days of Jerome, Doctor of the Church, the text itself had, however, been seen as evidence from Scripture for the superiority of celibacy to matrimony and accordingly been developed by Luther's opponents as a line of defence in favour of a life of celibacy over the state of marriage. The core of the text is therefore an argument about which style of living is truly conducive to chastity and which is actually detrimental to it.[78]

In 1 Corinthians 7, Paul resolves the confusion amongst the Corinthians about whether it is better to remain single in a culture that has been tolerating extra-marital fornication and adultery amongst other issues. Paul teaches them that everyone observing the word of God should live according to their disposition:

> For I wish that all men were even as I myself. But each one has his own gift from God, one in this manner and another in that. But I say to the unmarried and to the widows: It is good for them if they remain even as I am; but if they cannot exercise self-control, let them marry. For it is better to marry than to burn with passion. (1 Corinthians 7:7–9)

Paul also makes a clear distinction between his words and those of the Lord. This distinction, Luther claims, is passed over by the supporters of the Pope. It is not God who wants everyone to be like Paul, rather He has merely instated matrimony for those who are neither able to nor want to lead a celibate life, because singleness without

---

[78] Beyer (1999: 65).

celibacy is sinful. "But even if you do marry, you have not sinned; and if a virgin marries, she has not sinned" (1 Corinthians 7:28). The state of marriage, once attained, is to be kept, because it puts an end to unchaste living, which he believes is indeed harmful to the soul, for it is not God's will.

Luther repeats a considerable number of arguments from previous writings, especially 'De votis monasticis', and incorporates Paul's letter to the Corinthians into his argument. He stresses that there is no difference between the bearing that celibacy and matrimony have on salvation. He concludes that it is good not to marry unless it is necessary; but it is necessary where God does not give the rare and noble gift of chastity, for no human is created to be chaste, but each and every one of us is created to have children and to bear the burdens of matrimonial life.[79]

11. 'An die Herren Deutschordens' (1523)

Luther's open letter to the Order of the Teutonic Knights 'An die Herren Deutschordens, dass sie falsche Keuschheit meiden' (Appeal to the Knights of the Teutonic Order to avoid false celibacy) of 1523 addressed the well-established topic of vows on new grounds. The open letter is a response from Luther to the Grand Master Albrecht von Brandenburg (1490–1568), who was keen to reform his religious Order into a purely secular duchy. This pamphlet required Luther to be more adaptable in his tone, as he was addressing representatives of a secular and political institution which "at the same time is supposed to be religious, to vow and keep celibacy, poverty and obedience like

[79] WA 1,12, 141. *So ist nu dis die summa dis Capitels / Gutt ists nicht freyen / es sey den nott / Nott aber ists / wo Gott die seltzam edle gabe der keuscheyt nicht gibt / den keyn mensch ist zur keuscheyt geschaffen / sondern allesampt sind wyr geschaffen kinder zu tzeugen / vnd die můhe des ehlichen lebens zu tragen* (k2v).

other monks."[80] Luther hoped that the knights would set a good Christian example for others to follow.

Beyond his allusions to the concerns already voiced in his earlier pamphlets, Luther introduces new arguments tailored to his addressees, concerning: wealth and the sense of obedience in the ranks of the knights. Luther writes that wealth, in the form of goods and land, provides the security of meeting daily needs, whereas poverty is what ties members of the mendicant orders to their convents. He suggests that there is therefore no requirement for knights to pledge poverty because doing so would make them unfit for their role as protectors. He declares that the significance of this task requires the Teutonic Order not to wait for any ecclesiastical council to decide whether they should be allowed to marry. Continuing to mock councils and papal decrees, Luther insists that there is no certainty that their decisions will be compatible with Scripture, since he points out that they have been wrong before, especially over monastic vows. Thus, he concludes that the knights' vow of obedience requires them to adhere to the word of God, stating "It is not good that man should be alone" (Genesis 2:18).

The pamphlet's conclusion reads as though Luther were sending the Knights into battle because of a series of imperatives exhorting them not to linger any longer, but to become trail blazers (c3v).

12. 'Dass Eltern Kinder nicht zu Ehe zwingen' (1524)

In a short open letter dedicated to Hans Schott, a Saxon knight, 'Dass Eltern Kinder nicht zu Ehe zwingen' (That Parents shall not force their children to marry), Luther returns to the question of the duties of children towards their parents and discusses whether it is right for parents to compel their children to marry or not.

---

[80] WA 1,12, 232. *vnd soll doch zu gleych auch geystlich seyn / keuscheyt / armut vnd gehorsam geloben vnd hallten / wie ander mu͂nich* (a1v).

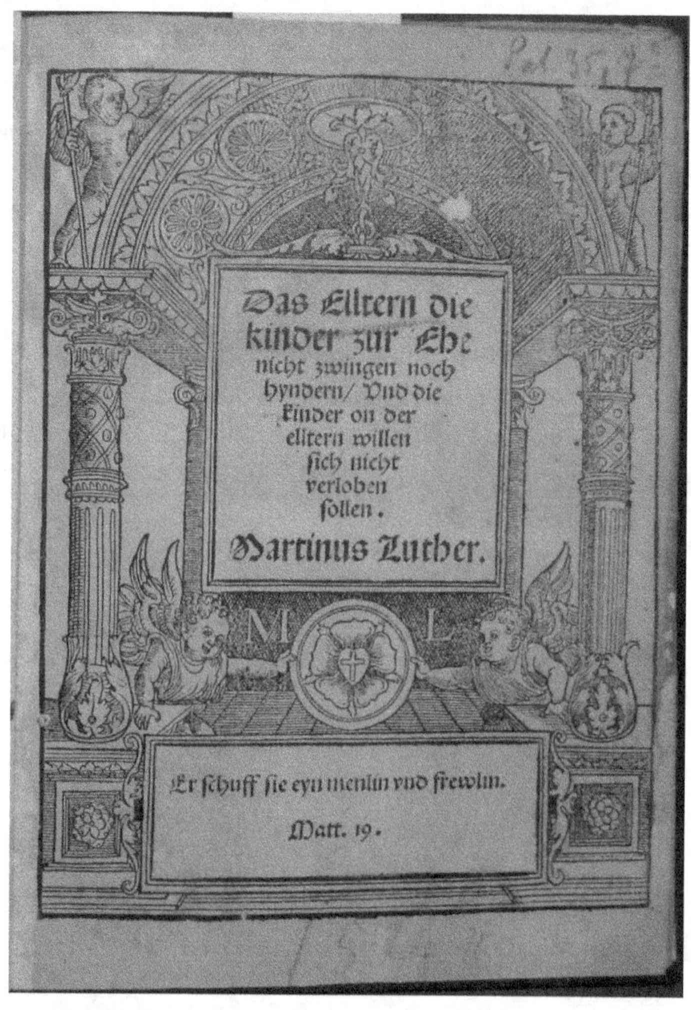
Das Eltern die kinder zur Ehe nicht zwingen noch hyndern/ Vnd die kinder on der eltern willen ſich nicht verloben ſollen.

Martinus Luther.

M L

Er ſchuff ſie eyn menlin vnd frewlin.

Matt. 19.

Ill. 8: Titlepage of 'Dass Eltern …' with Genesis 1:27: "He created them as man and woman" and reference to the marriage law in Matthew 19
Taylor Institution Library, Arch.8°.G.1524(7)

Luther states that children are to obey their parents in Christian matters. He argues that no parent – especially fathers – should compel their children to marry against their will, since he claims that the main condition for marriage is the mutual consent of the engaged couple. In such a case, Luther argues that the son or daughter should be allowed to escape their parents' guardianship and to seek help from other Christians and the authorities.

Moreover, he declares that it is not up to parents to decide that their children – especially daughters – should lead a monastic life. Luther thus touches upon the custom of noble families to send their daughters to convents to save money on dowry. He accepts that parents may object to their children's choice of partner in marriage, but not to their choice to get married at all:

> For just as the father may demand that his child do not eat or drink this or that, or not sleep here or there, so he cannot keep his child without food or drink. Indeed, he is obliged to provide his child with food, drink, clothes, sleep, and everything else required for the child's needs and well-being. And where he does not do so, he is no father, and the child must and shall fend for itself. Likewise, he has the authority to deny their child from taking this or that person in marriage, but he has no authority to dictate that they do not take anyone at all in marriage. Instead, he is obliged to give the child someone who is good and suitable for them or ensure that this person is suitable. If he does not do so, the child must and shall fend for itself.[81]

This short pamphlet re-affirms Luther's argument from *Reason and Justification* that it is appropriate for children to disobey their parents if their decisions are harmful to their children's soul and conscience, and that it is every Christian's duty to help these children in such cases.

---

[81] WA 1,15, 168. *Denn gleich wie der vater mag gebieten / das seyn kind dis odder das nicht esse odder trincke / hie oder da nicht schlaffe / So kan er doch nicht weren / das es gar on essen vnd trincken vnd schlaff bleybe / Ja er ist schůldig dem kinde / essen / trincken / kleyder schlaff / vnd alles zu versorgen / fur des kindes nott vnd zu seynem besten / Vnd wo er das nicht thet / so ist er nymmer vater / vnd mus vnd soll es das kind selbs thun. Also auch hat er die macht zu weren / das seyn kind / disen odder den nicht neme / aber gar keynen zu nemen hat er nicht die macht / sondern ist schuldig dem kinde eynen zu geben / der yhm gut vnd fůglich sey / odder sich versehe / das er yhm fůglich sey / Thut ers nicht / so mus vnd soll das kind selbs sich versorgen* (b1r–b1v).

13. 'Wie Gott einer ehrbaren Klosterjungfrau ausgeholfen hat' (1524)

In 1524, an account by Florentina von Oberweimar, a former nun, gave Luther the chance to generalize the case and claim the overall unruly state of convents and its harmful effects which he published as 'Wie Gott einer ehrbaren Klosterjungfrau ausgeholfen hat. Mit einem Sendbrief Martin Luthers' (An Account of how God helped out an Honourable Nun. With an Open Letter by M. Luther). Luther used Florentina's account of her convent life as evidence for his criticism:

> For it is not only from this account of Florentina, but also from the testimony of many other people, that we see clearly what devilish things nunnery and monkery are […]. I will say it once more: God does not want to have unwilling service. I will say it for a third time, I will say it for a hundred thousand times: God does not want unwilling service.[82]

Florentina's own preface of the text reveals that she wishes to defend her honour despite (and because of) her departure from the convent while her former abbess spreads defamatory statements about her. She then gives a brief account of the circumstances of her family's decision to bring her up in a convent which she entered at the age of six. She writes that, at the age of eleven, she was consecrated without knowing about the consequences. After she had turned fourteen, she felt that she did not have what it took to be a nun and thus unsuccessfully urged her family to withdraw her from her convent. When the abbess found out about it, she told Florentina that there was no way she could renounce her vows and that she had to remain a nun for the sake of her promise to God.

---

[82] WA 1,15, 87–88. *Denn nicht alleyn aus diser Florentina geschicht / sondern auch aus vieler andern zeugnis / man wol sihet / wilch eyn teuffelisch ding die nonnerey vnd muͦncherey ist* […]. *Jch sags abermal / Gott will nicht gezwungen dienst haben. Jch sags zum drytten mal / Jch sags hundert tausent mal / Got will keynen gezwungen dienst haben* (a3r).

Florentina claims that without knowing what she had vowed before she was mature enough to understand it, she had to surrender to the "Babylonian captivity" (*Babilonische gefengknis*; b1r). She complied with the abbess's demand against her own will because there was no chance to say or do anything against it. Certain that she would receive punishment rather than advice from the abbess, "I wrote to the profoundly learned Doctor Martin Luther, revealed my heart to him and sought comfort, help and advice from him" (*hab ich an den hoch gelarten Doctor Martinum Luther geschrieben / yhm meyn gemuͤt zu erkennen gegeben / von yhm trost / vnd hůlff vnd radt begeret*, b1v).[83]

She writes that some of her fellow nuns reported this to the abbess, who punished Florentina by having her repeatedly confess her trespasses and watching over her penance. She was obliged to show humility and to be regularly disciplined. She reported that her punishment was increased after writing a letter to a cousin asking for help which was disclosed to the abbess, who had Florentina physically punished until "none of them was able to beat [her] any longer" (*das yhr keyne mehr zu schlagen vermochte*; b2v[84]). The abbess instructed that Florentina was to be kept under surveillance at all times without speaking to anyone: "The person assigned to watch me had to walk by my side. I was to surrender to such captivity all my life, etc." (*Die person die mir zu deputyrt / můst bey meyner seytten gehen / yn solche gefengnis sollt ich mich meyn lebenlang geben etc.*; b3r[85]).

Florentina goes on to describe her escape, which she considers to be of God's miraculous making. One day, the door to her cell remained unlocked after a meal. She reports that she managed to escape from the convent without being seen because most of her sisters were also in their cells. On a final note, she appeals to all Christians to believe in her innocence.

---

[83] WA 1,15, 91.

[84] WA 1,15, 92.

[85] WA 1,15, 93.

Luther's final note on the text turns this first-hand account of a case, which in fact contravened church law on the legal age for taking vows,[86] into a wholesale condemnation not only of the "venomous, evil, acrimonious, false, lying" (*gifftig / boͤse / bitter / falsch / lugenhafftig*) nuns claiming to be the "tender brides of Christ" (*zarten breutte Christi*) but of everybody supporting the system of convents which he calls "pits of murder of body and soul" (*mord grůben leybs vnd seelen*), whether princes, family or friends. In an effective preacher's gesture, he ends the whole pamphlet with a resounding 'Amen'.

14. 'Ein schöner Sermon von dem Ehestand' (1525)

In 1525, the year of Luther's marriage to Katharina von Bora (one of the nine nuns mentioned in 'Ursache und Antwort'), he summarized his praise of the estate of marriage in comparison to monasticism in a series of sermons which also include advice on the characteristics of a consensual Christian marriage, 'Ein schöner Sermon von dem Ehestand' (A fine sermon on the estate of marriage) and the so-called 'Fastenpostille' (Lent exegesis), a sermon for the second Sunday after Epiphany. The encouragement in these texts draws on a number of honours that the Lord bestows upon married people, while also referring to and explaining the wedding feast at Cana attended by Jesus, His mother, and the disciples (see John 2:1–11).

Luther sharpens some of his earlier arguments with reference to God's will that man should not be alone. He insists that the estate of marriage is not man-made, but was constituted by God in Paradise before Adam and Eve were expelled from it. According to Luther, it would therefore be disrespectful not to honour marriage, since almost all the patriarchs and prophets were married. In fact, he argues, there is a much longer history and tradition of marriage than of monasticism and should thus be more highly valued. He declares that

---

[86] See Schlotheuber (2004) for an in-depth discussion of the legal age of maturity and the question of when it was permitted for girls and boys to swear.

monks and nuns, on the other hand, can only invoke and quote saints like Francis and Benedict in their defence. Moreover, they miss the opportunity to be delivered through procreation and the Christian upbringing of children. Luther emphasizes that Jesus Himself was born of a married woman, and His presence at the wedding feast at Cana including His miracle shows that He cares for married people.

15. 'Ursula von Münsterberg: Christlich Ursache' (1525)

In 1528, the high-profile case of Ursula von Münsterberg, a duchess related to the anti-Reformation rulers of Saxony, gave Luther another opportunity to attach his anti-monastic statements to an ego-document, even though he claims that by this point it has become so commonplace that children are singing ballads about it in the streets (*die kinder allenthalben auff der gassen gnůgsam dauon singen*, e3r). In his afterword, he is still keen to make this public to "abundantly heap such texts and examples upon" the sceptics (*mit solchen schrifften vnd exempeln reichlich vberschuͤtten*; f3v),[87] and to encourage the weaker people "against all those who speak or write slander" (*widder alle falsche meuler vnd schreiber*; f4v).[88]

The pamphlet begins with an address to Ursula's male relatives, asking for sympathy for her and her fellow nuns' decision to have left the convent. They intend to prevent any allegations that "it had happened out of a whim of levity, God forbid!" (*es geschehe ein solches aus leichtfertigem vorwitz / da Gott fur sey*; a2r).

Ursula von Münsterberg issues the text like a proclamation, prefacing all her titles with the formula 'by God's grace' (*Von Gottes gnaden Ursula geporne Hertzogin zů Moͤnsterberg vnd Troppaw / Graͤffin zů Glotz etc.*) and also names her two companions. The text opens with a quotation from Paul's letters whom the printer prominently placed in the opening initial, giving the text visibly scriptural authority. The

87 WA 26, 631b.

88 WA 26, 633b.

text is written in the first person plural which aligns both with the practice of letter-writing in convents and with the status of the duchess.[89]

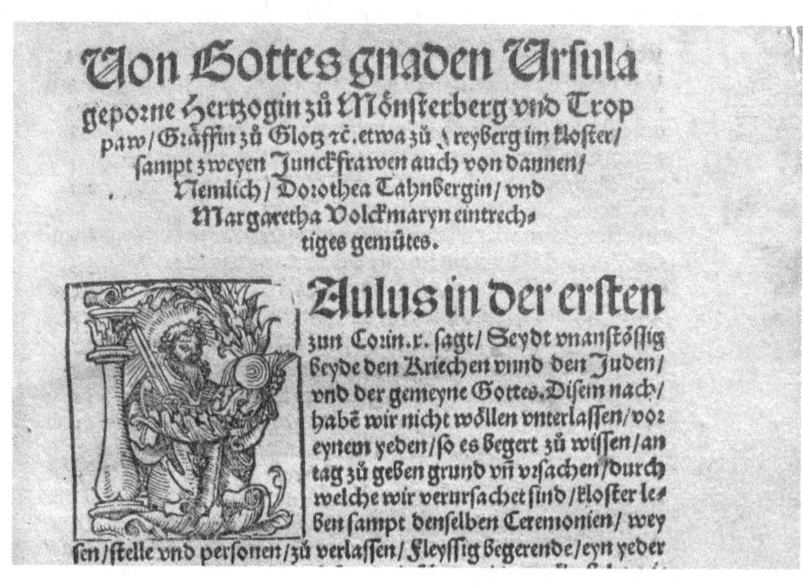

Von Gottes gnaden Urſula
geporne Hertzogin zů Mönſterberg vnd Trop
paw/ Gräffin zů Glotz rc. etwa zů Freyberg im kloſter/
ſampt zweyen Junckfrawen auch von dannen/
Nemlich/ Dorothea Tahnbergin/ vnd
Margaretha Volckmaryn eintrech-
tiges gemůtes.

Aulus in der erſten
zun Corin. x. ſagt/ Seydt vnanſtöſſig
beyde den Kriechen vnnd den Juden/
vnd der gemeyne Gottes. Diſem nach/
habē wir nicht wöllen vnterlaſſen/ vor
eynem yeden/ ſo es begert zů wiſſen/ an
tag zů geben grund vñ vrſachen/ durch
welche wir verurſachet ſind/ kloſter le-
ben ſampt denſelben Ceremonien/ wey
ſen/ ſtelle vnd perſonen/ zů verlaſſen/ Fleyſſig begerende/ eyn yeder

Ill. 9: Header with the titles and names of the three nuns, initial with St Paul
Bodleian Library: Antiq.e.G.1529.1, fol. a3r

The former nuns explain their motives in seven articles which, for a large part, share Luther's arguments from earlier publications. However, they add a note of experience, including their humility at having been misguided about, and disrespected, the word of God

> by the very fact that we, by joining an order, sought to bless ourselves, to exculpate us from our sins, to be blessed above everyone else, and we dared to do so not through Christ, who was sent and ordained by God to do it, but by our own actions.[90]

---

[89] On forms of address in nuns' letters see Netzwerke der Nonnen (2023), 3.4.

[90] *Eben ynn dem da wir durch annehmen des ordens / vns haben wollen seligen / sunde tilgen / heiligkeit vber alle ander zu erlangen / vns vnterstanden / vnd das nicht durch*

This is described as an act of utter blasphemy: "Is this not equal to what the devil did when he wanted to be equal to God, for which he was cast out?" (*Jst das nicht eben dem gleich / das der Teuffel gethan hat / da er Gott wolte gleich sein / vnd derhalben verstossen ist?*; b1v). They go on to argue that such service is only done to please others and to feel superior to them "while it was permissible for us to praise ourselves to be the brides of Christ" (*haben vns dennoch wol dů̈rffen rhů̈men / Wir sind breute Christi*; b2v). They state that there should be no encouragement to acquire such an attitude of pride, which they believe only leads to devotion to good works rather than to God. The danger here, as the escaped nuns argue, is that people in religious orders may consider their works equivalent to salvation.

> We wanted to make all these things known to you, dear friends, you who are our brothers and sisters in Christ, of one faith and one baptism, so that you might understand that our leaving the order was not due to a reckless temper, but due to weighty, important and serious matters [...].[91]

It was not faith alone for the sake of which Ursula and the others were willing to renounce their vows, but the duty to be openly committed to the faith, as they explain with biblical references. They go on to criticize priests and theologians who can read and explain so many scholarly books, but withhold the word of God from nuns, who Luther claims are unaware of their own idolatry.

Ursula and her fellow nuns argue that it is impossible for nuns to practise charity whilst imprisoned in convents, even though it is demanded by God. They emphasize that not helping and serving others, especially the needy, harms the soul and conscience. They feel

---

Christum / der zu solchem von Gott gesandt vnd verordent ist / sondern durch dis vnser werck (b1v).

[91] *Solches alles / lieben freunde / die yhr seid vnser brů̈der vnd schwestern ynn Christo / eines glawbens vnd einer Tauffe / haben wir euch offentlich wollen an tag geben / auff das yhr erkennen mů̈get / das die verlassung vnsers ordens nicht her fliesse aus einem leichtfertigen gemů̈te / sondern aus mechtigen wichtigen vnd ernsten sachen* (c2r).

safe in God, while they are scorned by those who do not understand their discomfort in religious orders, and ask all Christians to believe their account, which they also wish to be seen as a warning, because they stress that life in the convent was more than they could bear.

Finally, they emphasize their independence in writing this open letter by dating it before they left the convent. More nuns from the same convent would follow suit soon afterwards.

16. 'Von Ehesachen' (1530)

By 1530, Luther seems to have been regarded as an expert on marriage, because many ministers and representatives of secular authorities had sought his advice on how to deal with specific questions relating to marriage. He ultimately responded to their queries with a long pamphlet, 'Von Ehesachen' (On Questions of Marriage) (1530), although he states at the beginning of the text that he was hesitant to do so. He claims not to consider himself well enough trained in the law, although it should be noted that in earlier years "the publications and sermons of reformers focused on unresolved conflicts over jurisdiction."[92] Luther argues that the New Testament offers little in the way of established frameworks of rules for such special cases, but writes that he understands that people are in need of guidance. Therefore, he focuses on how to soothe wounded souls and consciences.

Luther writes that he is aggrieved to find "consciences in endless confusion" (*unzeliche verwirrunge der gewissen*; c3r).[93] He repeats and reinforces many arguments from earlier sermons on marriage, but also specifically addresses legal action relating to – and punishment for – un-Christian behaviour before, during and after marriage. He is urged to return a verdict on how a righteous and rightful marriage

[92] Plummer (2012, p. 97).
[93] WA 30.3, 215.

can be established and maintained after illegal engagements, adultery, abandonment of spouses and children, and many other specific incidents.

Once more, Luther emphasizes that "forced engagements should not count for anything" (*Getzwungen verloͤbnis solten nichts gelten*; a3v[94]). Nevertheless, he concedes that parents should have the greatest power over their children's marriage, because he considers Christian parental blessing to be indispensable. He argues that secret engagements and marriages should not be valid:

> What is more, even these days the Pope forbids such engagements, so that they do not take place, but, on the other hand, once they have taken place, he wants them to be seen as valid and binding. And thus, he alone turns it into a sin of disobedience, rewarding them with the joys and pleasures of the disobedient, so that they obtain what they desire with sins of disobedience, which is against everything that is lawful and right.[95]

He argues that an official engagement should take precedence even if it was preceded by a secret one, unless the bride (to be) has been dishonoured by pre-marital intercourse, which Luther argues would oblige the man involved to take care of her, especially if she fell pregnant. Luther suggests that this entanglement of special and unusual cases makes it so difficult to reach to a just verdict.

> Such awkward cases surely rather arise from such awkward laws and rules. And what good shall come of such mad, improper,

---

[94] WA 30.3, 207.

[95] WA 30.3, 208. *Ja auch noch heutiges tages der Bapst solche verloͤbnis verbeut / das sie nicht sollen geschehen / Aber widderumb wenn sie geschehen sind / wil er sie gehalten haben / das sie gelten vnd binden sollen / Vnd macht also allein ein sunde des vngehorsams daraus / Vnd belonet die selbigen mit freuden vnd wolgefallen der vngehorsamen / das sie yhren willen erlangen mit sunden des vngehorsames / welchs widder alle billigkeit vnd recht ist* (a4v).

> unnatural and ungodly laws?[96]

Luther criticizes the papal approach to dealing with these entanglements. He does not believe that secretly engaged people are brought together by God:

> Say, how do you know that it was God who brought you together? Is there a sign that shows that God did it and not you who did it yourself without God?[97]

According to Luther's reasoning, it is possible to suspend secret engagements because they do not conform to the word of God. If somebody becomes officially engaged to tow people, Luther concludes that only the first engagement is valid because it was witnessed by others and instituted by God. He emphasizes that those who have already been joined by God by becoming engaged cannot become engaged to anyone else.

Luther goes on to depict other scenarios that call for punishment because of their un-Christian nature. He states that the cases to which he alludes are not hypothetical; instead, the suggests that they have been disclosed to him for various reasons, but he is not keen to provide legal advice in every case. He professes to be content to advise ministers on how to support the people involved, while conceding that it is impossible to relate all cases (*Denn alle ſelle zu erzelen / ist vnmůglich*; e1r[98]). Luther considers it a serious disgrace when a fiancé(e) or spouse enters a convent in order to annul an engagement or marriage:

> But if it is a legitimate marriage, Church law should not permit, nor should it otherwise be valid, that a fiancé or fiancée might leave

[96] WA 30.3, 210. *Solcher vngeschickter ſelle / begeben sich wol mehr / aus solchen vngeschickten gesetzen vnd geboten. Vnd was solt guts aus solchen tollen / vnbillichen / vnnatůrlichen / vngottlichen gesetzen ſolgen?* (b2v).

[97] WA 30.3, 214. *Sage / wo bey weistu / das euch Gott zusamen geſuget hat? gib des ein warzeichen / das Got / vnd nicht du selbs / on Got gethan hast?* (c1v).

[98] WA 30.3, 222.

> the other and run away to a convent; for they are now a wedded spouse and have no power to take religious orders or to remain a virgin without the other's consent [...].[99]

At this point, Luther briefly returns to his criticism of monasticism, emphasising that it must not prevent marriage "because monastic life, as it has been practised hitherto, is condemned" (*weil kloster leben / wie es bisher gehalten / verdampt ist*; f4r[100]). He argues that such a state is commendable only for those who can truly devote themselves to God, and that it should not be seen as a convenient excuse to renounce one's spouse. Similarly, he urges that children whose parents misuse the word of God to either force them into or prevent them from marrying should not seek refuge in convents, but ask their families and friends and the authorities for help.

Luther's line of argument concerning matrimony and monasticism was completed with the pamphlet 'Von Ehesachen', but in the following years, Luther occasionally returned to the subject of the Christian marriage in a number of sermons, essentially repeating his advice from earlier texts.

At the heart of Luther's criticism was the notion of a prevalent but wrong attitude to God promoted by the Church centred around people seeking to attain assurance of salvation by themselves through good works, rather than trusting that God will deliver them through faith.

---

[99] WA 30.3, 231. *Jsts aber ein rechte Ehe / so solt das geistliche recht nicht haben zu gelassen / vnd sol auch noch nicht gelten / das solcher verlobert odder verlobte eins das ander liesse / vnd ynns kloster lieffe / Denn es ist nu ein ehelich gemahl / vnd hat nicht macht / geistlich zu werden odder iungfraw zu bleiben / on des andern willen* [...].

[100] WA 30.3, 231.

3. Counter-Arguments and Afterlife

Luther's writing on marriage proved highly controversial and provoked immediate reactions; the two texts edited in this volume were especially singled out for counter-attacks.

1. Countering the 'Mönchkalb' & 'Ursache und Antwort'

For Luther's 'Mönchkalb' in quick succession four Catholic counter-interpretations were offered. The first off the mark was Hieronymus Emser who in his 'Wider den falsch genannten Ecclesiasten und warhaftigen Ertzketzer Martinum Luther' (Against Martin Luther, wrongly called a preacher, in reality an arch-heretic, 1523/4) lists the Kalb zu Freyberg as one of many signs which Nature "who does nothing without cause" (*nichtzst vorgebens thut*, t1r) produced in Saxony to chastise the stubborn monk Luther who mainly spread his heretical teaching in Saxony. Also in 1523, Johannes Cochläus turned Luther into a 'cowled minotaur' in his 'Adversus cucullatum Minotaurum Wittenbergensem' and in 'Eine christliche Vermahnung der heiligen Stadt Rom an das Deutschland' (A Christian reproach by the holy city Rome to the German land) claims that all one hears of nowadays is the "half monkish calf, this Saxon Apis" (*diß halb münchisch kalp / diser sachsiß Apis*, f2r).[101]

Cochläus was also involved in a counter-attack against 'Ursache und Antwort'. Luther's justification of the nuns leaving the convent was immediately challenged by Johann Dietenberger, with Johannes Cochläus providing the German translation of the text: 'Antwort, dass Jungfrauen die Klöster und klösterliche Gelübde nimmer göttlich verlassen mögen' (Justification why it never pleases god that nuns leave their convents and vows, 1523). Dietenberger's approach in the pamphlet is to frequently quote from Luther's text to expose what he sees as fallacies and lies, followed by ecclesiastical counter-

[101] See WA 11, 360 for further examples of reactions against Luther's interpretation of the monstrous birth.

arguments. According to Dietenberger's reasoning, there is no noble cause or Christian intention to leave the convent and renounce one's vows. He sometimes uses quotations the wording of which is easier to twist, especially if there are a few omissions.

Dietenberger makes it very clear that Luther is fatally mistaken: "It is not enough for him to be wrong; he cannot help but lead others astray too" (*Jm ist nit genůg / dz er in irrung geet / můsz auch ander in irthum bringen*; a2r). Dietenberger explains that this is the reason for him to write his pamphlet: "so I have written this pamphlet, for the honour of God and for the consolation of all religious people, arguing with Scripture and truth against the heretical pamphlet" (*so hab ich got zů eren / vnnd allen geistlichen zů trost disz buͤchlin geschrieben / mit schrifft vnd der warheit nider gelegt / das ketzerische büchlen*; a2v). Luther, as Dietenberger criticizes, is misleading the people, contributing only to their dishonour and to the defamation of the word of God as represented by the Church. In such "devilish counsel" (*teüffelischem rath*), it is impossible to bring about the "greatest good of our neighbour" (*des nechsten bestes*; a3r).

The only consequence of this action is to forfeit one's salvation by renouncing one's vows, which bestow an angelic state upon religious people. It is therefore appropriate for parents to refuse their children's request to leave the convent, because they do not want to see their children condemned. Dietenberger warns that anyone who follows such a devilish counsel will be despised by God, such as Luther and his followers already are.

> How could they [the apostate nuns] not have been failed in their plea by their pious and Christian parents, or left without any help or advice from anyone except you [Luther] and others, who you are abhorrent to God, honour and all discipline?[102]

---

[102] *Wie sollten sie von jren frummen Christlichen eltern in diser bitt nit verlassen werden / vnd von niemants kein hilff oder rath haben / dan allein von dir vnd anderen / die got / der eren / vnnd aller zucht zůwideer seind* (a3v).

The increasing polemics underlines Luther's alleged lack of knowledge of the word of God, with which he prepares many souls for their damnation: For how could God be more blatantly denied than by renouncing holy vows?

> Tell me, you blind madman, what can be righteous and honest that is abhorrent to God, irksome and damnable to one's neighbour? Is this the way to bring about the greatest good for one's neighbour?[103]

Similarly to Luther, Dietenberger also refers to some of his other texts opposing Luther[104] and goes on to put monastic vows on the same level as godly vows: "[I] have sufficiently demonstrated this in other books" (*hab das gnůgsam in meinen anderen büchern angetzeigt*; a4r), and "as I have sufficiently proved in other books of mine" (*wie in andern meinen büchern ich gnůgsamlich beweiszt hab*; b2v). This should be proof enough that the word of God in particular goes forth in convents. His response to Luther's 'De votis monasticis' from 1522 only followed in 1524 ('De votis monasticis Luteri').

Dietenberger, bluntly speaking, puts Luther down as a liar, and repeatedly uses derivatives and compounds with this word stem along with pejorative attributes, e.g. "insolent lies" (*eytel lugen*; b1r), "Fie, fie, you reeking, abysmal liar" (*Pfu pfu dich stinckenden / heillosen lügner*; b1v), "impertinent lying toad" (*vnuerschemptes lügenmaul*; b1v), "blather of lies" (*lügenschwetz*; c1r), etc. It is only just not to follow Luther's "babbling" (*blapperey*; b2r) and not to commit oneself and one's children to the devil.

He also mockingly touches upon Luther's vows as a former Augustinian: "How then do you write about yourself? Like this: I took my monastic vows with displeasure and not through God. But how does

---

[103] *Sag doch du blinder doller kopff / was kan da doch recht vnnd redlich sein / dz got zůwider / gegen dem nechsten ergerlich / vnd jnen selber verdamlich ist. Jst das gottes eer / vnd des nechsten bestes gesůcht?* (a4r).

[104] Probably a reference to Dietenberger's 'Schlussrede'.

this concern other pious people in convents?" (*Wie schreibestu nun von dir selbst? Also. Mein kloͤsterliche gelübdt ist mit vnwillen vnnd nit ausz got geschehen. Was geet aber disz nun andere frumme kloͤsterleüt an*?; b3v). Dietenberger does not consider unwilling service to be widespread since it is the Holy Ghost that bestows the aptitude and love of such a life upon religious people, so there are not many "who keep God's commandments, service and vows with force, sadness and displeasure" (*die mit gezwang / traurigkeit / vnwillen gottes gebott / dienst / vnd gelübde halten*; b4r).

It is, however, not Dietenberger's intention to justify parents who compel their children to a life in a convent: "I do not approve of it; it rarely does any good" (*Lob das nit / es kumpt selten gůtes darausz*; b4v). On the other hand, he does not fail to emphasize that the upbringing of children in convents is commendable:

> But it is good to educate the children to God at an early age, and to leave them with the pious people in convents to be raised in discipline, virtue, doctrine and the fear of God [...]. Therefore, young sons and daughters should not be prevented from serving God in convents.[105]

Dietenberger's conclusive concession is to allow those who have been forced into the convents to leave them with the help of secular and ecclesiastical authorities, and to "devote themselves to another respectable state" (*sich in einen anderen erlichen standt ergeben*; c1r).

Other publications of the 1520s reacted more indirectly to the debate, e.g. Johann Eck's '160 Conclusiones' in praise of the monastic life in 1527. More generally, the Catholic response centred on Luther being *meineidig* (perjurious) which was a serious crime.[106]

---

[105] *Jst es doch gůt / dz man die kinder zů got in jungen tagen ziehe / vnd sie lasz bey den frummen kloͤsterleüten in züchten / tugenten / lere / vnd gotszforcht ertzogen werden [...]. Also sol man kein junge knaben oder toͤchter hindern / gott in den kloͤstern zů dienen* (b4v).

[106] With thanks to Edmund Wareham for these references.

2. The Afterlife of the Debate on Marriage

The break with the Catholic Church required the emerging Protestant denomination to set up new legal and administrative structures, leading to the establishment of the consistory as the authority governing ecclesiastical matters in Wittenberg in 1539.[107] It gradually took shape, with Protestant scholars of law and theology, notably Philipp Melanchthon, contributing to the debate. The rulers of the German principalities and duchies held the most power within this new ecclesiastical institution, including the power to confirm or reject any appointment to the consistory. Moreover, the consistories remained largely separate from the secular courts with only occasional overlaps in their areas of jurisdiction, suggesting that the new consistories were not intended to replace the authority of the existing secular courts.

In respect of matters relating to marriage, the Wittenberg consistory was granted jurisdiction over decisions on the lawfulness of marriage vows, advice and support for wrongfully deserted spouses, marital strife, adultery, impregnation of virgins, incest, public usury, violence of children against their parents, infanticide, mockery of the Gospel, and associating with Jewish men and women in secret.[108]

After Luther's death in 1546, Protestant scholars were eager to formulate a consistent Lutheran doctrine. However, this proved difficult because Luther had left no specific constitution for the Protestant denomination. His texts, especially on marriage, did not form a continuous series and thus did not lend themselves easily to the development of a foundational doctrine. Essays and treatises by later scholars attempted to systematize the essence of Luther's theology which led to a rather complex set of elaborate caselaw.[109]

---

[107] See Appold (1999: 195) and Lück (1999: 161).
[108] Lück (1999: 165).
[109] Appold (1999: 196).

A prominent text representing this shift from Luther's case-by-case approach to questions of marriage and vows towards a more doctrinally established form of Lutheranism are the *Loci Theologici* ('Theological Premises') by Johann Gerhard (1582–1637), a theologian from the University of Jena. The seventh volume (1620) is dedicated to marriage, developing and defending Luther's views on marriage. In particular, Gerhard elaborates on how marriage is simultaneously a religious and a secular institution. He argues that it is the act of mutual agreement in public that makes marriage a (legal) matter of the world, while he stresses that husbands and wives are also partners in piety and prayer, and are supposed to support each other and share the burdens of life as well as rejoicing in its happiness together. Gerhard describes and explains the "ultimate purpose of marriage" in God's creation (*De causa finali conjugii*).[110] Gerhard's comprehensive texts on marriage include a defence of sexual intimacy. Like Luther, he is prepared to see it as a natural disposition which can be kept in check and moderation in marriage, preventing 'fornication'.[111]

Luther's views continued to cause controversy; a particularly elaborate set of Catholic counter-arguments to Luther's 'Ursache und Antwort' was conceived by Alois Merz (1727–1792), an anti-Protestant as well as anti-Enlightenment Catholic theologian, in a 1765 pamphlet 'Frag, Ob D. Luther nicht unverantwortlich gehandelt, da er die Mönche und Nonnen zur Ehe angehalten hat' (Enquiry as to whether Dr Luther May Have Acted Irresponsibly in Urging Monks and Nuns to Marry). The text corroborates the Catholic doctrine of the sanctity of monastic life. Merz accuses Luther of leading the people into temptation by luring them away from Catholicism and, in particular, from monastic vows. He argues that these vows could evidently be kept, as shown by the lives of many holy people in religious orders before his time: "I can fathom it all the less because it must have been possible for the Reformer himself,

---

[110] See *Loci Theologici* VII, 613–636.

[111] Appold (1999: 194).

who lived without being married until the forty-fourth year of his age."[112]

Looking at this line of male theologians and their writings, whether Protestant or Catholic, could lead to the assumption that monasticism right in the 1520s had become the clear denominational dividing line. However, the reality of life in convents and religious communities developed in a far more complex and nuanced way than Protestant historiography and Catholic stereotypes alike were prepared to admit.[113] There was a certain confessional fluidity with hybrid practices of permissible devotional diversity in religious houses for women in sixteenth-century Germany. Only 55% of the convents in Protestant areas closed in the early years of the Reformation; of those which made it to 1555, 63.4% (213 of 336) survived to 1590.[114]

The nuns of the Lüneburg convents, who equally eloquently wrote about the institution of marriage in paradise and their own wish to be married only to Christ (and vigorously defended their right to do so in well-endowed convents without secular interference from the local duke or town council) were successful in their fight for a self-determined life as a religious community – and they remain there to this day, extant as 'Protestant convents'.

---

[112] Merz (1765: 8): *ich fasse es um so weniger, weil es dem Reformator selbst hat muͤssen moͤglich seyn, indem er bis in das ein und vierzigste Jahr seines Alters ehelos gelebt hat.*
[113] See Lähnemann (2016).
[114] See Plummer (2022).

2. The Publications

The media pressures of the time necessitated the production of pamphlets and treatises to provide rapid responses to contemporary events and publications. Luther's growing prominence as a publicist coincided with a peak in production between 1520 and 1525, and his name was already being used as a marketing device, as was the reference to Wittenberg as the place of printing of his pamphlets, although these labels were also used on pirated copies to increase sales.[1]

Luther used a variety of short publication formats as the basis of his pamphlets, which he refers to using the word *büchlin* (literally 'booklet'; as in *Reason and Justification,* a2v).[2] A steady stream of his German sermons appeared, beginning with the German version of the 95 Theses as 'Sermon von Ablass und Gnade' (1518).[3] Increasingly, as in 'Ursache und Antwort', Luther used open letters as a framework in which he could argue more polemically against the shortcomings of ecclesiastical politics, most prominently in his 'Sendbrief vom Dolmetschen'. Luther wrote that he preferred shorter publications to larger book formats to enable his writings to reach a wider audience: *I only make short sexterns*[4] *and German sermons for illiterate laypeople*, and followed this statement with a slightly condescending comment on other learned clergymen: *Whether producing large and numerous*

---

[1] See Kaufmann (2022: 83–85).

[2] The NHG expression *Flugschrift* (literally 'flying text' i.e. not bound into covers) is a loan translation (alongside *fliegendes Blatt*, *fliegende Schrift*) from French feuille volante (dwds.de s.v.) and seems to be referenced no earlier than in the second half of the eighteenth century (see Schwitalla, Johannes: Flugschrift. Max Niemeyer: Tübingen 1999, 2–4).

[3] See Sermon von Ablass und Gnade. Sermon on Indulgences and Grace. 95 Theses. Eds. Howard Jones, Martin Keßler, Henrike Lähnemann, and Christina Ostermann. Taylor Institution Library: Oxford 2018. https://editions.mml.ox.ac.uk/editions/ablassgnade5/

[4] In bookbinding: a quire of "six gathered sheets folded in two for binding together", OED, s.v.

books is an art form and conducive to improving Christendom, I will leave to others to decide.[5]

Small Reformation pamphlets were a good business model for the printers, as is apparent in the Wittenberg 'Deutung der zwo greulichen Figuren', for which demand was so high that it was simultaneously printed on two presses.[6] The Erfurt printer Wolfgang Stürmer's 'Mönchkalb' edition developed as the result of a serialisation of the two aforementioned monster-related pamphlets. Such short texts did not need a large and well-equipped workshop and could be printed on demand as and when required.

In general, the latest contemporary controversies contributed to an increase in printed products and the speed of (re-)production. "Delayed reactions were tantamount to admitting inferiority and leaving the field clear for the competition."[7] The interest in Reformation ideas and the theological conflict they provoked was continually shared and extended beyond the initial reception in scholarly circles to a wider audience including preachers and clergymen, who, in turn, brought these ideas to the general public. The reception of Luther's texts became more widespread after he decided to produce bilingual publications of the same text in Latin and German, before turning almost exclusively to the vernacular, of which the 1523 pamphlets are a prime example. This was combined with an effort to write idiomatically in German, a stance which he emphatically defended in his 'Sendbrief vom Dolmetschen' (1530). The Bodleian Library holds a make-shift autograph booklet of Luther's in octavo format, small enough to carry around in a pocket, in which he collected

[5] On the deeds of kindness '*Von den guten werckenn*', WA 6, 203: *ich mach nur kleyn sexternlin und deutsche prediget fur die ungeleretenn leyenn.* [...] *Ob grosz und vil bucher machen kunst sey und besserlich der Christenheit, lasz ich andere richtenn.* See also Schwitalla 1999: 3.

[6] See Introduction 2.1.1. below.

[7] Kaufmann 2022: 11. "Verzögertes Reagieren grenzte an das Eingeständnis von Unterlegenheit und bedeutete, dem Gegner das Feld zu überlassen."

phrases, sayings, and proverbs which he then could use for writing in easily accessible and memorable German.[8]

The language of publication, Latin or German, was a choice that – to a certain extent – determined the breadth of reception of Luther's writings. It was customary for scholars to write their works in Latin, which limited their reception to a relatively small audience trained in classical languages. Even vernacular texts were drafted according to Latinate principles of rhetoric.

The successful circulation of German-language texts was based on pamphlets not simply being *read* but *read out*,[9] meaning that these pamphlets reached a far greater percentage of the population, particularly in towns, than those who could read (ca. 5% in towns, 1% overall).[10] The language of each pamphlet was tailored to different regional dialects, with *Reason and Justification* being published in Central and Upper German dialect forms as well as a Low German version.[11]

Pamphlets and sermons were also used as drafting material for other sermons by Protestant ministers – and referenced by Luther's opponents, e.g. Johannes Eck (1486–1543) and Johann Tetzel (1465–1519). Johann Dietenberger (1475–1537) challenged Luther's *Reason and Justification* in a pamphlet entitled 'Antwort, dass Jungfrauen die Klöster und klösterliche Gelübde nimmer göttlich verlassen mögen' (Justification Why It Never Pleases God that Nuns Abandon Their Convents and Vows) (1523). Each paragraph cites passages from Luther's pamphlet, which Dietenberger refers to as *lies*. Dietenberger's text was originally written in Latin, with the translator, Johannes Cochläus (1479–1552), stating in a short preface and dedication that

---

[8] Bodleian Library, MS. Add. A. 92, edited in WA 51, discussed in: Alexander Peplow's blogpost.

[9] See Introduction 3 below.

[10] See Schwitalla 1999: 27 and the research referenced there.

[11] See Introduction 3 for the dialect markers in this Wittenberg edition.

he “as a consolation translated into German a good and respectable pamphlet, well-founded on written sources”.[12]

Bilingual publishing[13] was practised on both sides. Luther repeatedly used a form of ‘co-publication’ of two versions of a text to cater for both the public interest in the vernacular and for scholarly use, cf. for example the ‘Sermon von Ablass und Gnade’ (Sermon on Indulgences and Grace, 1518), ‘Von der Freiheit eines Christenmenschen’ (1520) and ‘Passional Christi und Antichristi’ (Passional of Christ and Antichrist, 1521) with different paratexts. He sometimes reworked the texts for his German editions to provide more clarity. Moreover, the form and structure of his early German texts were still indebted to the Latin rhetorical tradition before he succeeded in establishing a distinctly German style of writing.

This can be seen in the pamphlets ‘Mönchkalb’ and ‘Ursache und Antwort’, both of which were intended for a German-speaking audience. Luther even urged Philipp Melanchthon to adapt to a less Latinate style of writing for their joint publication of the two monsters in ‘Deutung der zwo greulichen Figuren’.

Conceived as German texts, these were intended for a ‘local’ rather than a ‘global’ audience. However, the vernacular audience in question would certainly have been wider, whereas the number of readers participating in global or Latinate reception would have been comparatively limited.

Luther eventually dominated the entire German-speaking book market due to the amount of his reprinted texts, and spread into other European countries with his Latin writings and, shortly afterwards, some translations into vernacular languages. However, his opponents

---

[12] Dietenberger Johann / Cochläus, Johannes: *Antwort das Junckfrawen die kloͤster vnd kloͤsterliche gelübt nümer goͤtlich verlassen moͤgen.* Strasbourg 1523, a1v: *zů trost verteütscht ein gůt redlich vnd mit schrifften wol gegründt büchlin.*

[13] See for example Bubenheimer (2021: xxv –xxxii).

only achieved meagre print runs, rarely exceeding regional circulation. Therefore, it became increasingly difficult for them to find printers willing to publish their texts.[14]

1. 'Mönchkalb'

Martin Luther's works became a European success thanks to their Latin versions. Many texts were either originally conceived in Latin or published more or less simultaneously in both languages, such as 'Von der Freiheit'. Whilst 'Ursache und Antwort' was never translated into Latin, the 'Mönchkalb' – as the second panel of the monster diptych – was incorporated into the second volume of Luther's complete works, printed in the year of his death, without naming the translator who added a number of scholarly elements to the text. This collection underwent a number of editions. Indeed, there are no fewer than eleven copies of the Latin version in Oxford: seven from 1551, three from 1562, and the Taylorian copy from 1572.

One of the early editions formed the basis for the French translation printed by Crespin in Geneva in 1557 and combined with a further anti-papal treatise. The French version, in turn, formed the basis of the English version of 1579 which added a translator's preface stressing both the apocalyptic and anti-papal aspects of the monsters.

1. German editions

The following copies of 'Papstesel' and 'Mönchkalb' are in Oxford:

1. The pamphlet was first published as a double-bill with Melanchthon's interpretation of the pope-donkey in Wittenberg. One of the Bodleian copies belongs to the first print-run of the first edition (A1), which can be spotted on the title-page, since the place name 'Freiberg' is spelled with a lower case letter. It shows further signs of being printed hastily; some of the letters are fairly faint whilst the

[14] Kaufmann (2022: 111).

frame is printed too dark, and some smudges and traces of offset are visible on a2v. A corner of fol. a2 is torn off (Ill. 6). Both of the beasts are facing left, which is in accordance with the standard iconography of Villains moving against the direction of reading. However, the image of the monk-calf runs counter to the description of it given in the text which has it lifting up its front right leg as though preaching, while Cranach's woodcut depicts it with a raised left hoof. The direction of the pope-donkey in the woodcut is consistent with that laid out in the text which describes the front right leg as ending in an elephant hoof and the front left ending in a human hand.

> [Wittenberg: Johann Grunenberg, 1523]
> Title: Deuttung der zwo grewlichen || figuren Bapstesel zu Rom vnd Munchkalbs || zu freyberg in Meyssen funden || Philippus Melanchthon || Doct. Martinus luther. || Wittemberg
> Imprint: M. D. xxiij
> 8 fols in 4to. Quire signatures: Aij, Aiij, B, Bij, Biij
> Bodleian, Tr.Luth. 95(15). VD16 M2987.

A comparison of the Bodleian copy with other copies from the same Wittenberg workshop of Johann Grunenberg shows how high the demand for the text was. There are copies which have the identical quire B to the Bodleian copy and a newly typeset quire A, correcting typographical errors, such as by spelling Freiberg with an upper case letter; and there are other copies which retain the earlier version of quire A, but have a newly typeset quire B. This indicates that the workshop produced a second set of type in the process of printing to be able to print simultaneously on two presses, probably to meet the high demand for the monster publication.

2. The second copy in the Bodleian Library is an Augsburg reprint (D) which also shows signs of being hastily printed: the text block on b2r/v is not aligned properly, and the ink from b3v has bled through to b3r. The woodcuts have been copied from the Wittenberg editions AB, including the direction in which both beasts are facing. The copy formed part of an earlier *sammelband,* as the red leather tab shows.

[Augsburg: Heinrich Steiner, 1523]
Title: Deüttung der || Zwů grewlichen figuren Bapst- || esels zů Rom vñ Münchkalbs zů Frey- || berg jn Meyssen funden || Philippus Melanchthon || Doct. Martinus Luther. || Wittemberg
Imprint: M. D. xxiij
8 fols in 4to. Quire signatures: Aiij, B, Bij, Biij
Bodleian, Tr.Luth. 26 (66). VD16 M2980.

3. The Taylorian edition 'a' of the 'Mönchkalb' was the first to be issued as a stand-alone edition, with the 'Papstesel' also issued by the same Erfurt printer, Wolfgang Stürmer, who specialised in affordable popular editions of vernacular texts.[15] His monk-calf is a mirror-image of that depicted in the Wittenberg editions. This could be explained as a common effect when doing cheap reprints which copy an earlier version without paying attention to the effect on direction. However, in this case, it is more likely the result of a close reading of the description, since it produces the desired effect of having the calf lift its right 'arm' rather than the left one as described on 3v: "Thirdly, the calf has the overall posture of a preacher: it is […] lifting its right paw as a preacher raises his right hand, and is pulling its left one towards itself, throwing up its head, its tongue showing in its mouth, and it is fashioned in every respect as if it were standing and preaching." The donkey in the separate twin edition retained the correct original position with a human left hand and looking to the left. All following editions keep the pairing accordingly: the calf gesturing with the right hand to the right, the donkey facing left.

[Erfurt: Wolfgang Stürmer, 1523]
Title: Deuttung der grewlichen figur des || Munchkalbs tzu Freyberg in || Meyssen gfunden. || D. Martin. Luther.
4 fols in 4to. No quire signatures
Taylor Inst. Library, ARCH.8°.G.1523(8). VD 16 L 4424

[15] See Ristic (2023) for an in-depth analysis of the print features, watermark, and typographical features of the Taylorian copy.

The Taylorian copy belongs to the numerous Reformation pamphlets bought in 1878 on behalf of Friedrich Max Müller from the University Library.[16]

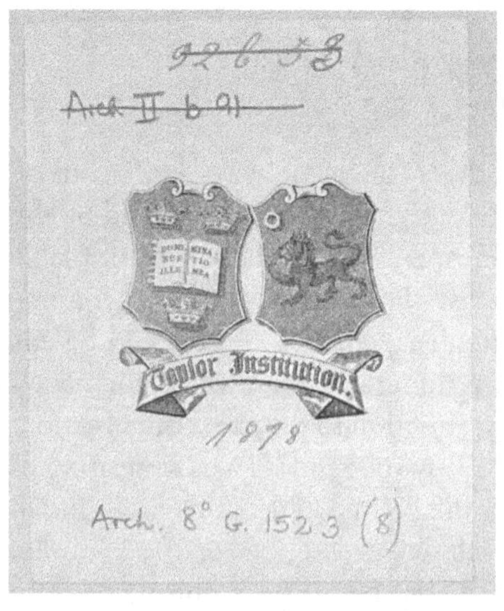

Ill. 10: The succession of Taylorian shelfmarks on the copy of the 'Mönchkalb'
92 b. 53 (also on the cover)
Arch II b 9
Arch.8°.G.1523(8)

It is a special case in that it has an identical twin which remained in Heidelberg. Both copies of the same Erfurt edition were once part of the library of the Cistercian Abbey of Salem which was only dissolved in 1802, with the library falling to the Duke Ludwig von Baden and being sold by him in 1826/27.[17] This is the rather astonishing case of two copies of this strongly anti-monastic pamphlet being circulated, heavily used and then integrated into the library of a working library of a Catholic house, with annotations in all probability being made by users there such as the contemporary manicule. It is an interesting thought that it might have been one of the Cistercians in Salem who drew in the pointer to the underlined phrase "it is not possible that such a large group should all be chaste".

---

[16] See Krümpelmann (2020: xl), Lähnemann (2022: xlif) on the acquisition policy.
[17] See the documentation of the 'Bibliotheca Salemitana – digital' by UB Heidelberg.

schen sind eben als yr/vnd ia so hartt verpunden sind/dem
natturlichen orden alß alle ander/vnd nicht müglich ist/dz
ein solch grosse mengen/soltē keusche odd willigklich Junck
frawen seyn. Jch wil das meine thân vnnd euch alle gewar
net habenn.

Ill. 11: Manicule on Taylor Inst. Library, ARCH.8°.G.1523(8), 4v

It must have been a Heidelberg librarian who marked up the twin pamphlets with pencil as 'Sal. 33, 13b', just distinguishing them by underlining the 'b' once in the copy which remained in Heidelberg and twice in the one put up for sale – presumably because it was the grubbier copy with worn-away corners and the afore-mentioned manicule, additions which actually increase its interest as cultural object for studying.

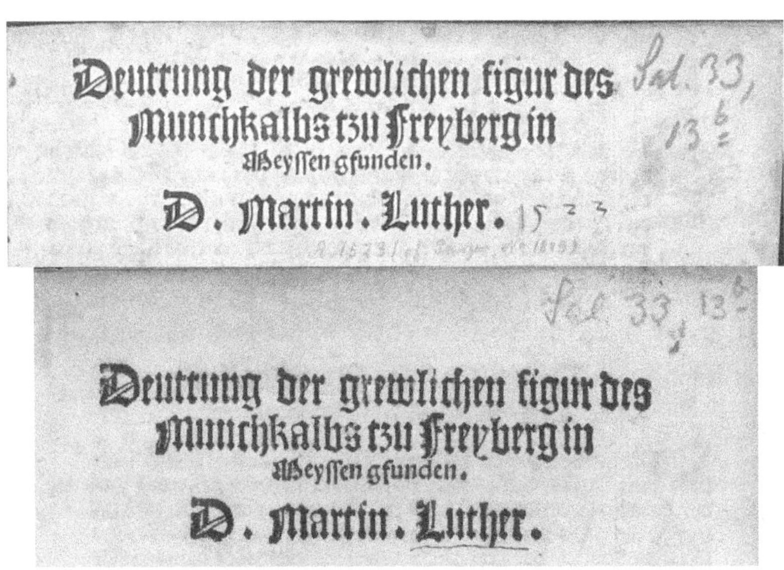
Deuttung der grewlichen figur des Munchkalbs tzu Freyberg in Meyssen gfunden.
D. Martin. Luther.

Deuttung der grewlichen figur des Munchkalbs tzu Freyberg in Meyssen gfunden.
D. Martin. Luther.

Ill. 12: Above: Taylor Inst. Library, ARCH.8°.G.1523(8)
Below: UB Heidelberg, Salem 72,4/A RES VD16 M 2984

Salem also had a copy of the companion-piece, the broadside version of the 'Papstesel' by Wolfgang Stürmer who simply used the same simplified woodcut twice, on 1r and 1v, the two sides of the sheet.

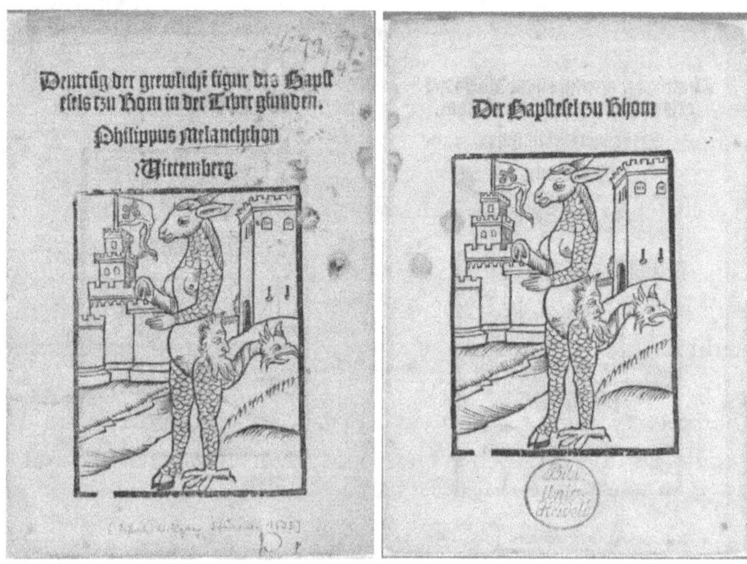

Ill. 13: The same simplified pope-donkey woodcut used twice by the Erfurt printer
UB Heidelberg, Salem 72,4/A RES VD16 M 2984

4. Finally, the Taylorian also holds a copy of the later stand-alone edition of the Pope-Donkey, edition 'δ' (see Ill. 3). Philipp Melanchthon had made substantial additions to the text and Martin Luther had added half a sheet (c1 and c2) confirming this, which, on the titlepage, is referred to as his 'Amen' in which he further stressed their anti-papal reading of the sign. This expanded the pamphlet from one to three full quires. The woodcut is a very close copy of the older Wittenberg editions. The border in the Taylorian copy is broken in several places, which shows that it had already seen heavy usage despite being a replacement woodcut.

Wittenberg: Nickel Schirlentz, 1535
Title: Der BapstEsel durch || M. Philippum Melach-||thon gedeutet vnd || gebessert. || Mit D. Mart. Luth. Amen. || Wittemberg
Imprint: 1535
10 fols in 4to. Quire signatures Aij, Aiij, B, Bij, Biij, C, Cij
Taylor Inst. Library, ARCH.8°.G.1535(9). VD16 M 2990

2. Latin editions (1545, 1551, 1562)

The 'Mönchkalb' was presumably translated into Latin specifically for the Collected Works by Martin Luther which first came out directly after his death. They present Luther as a scholar and theologian of European standing. This is apparent in the learned apparatus added into the text with printed marginalia, occasional use of Greek terms such as ἐξηγητής for the German word *deutter* (interpreter, 2r). The basis for the text is the expanded version of the double-bill from 1535, which combined the extended 'Papstesel' including Martin Luther's 'Amen' with the 'Mönchkalb'. The two monsters are, apart from the title-page, the only woodcuts in the volume. The different ratio of the pages in the folio format of the massive volumes prompted a reformatting of the woodcut (18.2×11.2cm), one and a half times higher than the Erfurt 'Mönchkalb' (12.2×9.3cm) whilst only slightly enlarging the width of the textblock. The calf now has nearly human proportions, with longer legs and a stretched body; background elements have been removed to focus completely on the towering figure. These proportions remain the same throughout the different editions of the Collected Works, with nearly identical new woodcuts being used for later editions.

No copy of the first edition of Martin Luther's Latin works appears to be in Oxford. The second edition was issued in 1551:

> Wittenberg: Erben von Peter Seitz, 1551
> Tomus secundus omnium operum reuerendi domini Martini Lutheri doctoris theologiae, … VVitebergae
> Imprint: M.D.LI
> Title: Interpretatio Mo-||nachouituli Monstri Fri-||bergae editi: || Per || Martinum Lutherum. fol. 399r–401v
> 597 leaves in folio. fol. 396v–398v.
> Balliol College Library, St Cross – 540 e 2
> Jesus College Library, F.15.10.
> Worcester College Library, Special Collections – D.3.4

TOMVS
SECVNDVS OMNIVM
OPERVM REVERENDI DOMINI MARTI-
ni Lutheri, Doctoris Theologiæ, continens monu-
menta, quæ de multis grauissimis controuersijs
ab anno xx. usque ad xxvij. annum
edita sunt.

CATALOGVM AVTEM SINGVLARVM
partiū inuenies in fine huius Voluminis. Ac series operū osten-
det paulatim plures controuersias, ab hostibus Euangelij motas,
Luthero præbuisse occasionem plures errores taxandi. Initio
doctrina de iustificatione patefacta est, quæ hic sepe repeti-
tur. Deinde accesserunt Disputationes de usu Sacramentorum
de potestate Ministrorum Euangelij, de applicatione Cœnæ
Domini, de discrimine legum diuinarum & ceremoniarum
humanarum, de uotis. Hæ tam uariæ controuersiæ
in hoc Volumine continentur, quarum
explicatio ualde illustrat Euan-
gelium.

VVITEBERGÆ
EXCVDEBAT LAVRENTIVS
SCHVVENCK,
ANNO M. D. LXII.

Ill. 14: Taylor Inst. Library, U.S.R.2.D. v. 2

The third edition was issued eleven years later by a different printer. Like its predecessors, it is a monument of presenting Martin Luther as the new church-father, kneeling together with the Elector of Saxony beneath the crucifix and the symbols of the four evangelists in the title-border.

> Wittenberg: Lorenz Schwenk, 1562
> Tomus secundus omnium operum Reuerendi Domini Martini Lutheri Doctoris Theologiæ, continens monumenta, quæ de multis grauissimis controuersijs ab anno xx. usque ad xxvij. annum edita sunt
> Imprint: M.D.LXII
> Title: *Interpretatio Mo-||nachouituli Monstri Fri-||bergae editi: || Per || Martinum Lutherum.* fol. 399r–401v
> 512 leaves in folio.
> All Souls' College Library, Great Lib. Gallery – w.infra 1.2
> Christ Church Library, Special Collections – G.3.4.2
> Lincoln College Library, Senior Library – L.6.10
> Magdalen College Library, Old Library – Q.8.6
> Merton College Library, Restricted Access – 87.G.2
> St John's College Library, M.1.17
> Taylor Inst. Library, U.S.R.2.D. v. 2
> The Queen's College Library, Upper Library – 64.D.11
> University College Library, Rare Books – G.26.2

The Taylorian copy, which formed the basis for the text quadrilingual edition, actually was also once part of a college library since it has a 'cancelled' stamp from Christ's College Cambridge on the title-page.

The number of copies in Oxford speaks to the interest across Europe following the continental debate and having up-to-date information on controversial issues during the course of the 16th century.

INTERPRETATIO MO- 399
nachouituli Monſtri Fri-
bergæ editi:

Per

Martinum Lutherum.

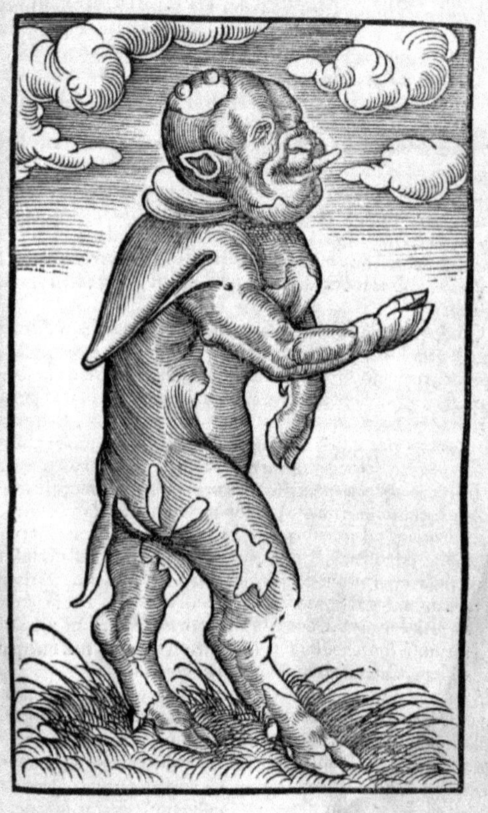

Xx iij PRO.

Ill. 15: The elongated monk-calf. Taylor Inst. Library, U.S.R.2.D. v. 2, fol. 399r.

3. French edition (1557)

The French edition is part of a composite publication with another Protestant treatise. The translator, possibly Jean Crespin himself, probably used the first Latin edition of 1545 since, on p. 33, he writes of the *voix tresclaire* (very clear voice) of the Gospel which translates *clarissima vox* of the first edition, a free rendering of the original *helle warheitt deß Euangeli* (2r, the bright truth of the Gospel), rather than the later *charissima vox* (dearest voice). The oblong proportions of the woodcut from the Latin edition (see Ill. 13) are retained despite the return to the quarto format, typical for the pamphlet format (see Ill. 2a). This leads to the calf bumping its head on the upper woodcut border and being overall much more tightly framed.

> Philipp Melanchthon and Martin Luther
> [Geneva]: Chez Iean Crespin
> Title: De deux monstres prodigieux, à savoir, D'un Asne-Pape, qui fut trouué à Rome en la riuiere du Tibre, l'an M.CCCC.XCVI. et D'un Veau-moine nay à Friberg en Misne, l'an M.D.XXVIII. … Avec quelques exemples des iugemens de Dieu en la morte espouantable, & desespoir de plusieurs, pour auoir abandonné la verité de l'Euangile
> 87 fols in 4to. Quire signatures A-L^4.
> New College Library BT1.17.6(1)

This formed the basis for the following translation into English.

4. English edition (1579)

The English version was translated 'out of French', as John Brooke 'of Assh, next Sandwich' states on the title-page. He adds a preface stressing the apocalyptic and anti-papal elements of the text, but does not take over any of the additional French text. The woodcut has been returned to the squarish format of the German edition which leads to the calf being squashed by the woodcut borders on all sides (18.2×11.2cm). Since the monk-calf is placed on a verso-page, this has the nearly comic effect of making the text on the right hand side look like the speech of the monster whose right hoof, interpreted by Luther as lifted for preaching, points directly to the initial 'A' which starts the text with *As touching*.

Ill. 16: The *Moonkish Calfe* with its cowl-like neck-flap and patchy skin
Bodleian Library, Douce B subt. 268, fol. 11v/12r

London: Thomas East, dwelling by Paules Wharfe, 1579
Title: Of two Woonderful Popish Monsters, to wyt, Of a Popish Asse which was found at Rome in the river of Tyber and of a Moonkish Calfe, calved at Friberge in Misne Which are the very foreshewings and tokens of Gods wrath, against blinde, obstinate, and monstrous Papistes. Witnessed, and declared, the one by P. Melancthon, the other by Martyn Luther. Tr. by I. Brooke.
22 fols in 4to. Bodleian Library, Douce B subt. 268

The Bodleian copy shows signs of heavy use. It has a ownership mark by Rev. Henry White of Lichfield (1762–1836)[18] who wrote his name, the acquisition date 11 November 1818 and the remark 'extra rare' on a front flyleaf; he or Francis Douce (1757–1834), via whose collection it came to the Bodleian, was probably responsible to repairs which closed a large tear on b1r and drew the missing part of the damaged woodcut initial in ink; other pages were backed with additional paper and ink marginalia have been partly cleaned off but are still visible on the front and final page. The translator's preface from another copy of the same edition is bound into the New College copy of the French edition.

2. 'Ursache und Antwort'

Nine versions of 'Ursache und Antwort' are currently known to exist. A1[19], of which the Taylorian copy, the basis for our edition, is an example, was printed by Lucas Cranach the Elder and Christian Döring in Wittenberg. This was obviously put out in great haste since press corrections resulted in *A2*, of which a copy is in the Bodleian Library. This corrected a number of typographical errors, the most noticeable being on the title page of *A1*, where *Vrsach* had been spelled with a final *b* instead of *h*, but kept the type standing, and *B*, a newly typeset edition which corrected several further typographical errors whilst keeping the same title border, ornamented pillars with floral decoration, and cherubs holding leaf-shaped empty shields. Further editions were printed in Erfurt by Matthes Maler (*C*) and Ludwig Trutebul (*D*); in Augsburg by Heinrich Steiner (*E*) (VD 16 L 6882), another edition of which the Bodleian holds a copy, and Siegmund Grimm (*F*); and in Basel by Adam Petri (*G*). Furthermore, a Low German edition (*H*) was published by Melchior Lotter in Wittenberg.

[18] Dates according to his memorial in Lichfield Cathedral on https://epigraphs.net/.
[19] Sigla are based on the *Weimarer Ausgabe* of Luther's works, WA 11, 389–91.

The following copies of 'Ursache und Antwort' are in Oxford:

1. The Taylorian copy of A1 forms the basis for this edition (see facsimile); it has torn bottom right-hand corners, an ink note *Taylor Institution 1876* above the title woodcut, the old shelfmark *91.a.5^{bb}* in pencil below the border, a rust stain on the title page, and a manicule on a1v:

> Wittenberg [: Cranach and Döring] 1523
> Title: Vrsacb.[!] vnd antt=||wort. das iungk=||frawē. kloster. got=|||lich. v̉lassen mugē.|| Doctor Martin⁹ || Luther. || Wittemberg.
> Imprint: M.D.xxiij.
> 6 fols in 4to. Quire signatures: Aij, Aiij, B, Bij
> Taylor Inst. Library ARCH.8°.G.1523(34); VD 16 L 1888.[20]

2. The Bodleian copy of A2, the corrected version of the first edition, shows an ink note *94.9* below the title border, given the sequence in one of the later *sammelband* editions of Lutheran pamphlets, originally 84 bound volumes of 'Tractatus Lutherani' bought at Sotheby's in 1818, which came from a private collection in Augsburg. Tr. Luth. 94 is one of the additional volumes; the collection was expanded to 538 volumes, comprising all 2,513 published Reformation items.[21]

> Wittenberg [: Cranach and Döring] 1523
> Title: Vrsach. vnd antt=||wort. das iungk=||frawē. kloster. got=|||lich. v̉lassen mugē.|| Doctor Martin⁹ || Luther. || Wittemberg.
> Imprint: M.D.xxiij.
> 6 fols in 4to. Quire signatures: Aij, Aiij, B, Bij
> Bodleian Library, Tr. Luth. 94 (9), VD 16 L 1889.

[20] References to the *Verzeichnis der im deutschen Sprachbereich erschienenen Drucke des sechzehnten Jahrhunderts,* the modern standard reference work on sixteenth-century printed books and pamphlets from the German-speaking world, are given in the following as 'VD 16' followed by the number; online under https://gateway-bayern.de/VD16 followed by +, the first letter of the author's name, another + and the number.

[21] More on the collection history in the introduction to the 'Sendbrief vom Dolmetschen', fn. 7.

3. E is a reprint from Augsburg with a symmetrical title-border showing grotesques such as two crowned sphinxes suckling satyrs whilst cherubs dance on their backs; other cherubs are riding dolphins (Ill. 7). The title is typeset in three different-sized fonts: a large first line, a decidedly smaller second line, and then the small font also used for the body of the text. The text shows signs of having been hastily typeset, e.g. in the misspelling of 'Wittenberg' with a double-e instead of a double-t in the last line of text:

Hyemit beuilch ich euch Gott/ vñ grüſt mir ewer liebe Audi vnnd alle freŭnde ynn Chriſto/ Gegebenn zů Witeemberg am freytag inn der Oſterwochen. Anno 1 5 2 3

Ill. 17: Final paragraph of 'Ursache und Antwort' with the misspelled *Witeemberg*
Bodleian Library, Tr. Luth. 94 (9), b2r

The Bodleian copy is part of the original 84 volumes collected by Johannes Gottlob May (1754–1821), with an ink no. *N. 38* showing that it was part of a shorter *sammelband* before it became part of this collection; the later ink note *Fasc. 25.n.44* refers to this, in accordance with the Bodleian shelfmark. It also has water stains in the top right-hand corner and shows signs of having been carried folded down in the middle.

[Augsburg: Heinrich Steiner, previously attributed to Melchior Ramminger], 1523
Title: *Vrsach vnd* || *antwort. das Junck*=||*frawen. Klöster. Götlich* || *verlassen mügen.*|| *Doctor Martinus.* || *Luther.* || Wittemberg.
Imprint: *M.D.XXiij.*
6 fols in 4to. Quire signature: Aij, Aiij, B, Bij
Bodleian Library, Tr. Luth. 25 (44); VD 16 L 6882.

3. The Edition

The following is meant as a practical guide for studying early modern print publications and – preferably – for reading them aloud. Early modern German was written to be performed. Luther's audience would have had exposure to German verse and prose largely as listeners, whether through mystery plays, sermons, or public performance of the works of the 'Meistersinger'. The best approach to what may seem at first to be an impenetrable succession of clauses is therefore to read them aloud, particularly since Luther extensively argued for the importance of idiomatic expression and the 'street value' of language.

We have only lightly normalized the spelling, because the inconsistency is part of the reality of written German at the time. The short guide below is intended to help the modern reader to make sense of the facsimile and understand the transcription in order to enjoy the rhetorical flourish of Luther's style. The main rule of thumb is to pronounce the words like their modern German equivalents, regardless of differences in spelling.

1. Punctuation
   Early modern prints use full stops, brackets, question marks, and virgules as punctuation marks. The '/' Virgel (virgule or forward slash) is the main means of structuring sentences, and can stand for both a comma and a semicolon. It is best to treat a virgule like a musical caesura, to pause for breath.

2. Abbreviations
   Early prints took over from manuscripts some handy ways to save space. The main abbreviation mark is a bar (macron) over characters '–'. As a nasal bar above any letter replaces a following n such as 'warē' = waren or (mainly for Latin case endings) an m such as 'Jtē' = Item. The macron is also habitually used for 'vn̄' = und. Confusingly, the rounded z-form

'ʒ' stands both for z and for a number of established abbreviations, particularly in 'dʒ' / 'wʒ'= das / was and 'qʒ' = que. In the transcription, ʒ has been rendered as z where it stands for the affricate sound /ts/ and has been resolved where it is used as abbreviation. Occasionally a hook is used for the -er ending, e.g. 'd'' = der; this has also been resolved in the transcription.

3. u/v/w – v/f – i/j/y, and different s– and r–forms
   The Roman alphabet had only one symbol for u and v and one for i and j. u/v/w are interchangeable, as are i/j/y, and v/f are both used for f, e.g. 'vnd' = und; 'zuuor' = zuvor; 'new' = neu; 'vleissig' = fleißig; 'jch' = ich. In most cases, letters are pronounced as in the equivalent modern German word.
   The two typographically different forms for s (long ſ versus round s) and for r (the round form of r = 2 being mainly used after characters with a rounded right-hand border such as o or – in some fonts – h) in the print have not been distinguished in the transcription because they are simply graphic variations.

4. Umlauts
   The umlaut sound would have been in the same position as in modern German, but there is no strict rule for writing it. East Central German is slightly delayed in adopting secondary umlaut, but spelling of 'Räuber' as *reuber* indicates that, in 'Ursache und Antwort' A1, the umlaut was implied and that the lack of umlaut marker is due to the absence of type with superscript. This means that 'konige' = *Könige* and 'furet' = *führet*; 'vber' = *über*. In most cases, an umlaut should be used wherever one occurs in modern German.

5. Double versus single consonants and s/ß, k/ck, z/tz, r/rh, t/th
   There is no consistency in writing single and double consonants such as f/ff or n/nn, nor is there a difference in pronunciation, i.e. 'gottlich' and 'gotlich' are pronounced the same.

This also applies to s and ß (the latter started out as a ligature of long ſ and z to indicate a double consonant), to k and ck (the spelling for double k), and to z and tz. Note that z always sounds like modern German z, i.e. /ts/, not like English z. The spelling of initial r and t as rh ('verrhaten') and th ('thun') is a common feature of Humanist writing, inspired by the transliteration of Greek rho (ρ) and theta (θ) into German as rh and th. This spelling convention continued until 1902, when the 'h' following a 't' was dropped in all words of German origin - such as *das Thier,* which became *das Tier* (animal) - as part of a drive for standardized spelling across the constituent states of the German Empire of 1871–1918. Again, almost all consonants can be pronounced like their modern German equivalents.

6. Use of h and e after vowels; long and short vowels
   While in medieval German each letter would have been sounded, e.g. 'lieb' would have had a diphthong in the middle, 'e' after other vowels had become silent in the sixteenth century. This is evident from the use of e after i where there never was a diphthong, e.g. the word 'diesen'. The same applies to h. In most instances a following e or h indicates a long preceding vowel, but this is not consistent, e.g. 'jhm' can stand both for modern *im* and *ihm*. Do not therefore pronounce h and e after vowels, but use long vowels as in modern German.

7. Word division and 'Zusammenschreibung'
   Hyphens in the form of '=' are used frequently but not consistently to indicate the continuation of words across line-breaks; if typesetters ran out of space in a line, they would assume that the reader would be able to link words without this visual prompt. Clear single words have been joined in the transcription, e.g. 'od|der' as 'odder', but the irregular use of spaces between compounds such as 'lester meuler(n)' for

Lästermäuler and 'eraus (tzu) komen' for heraus(zu)kommen has not been normalized.

8. Capital letters
   Capital letters are used as in English to indicate the beginning of new sentences and for proper names but also for emphasis in words such as 'Nonnen', 'Ebte' or 'Ergernis'; these have not been normalized since they highlight key terms.

9. Syncope, apocope, and contraction
   Unstressed vowels are sometimes absent where we should expect them in NHG, either mid-word (syncope), e.g. 'gsagt', 'gnug', or at word-end (apocope), e.g. 't(h)u', 'sach' (note that the opposite also happens, e.g. 'bedrenget', 'gehet'). Such vowel loss can cause confusion, e.g. 'gelob(e)t', which looks like a present, may stand for the preterite 'gelob(e)te'. Sometimes a consonant is lost along with a vowel, especially a repeated consonant, e.g. 'laut' for 'lautet', 'veracht' for 'verachtet', 'verstorben' for 'verstorbenen'. Vowel loss also occurs by contraction between words, e.g. 'ers' for 'er es', 'nympts' for 'nimmt es', 'zun' for 'zu den'.

10. Zero inflections and absence of ge- prefixes
    Some neuter plurals have a zero-inflection in ENHG and look like singulars, e.g. 'das/die werk', 'das/die wort'. Strong adjectives in the nominative and accusative singular could also be zero-inflected, e.g. 'ein solch fein hubsch new deutsch Testament', 'solch vnleidlich tyranney'. The past participles of some ENHG verbs may be formed without the ge- prefix, notably komen, troffen, gangen (and its compounds), geben, and (even outside the passive) worden.

11. Omission of auxiliaries and personal subject pronouns
    The auxiliaries haben and sein are sometimes omitted, especially in subordinate clauses, e.g. 'damit er … nichts dauon gesagt' (NHG gesagt hat), 'das die kinder zuuorn selbs yhr

Eldern vnd freundschafft [....] mit vernunfftigen gnugsamen vrsachen angetzeygt' (NHG angezeigt haben). Personal pronouns are also sometimes left out where they would appear in NHG, e.g. 'Vnd werden doch ynn den hohisten kampf gestellet' (NHG Und sie werden in den höchsten Kampf gestellt'.

Sample transcription

Ill. 18: 'Ursache und Antwort', first paragraph of a2r

¶ Hie werdet yhr aber mal ſagen/ Das iſt warlich
heymlich gehallten vnd wol verporgen/ ia verrhaten
vñ verkaufft/ das auff mich erhetzet werde das gantze
kloſter tzu Nymptzſchen/ weyl ſie nu horen/ das ich der
reuber geweßen byn. Antwortt ich ia freylich eyn ſe=
liger reuber/ gleich wie Chriſtus eyn reuber war yñ der wellt/
da er durch ſeynen todt dem Furſten der wellt/
ſeynen harnſch vnd haus geredt nam [...]

The equivalent modern German text with normalized punctuation, capitalization, no abbreviations, and umlaut:

Hier werdet Ihr abermal sagen: Das ist wahrlich heimlich gehalten und wohl verborgen, ja verraten und verkauft, dass auf mich erhetzt wird das ganze Kloster zu Nimbschen, weil sie nun hören, dass ich der Räuber gewesen bin! Ich antworte: ja, freilich, ein seliger Räuber, gleich wie Christus ein Räuber war in der Welt, als er durch seinen Tod dem Fürsten der Welt seinen Harnisch und Hausgerät nahm [...].

4. Bibliography

The bibliography is a combination of full references for short titles used in the footnotes of the introduction and some general introductory books. This is obviously not exhaustive and is designed mainly for anglophone students of historical linguistics.
Further resources are available at the Reformation editions website of the Taylor Institution Library https://editions.mml.ox.ac.uk/topics/reformation.shtml

1. Abbreviations

BBKL *Biographisch-Bibliographisches Kirchenlexikon,* ed. by Friedrich Wilhelm Bautz and Traugott Bautz. Herzberg: Verlag Traugott Bautz, 1990ff (Online available as https://bbkl.de).

DWB *Deutsches Wörterbuch*, ed. by Jacob Grimm and Wilhelm Grimm, Leipzig: Hirzel 1854–1961.

DWDS *Digitales Wörterbuch der deutschen Sprache*. https://www.dwds.de/

LStA *Martin Luther: Studienausgabe*, ed. by Hans-Ulrich-Delius. Berlin 1979–1999.

NDB *Neue deutsche Bibliographie.*

PL *Patrologia Latina.*

VD16 *Verzeichnis der im deutschen Sprachbereich erschienenen Drucke des 16. Jahrhunderts (VD 16)*: https://vd16.de (Full bibliographic reference for all Reformation pamphlets with linked-in digitized copies, continually updated; links: http://gateway-bayern.de/VD16+[letter]+[number]).

TRE *Theologische Realenzyklopädie,* ed. by Gerhard Müller. Berlin; New York: Walter de Gruyter 1976–2004 https://doi.org/10.1515/tre.

WA *Martin Luther: Werke. Kritische Gesamtausgabe* [*Weimarer Ausgabe*]. Weimar 1883ff (Comprehensive edition in original spelling).

WA.B *Martin Luther: Werke. Kritische Gesamtausgabe. Briefwechsel.*

WA.T *Martin Luther: Werke. Kritische Gesamtausgabe. Tischreden.*

Works *The Works of Martin Luther* vol. 44: *Christian in Society 1*, Charlottesville: Fortress Press 1966.

2. Primary Works

The texts are listed in chronological order, with the title in the spelling of the edition which is quoted; if they are discussed in the introduction, the chapter-number is given.

Luther, Martin: *Ein Sermon von dem elichen standt Doctoris Martini Lutter Augustiner zu wittenburgk gepredigt im tausent funfhundert vnd neuntzehenden Jar*. Leipzig: Wolfgang Stöckel, 1519. VD16 L 6310. https://editions.mml.ox.ac.uk/editions/elichenstandt/.

Luther, Martin: *Eyn Sermon von dem Elichen standt vorendert vnd corrigiret durch D. Martinum Luther Augustiner tzu Wittenberg*. Wittenberg: Johann Rhau-Grunenberg, 1519. VD16 L 6317 = WA 2, 162–171. https://editions.mml.ox.ac.uk/editions/elichenstandt2/

Luther, Martin: *Von den guten werckenn. D. M. L.*: Vuittenberg [Wittenberg]: Melchior Lotter, 1520. = WA 6, 196–276.

Luther, Martin: *An den Christlichen Adel deutscher Nation: von des Christlichen standes besserung. D. Martinus Luther. Durch yhn selbs gemehret vnd corrigirt*. Wittenberg: Melchior Lotter d. J., 1520. VD16 L 3759 / VD16 L 3760 = WA 6, 381–469 and WA 6, 484–573. [Augsburg: Melchior Ramminger 1520] Taylor Institution Library, Arch.8°.G.1520(5), VD16 L 3751.

Luther Martin: *De captivitate Babylonica ecclesiae praeludium Martini Lutheri*. Wittenberg: Melchior Lotter, 1520. VD16 L 4189 = WA 6, 484–573.

Luther, Martin: *Von der Babylonischen gefengknusz der Kirchen Doctor Martin Luthers*. [Transl. by Thomas Murner.] Strasbourg: Johann Schott, 1520. VD16 L 4195.

Luther, Martin: *Von der Freyheyt eynisz Christen menschen. Martinus Luther*. Wittenberg: Johann Rhau-Grunenberg, 1520. VD16 L 7198 = WA 7, 12–38.

Luther, Martin: *Ivdicivm Martini Lutheri de Votis, scriptum ad Episcopos & Diaconos Vuittembern[ses] Ecclesiae* [*Themata de votis*]. Wittenberg: Melchior Lotter, 1521. VD 16 L 5010 = WA 8, 313–335. Translated as *Doctoris Mar[tin] Lutther kurtz schluszrede von den gelobdten vnnd geystlichen leben der closter*. Erfurt: Matthes Maler, 1521. VD16 L 5012.

Luther, Martin: *De votis Monasticis Martini Lutheri Ivdicivm*. Wittenberg: Melchior Lotter, 1522. VD16 L 7322 = WA 8, 564–669. Translations: *Uon denn geystlichen vnd klostergelubden Martini Luthers vrteyll* (Justus

Jonas). Nickel Schirlentz: Wittemberg 1522. VD16 L 7327: https://gateway-bayern.de/VD16+L+7327. *Ein gar schon nutzlich buechlin / des hochgelerten vnd Christenlichen lerers Martini Luthers / von den gelübden der klosterlüten / ob sy ware gelübd syen vnd von wem sy ein vrsprung vnd anfang haben* (Leo Jud). Christoph Froschauer: Zürich 1523. VD16 L 7328: https://gateway-bayern.de/VD16+L+7328.

Karlstadt, Andreas: *Contra papisticas leges sacerdotibus prohibentes matrimonium, apologia pastoris Cembergensis, qui nuper suae ecclesiae consensu uxorem duxit* ['Against the Papist Laws Forbidding the Marriage of Priests, the Justification of the Pastor of Kemberg, who recently Married with the Consent of his Church'], Basel: Adam Petri, 1521. VD16 B 6100.

Karlstadt, Andreas: *Das die Priester Eeweyber nemen mögen vnd sollen* ['Why Priests Should Marry']. Strasbourg: Reinhard Beck, 1522. VD16 B 6106.

Luther, Martin: *Uom Eelichen Leben*. Wittenberg: Johann Rhau-Grunenberg, 1522. VD16 L 7032 = WA 10.2, 267–304. Taylor Institution Library, Arch.8°.G.1522(19).

Luther, Martin: *Ein Christliche und vast wol gegründete beweysung von dem Jüngsten tag*. Basel: Adam Petri, 1522. VD16 L 3931.

Melanchthon, Philipp: *Figur des Antichristlichen Bapsts und seiner Synagog* . Wittenberg: Johann Rhau-Grunenberg, 1523. VD16 F 1014.

Luther, Martin: *Dasz eine christliche versammlung odder gemeinde recht vnd macht habe, alle lehre zu urteilen vnd lehrer zu beruffen ein vnd abtzusetzen. Grund vnd Vrsach aus der Schrifft*. Wittenberg: Lukas Cranach d.Ä. / Christian Döring, 1523. VD16 L 4290.

Luther, Martin: *Von Ordnunng gotes dienst in der gemain*. Augsburg: Heinrich Steiner, 1523. VD16 L 7299.

Luther, Martin: *Das siebend Capitel S. Pauli zu den Chorinthern Ausgelegt durch Martinum Luther*. Wittenberg: Melchior Lotter, 1523. VD16 L 6683 = WA 12, 88–142.

Luther, Martin / Melanchthon, Philipp: *Deuttung der czwo grewlichen Figuren Babstesels czu Rom vnd Munchskalbs zu Freyberg ynn Meysszen funden*. Wittenberg: Johann Rhau-Grunenberg, 1523. VD16 L 4429 / M 2989 = WA 11, 357–385. See below Introduction 2.1.1. for the Bodleian copy of this edition.

Luther, Martin: *Deuttung der grewlichen figur des || Munchkalbs tzu Freyberg in || Meyssen gfunden*. (Separate edition of the second part of preceding title). Erfurt: Wolfgang Stürmer, 1523. VD 16 L 4424. Online edition by Katarina Ristic of Taylor Inst. Library, ARCH.8°.G.1523(8). Edited below 5.1. as bilingual edition with scholarly apparatus, 5.2. as quadrilingual edition, 6.1. facsimile.

Cochlaeus, Johannes: *ADVERSVS CVCVLLATVM Minotaurum Vuittembergensem*. Tübingen: Ulrich Morhart, 1523. VD16 C 4241.

Luther, Martin: *Vrsach vnd anttwortt das iungkfrawen kloster gotlich verlassen mugen*. Wittenberg: Lukas Cranach d. Ä. / Christian Döring, 1523. VD16 L 6888 = WA 11, 387–400 and edited below. See below Introduction 2.2. for the Taylorian and Bodleian copies of this edition.

Luther, Martin: *An die herren Deutschs Ordens / das sie falsche keuscheyt meyden vnd zur rechten ehlichen keuscheyt greyffen. Ermanung*. [Appeal to the Knights of the Teutonic Order to avoid false celibacy and embrace right matrimonial chastity]. Wittenberg: Johann Rhau-Grunenberg, 1523/1524. VD16 L 3779 = WA 12, 228–244.

Dietenberger, Johannes: *Antwort das Junckfrawen die klo̍ster vnd klo̍sterliche gelübt nümer go̍tlich verlassen mo̍gen*. Strasbourg: Johann Grüninger, 1523. VD16 L 6886 / VD16 L 6887.

Dietenberger, Johannes: *Doctor Joannes Dietenberger wider CXXXIX schluszrede Mar. Luthers / von gelübdnisz vnnd geistlichem leben der klosterlüt vnnd iunckfrawschafft etc. vertütscht durch Jo. Cochleum*. Strasbourg: Johann Grüninger, 1523. VD16 D 1481.

Emser, Hieronymus: *Wyder den falschgenanten Ecclesiasten / vnd warhafftigen Ertzketzer Martinum Luther*. Dresden: Emserpresse, 1524. VD16 E 1139.

Cochlaeus, Johannes: *Ein Christliche vermanung der heyligen stat Rom an das Teütschlandt*. Tübingen: Ulrich Morhart, 1524. VD16 C 4363.

Dietenberger, Johannes: *IOHANNIS DITENBERGII sacrarum literarum professoris de uotis monasticis liber secundus, editus in secundum de uotis monasticis Luteri iudicium*. Cologne: Eucharius Cervicornus, 1524. VD16 D 1479.

Luther, Martin: *Das Ellтern die kinder zur Ehe nicht zwingen noch hyndern / Vnd die kinder on der elltern willen sich nicht verloben sollen*. [That Parents shall neither compel their children to nor prevent them from marriage, and children shall not get engaged without the parents' consent]. Wittenberg: Lukas Cranach / Christian Döring, 1524. VD16 L 4301. Wittenberg: Lukas Cranach d. Ä. / Christian Döring, 1524. VD16 L 4301 = WA 15, 155–169. Taylor Institution Library, Arch.8°.G.1524(7). Open access.

Luther, Martin / Florentina von Oberweimar: *Eyn geschicht wie Got eyner Erbarn kloster Jungfrawen ausgeholffen hat. Mit eynem Sendebrief M. Luthers*. [An Account of how God helped out an Honourable Nun. With an Open Letter by M. Luther]. Wittenberg: Lukas Cranach d. Ä. / Christian Döring, 1524. VD16 O 91 / L 5911 = WA 15, 79–94.

Luther, Martin: [1525] *Ein schöner Sermon oder Predigt vonn dem Ehestand/ durch den Ehrwirdigen Vater Doctorem Martinum Lutherum/ Heiliger vnd seliger gedechtnis/ zu Wittenberg geprediget/ vormals deßgleichen nie ausgangen/ oder gedruckt worden*. [A Fine Sermon on the Estate of Marriage by the honourable Doctor Martin Luther, in holy and blessed Commemoration, held in Wittenberg, never before published or printed]. Berlin: Georg Buchholtzer, 1561. VD16 ZV 16255 = WA 17.1, 1–29. WA 17.2, 12–29; 60–70.

Luther, Martin: *Das Euangelion auff den andern Sontag nach Epiphanie. Johannis ij*. [The Gospel on the Second Sunday after Epiphany. John 2.] [Fastenpostille]. Wittenberg: Lukas Cranach d.Ä. / Christian Döring, 1525. VD16 L 3971 = WA 17.2, 60–70.

Eck, Johannes: *Ad Laudem D. O. M. ac sanctorum patrum qui vitam monasticam coluerunt, Conclusiones 160. sub Eckio Ingolstadii disputandae … De Votis*, Ingolstadt: Peter Apian / Georg Apian, 1527. VD16 E 257.

Ursula von Münsterberg: *Der Durchleuchtigen hochgebornen F. Vrsulen/ Hertzogin zu Monsterberg etc. Grefin zu Glotz etc. Christlich vrsach des verlassen Klosters zu Freyberg*. Wittenberg: Hans Luft, 1528. VD16 M 6729. Nuremberg: Georg Wachter, 1529. VD16 M 6731, Bodleian Library: Antiq.e.G.1529.1. = WA 26, 623–633.

Luther, Martin: *Von ehesachen*. Wittenberg: Hans Luft, 1530. VD16 L 7249 = WA 30, 198–248.

Melanchthon, Philipp / Luther, Martin: *De deux monstres prodigieux, à savoir d'un asne-pape qui fut trouvé à Rome en la rivière du Tibre l'an 1496, et d'un veau-moine nay à Friberg en Misne l'an 1528*. Geneva: Jean Crespin, 1557. Online edition of the second part by Ksenia Dugæva with a full facsimile of New College Library BT1.17.6(1). Edited below 5.2. as quadrilingual edition.

Melanchthon, Philipp / Luther, Martin: *De deux monstres prodigieux, à savoir d'un asne-pape qui fut trouvé à Rome en la rivière du Tibre l'an 1496, et d'un veau-moine nay à Friberg en Misne l'an 1528*. Geneva: Jean Crespin, 1557. Online edition by Elena Trowsdale with a full facsimile of Bodleian Library, Douce B subt. 268. Edited below 5.2. as quadrilingual edition.

Torgau Chronicle. *Chronik von Torgau bis zum J. 1627* – Mscr.Dresd.d.1.

Gerhard, Johann: *Locorum Theologicorum Cum Pro Adstruenda Veritate, Tum Pro Destruenda quorumvis contradicentium falsitate, per Theses nervose, solide & copiose explicatorum Tomus Septimus In quo continetur Caput 28. De Coniugio, Coelibatu & cognatis materiis. Tobias Steinmann: Jena 1620.* VD17 3:608872K.

Merz, Alois: *Frag, Ob D. Luther nicht unverantwortlich gehandelt, da er die Mönche und Nonnen zur Ehe angehalten hat. An den heiligen Osterfeyertagen beantwortet von P. Aloysio Merz.* Augsburg / Innsbruck: Joseph Wolff, 1765. VD18 14507072.

3. Secondary Literature

Appold, Kenneth G.: "Ehe und Erotik in der Theologie der lutherischen Orthodoxie." in: Treu (1999: 192–204).

Beyer, Michael: "Luthers Ehelehre bis 1525." in: Treu (1999: 59–82).

Bubenheimer, Ulrich: "Content – Sources – Author – Reception" in: Wareham & al. (2021: xx–lv).

Clemens, Dennis / Clemens, Hannah: "Introduction. The Historical and Philosophical Background." in: Jones (2020: xii–xxxviii).

Gößner, Andreas: "Nonnenklöster in Augsburg und Nürnberg – ihr Schicksal in der Reformation." in: Treu (1999: 105–112).

Jones, Howard et al: "Martin Luther: Sermon von Ablass und Gnade, 95 Thesen. Sermon on Indulgences and Grace and the 95 Theses." 2018 Open access.

Jones, Howard / Lähnemann, Henrike: "Martin Luther: Von der Freiheit eines Christenmenschen. On Christian Freedom." 2020 Open access.

Jones, Howard and Lähnemann, Henrike: "Martin Luther: Sendbrief vom Dolmetschen und Fürsprache der Heiligen. An Open Letter on Translation and Intercession of Saints." 2022 (Second edition).

Kaufmann, Thomas: "Die Druckmacher. Wie die Generation Luther die erste Medienrevolution entfesselte." Munich: C. H. Beck, 2022.

Kröker, Ernst: "Katharina von Bora. Martin Luthers Frau", Leipzig 1906.

Krümpelmann, Maximilian: "The History of the Taylorian Copies", in: Jones / Lähnemann (2020: xxxix–lxvi). Open access.

Lähnemann, Henrike: "Introduction 3: Publication", in: Jones / Lähnemann (2022: xxx–xliv).

Lähnemann, Henrike: "Der Medinger "Nonnenkrieg" aus der Perspektive der Klosterreform. Geistliche Selbstbehauptung 1479–1554", in: "1517–1545: The Northern Experience. Mysticism, Art and Devotion between Late Medieval and Early Modern. Antwerp Conference 2011", ed. Kees Scheepers et al., Ons Geestelijk Erf 87 (2016), 91–116.

Lück, Heiner: "Zur Grundlegung des evangelischen Eherechts in Wittenberg." in Treu (1999: 161–177).

Machilek, Franz: "Menschenwürde und Gewissensfreiheit. Caritas Pirckheimer und die Reformation in Nürnberg", in: Rainer Bucher et al. (eds): "In Würde leben, interdisziplinäre Studien zu Ehren von Ernst Ludwig Grasmück." Luzern (1998: 49-71).

MacKenzie, Paul (ed.): "Caritas Pirckheimer: a journal of the Reformation years", 1524-1528, Cambridge 2006.

Makowski, Elizabeth, "Apostate nuns in the later Middle Ages", Suffolk 2019.

Mühlen, Karl-Heinz "Zum biblischen Hintergrund von Luthers Freiheitsbegriff." in: "Martin Luther. Freiheit und Lebensgestaltung. Ausgewählte Texte", ed. Luther-Gesellschaft. Vandenhoeck /Ruprecht: Göttingen (1983: 7–17).

Mühlen, Karl-Heinz zur: "Taufe und Freiheit. Einleitung." in: "Martin Luther. Freiheit und Lebensgestaltung. Ausgewählte Texte", ed. Luther-Gesellschaft. Vandenhoeck / Ruprecht: Göttingen (1983: 18–20).

"Netzwerke der Nonnen. Edition und Erschließung der Briefsammlung aus Kloster Lüne", vol. 1. ed. Schlotheuber / Lähnemann, Tübingen: Mohr Siebeck, in press. Open access edition of the letters (introduction, facsimile, diplomatic transcription, critical edition and commentary) in the Digital Library of the Herzog August Bibliothek Wolfenbüttel.

Pfanner, Joseph (ed.): "Die "Denkwürdigkeiten" der Caritas Pirckheimer (Caritas Pirckheimer Quellensammlung 2)", Landshut 1962.

Plummer, Marjorie Elizabeth: "From Priest's Whore to Pastor's Wife: Clerical Marriage and the Process of Reform in the Early German Reformation", Routledge 2012. Introduction online.

Plummer, Marjorie Elizabeth: "Stripping the Veil: Convent Reform, Protestant Nuns, and Female Devotional Life in Sixteenth-Century Germany", Oxford: O.U.P., 2022.

Reich, Christa: "67 – Herr Christ, der einig Gotts Sohn", in: "Liederkunde zum Evangelischen Gesangbuch. Nr. 2.", ed. Hahn / Henkys, Göttingen: Vandenhoeck / Ruprecht, (2001: 48–54).

Ristic, Katarina: "A Monstrous Misbirth as History of the Book Project", Blogpost for the History of the Book Blog, posted 4 September 2023.

Schlotheuber, Eva: "Klostereintritt und Bildung. Die Lebenswelt der Nonnen im späten Mittelalter. Mit einer Edition des 'Konventstagebuchs' einer Zisterzienserin von Heilig-Kreuz bei Braunschweig (1484–1507). (Spätmittelalter, Humanismus, *Reformation* 24)", Tübingen: Mohr-Siebeck 2004.

Schlotheuber, Eva: "Per vim et metum – Die bitteren Klagen der Mädchen und Frauen an der römischen Kurie über ein erzwungenes Professgelübde", in: "Kirchlicher und religiöser Alltag im Spätmittelalter, Akten der internationalen Tagung in Weingarten 4.-7. Oktober 2007 (Schriften zur südwestdeutschen Landeskunde 69)", ed. Meyer, Ostfildern (2010: 165–176).

Schwitalla, Johannes: "Deutsche Flugschriften 1460–1525. Textsortengeschichtliche Studien", Max Niemeyer: Tübingen 1983.

Spinks, Jennifer: "Monstrous Births and Visual Culture in Sixteenth-Century Germany", London: Pickering / Chatto, 2009.

Treu, Martin (ed.): "Katharina von Bora. Die Lutherin. Aufsätze anläßlich ihres 500. Geburtstages", Wittenberg 1999.

Treu, Martin: "Katharina von Bora", Wittenberg: Drei Kastanien Verlag, 2016.

Wareham, Edmund et al: "Martin Luther: Passional Christi und Antichristi. Passional of Christ and Antichrist". 2021 Open access.

Wriedt, Markus: "Staupitz, Johann von", in: NDB 25 (2013), 95f.

Edition, Translation, Commentary of the 'Mönchkalb'

The edition is a semi-diplomatic transcription of *Deuttung der grewlichen figur des Munchkalbs tzu Freyberg in Meyssen gfunden*, Taylor Institution Library, ARCH. 8°.G.1523 (8), printed in 1523 by Wolfgang Stürmer in Leipzig (see Introduction 2). The paragraph structure of the pamphlet has been retained as far as possible; the page references are given as quire (the sheet folded to make up the four folios or eight pages of the quarto booklet) and folio with recto (front side) and verso (back side) e.g. the eighth page is a4v = first quire, back of the fourth folio.

The commentary to the edition consists of two sets of footnotes. Those on the edition side (left-hand pages) are not a full linguistic analysis, but are designed to help readers understand Luther's German and typographical features, comparing Early New High German (ENHG) forms with modern (NHG) usage and English parallels. The footnotes to the English translation (right-hand side) include biblical references and other background information.

The pamphlet is in a 19th century cover with a front flyleaf and a number of empty pages at the back, probably meant for notes on the pamphlet. On the upper pastedown, the shelfmark, ARCH. 8^{0}. G.1523 (8), can be found alongside the Taylor Institution crest and former shelfmarks.

(1r) Deuttung der grewlichen figur[1] des Munchkalbs tzu Freyberg in Meyssen gfunden
D. Martin. Luther.[2]

(1v) Deuttung des Munchkalbs Zu Freyberg Martin Luthers

Die Prophetische deuttung dises Munchkalbs wil ich dem geist lassen / den ich kein prophet bin / on daß gewiß ist / der gemeinen deuttung nach / yn allen wunderzeichen[3] / daß dadurch ein gros vnfall vnd verenderung zukunfftig[4] / Got tzu verstehen gibtt / der[5] sich auch gewiszlich deutschland[6] versehen mag / Welche aber die selben sei / vnd wie eß zu gehen werde / gepurt den propheten tzu sagen / Mein wundsch vnd hoffnung ist / daß der Iunst[7] tag sei. Den der zeichen biß her vil auff ein ander fallen / vnd gleich[8] alle welt in einer grossen woge steht / Die on grossen wandel nicht kan abgehn / Dartzu daß Euangelische liecht so helle auffgangen / welchem alle mall / gros verenderung / vmb der vngleubygen willen / erfolget[9] hatt

---

[1] ENHG *figur* reflects the use of Latin *figura* and means both a physical and imaginary representation of an object with symbolic meaning.

[2] Date *1523* added in the Taylorian copy by a contemporary hand.

[3] The clause *on daß … yn allen wunderzeichen* is part of a complex ENHG syntactical construction; NHG natural sentence structure would be *außer dass Gott in allen Wunderzeichen zu verstehen gibt, dass dadurch ein großer Unfall und Veränderung bevorsteht, deren sich auch….*

[4] = NHG *zukünftig*, meaning here 'about to come'.

[5] = NHG *deren*, referring back to *verenderung*.

[6] A *deuttsch land* C *deutsches land* a *deütschland* b *Teütslandt*. The concept of 'the German land' is to be taken in the same sense as in Luther's address to the princes of the 'German nation' (1520).

[7] CG *jüngst*, E *Jungs*. = NHG *Jüngster Tag*, literally 'the Last Day', i.e. the Day of Judgment or Last Judgement.

[8] = NHG *gleichsam*.

[9] = NHG *zur Folge*.

(1r) Interpretation of the gruesome figure of the monk-calf found at Freiberg in Meissen by Doctor Martin Luther

(1v) Martin Luther's Interpretation of the Monk-Calf at Freiberg

I will leave the prophetic interpretation[10] of this monk-calf to the Holy Spirit[11], for I am not a prophet, except to say that the generally accepted interpretation is that God is warning us in all miraculous signs of a great misfortune and change to come, and there is no doubt that also Germany should prepare itself for this. But what it may be and how it will take place is for the prophets to say. My wish and hope is that it is the Day of Judgement.[12] For there have been many signs one after the other and virtually the whole world is in a turmoil which, without great change, will not go away. Moreover the light of the Gospel has been dawning so brightly, and this has always been followed by an upheaval for non-believers.

---

[10] Luther is referring here to the interpretation of remarkable events as portents of woe (or even of the Last Judgement), along the lines of Pharaoh's dream of the fat and lean cows in Genesis 41. This type of interpretation was the fourth part of the four-fold interpretation of scripture and signs, in which a so-called anagogical reading was given, i.e. one foretelling things to come.

[11] Luther distances himself from this form of interpretation, typical of the spiritists, and claims to stick to the obvious literal meaning. This is, of course, a polemical device, for he goes on to do exactly what he claims not to do.

[12] For the apocalyptic tendencies in Luther's writing and the period more generally, cf. the introduction.

Ich wil nur des gewissesten geram[13] / vnd mit[14] antzeigen / warumb Got zu solchem zeichen ein munch kalb[15] genomen hat / vnd daß heilige kleid so verkerlich vnd grewlich schendet / so er doch eben so wol solch kunfftig vngluck hette durch ein wunder on munchkutten mugen angeben / Datzu nu auch zu landßberg ein pfaffenkalb hat geschaffen / vnd wil dyß iar nur mit geistlichen / heiligen wundertzeichen faren / damitt er yhe sich mercken lest / daz er deß geistlichen standen[16] sonderlich acht hat / vnd etwas ym syn hat auff die selben

Also thet er vortzeitten auch / Da er Danielis .viij. den grossen konig Alexander durch ein zigen bock ließ bedeutten. damit er anzeigt / vber die prophetische deuttung deß zukunfftigen fals / was die kriechen fur ein volck weren / nemlich / geylle vnd furwitzige leut / wie die geissen sind / die sich mit irer vernunfft hoch tzusteigen vnd allerley vermassen[17].

Also hat er auch hie im Munchkalb vber die prophetische deuttung an tzeigt / was die Munche fur leut sind / Unnd villeicht auch: das solch vnfall vber die welt komen werde / vmb der geystlichen missethat willenn / die[18] durch yhr fleyschliche lere den[19] (2r) glauben vertilget vnd die welt zu kalb fleisch gemacht haben / Ein annder gebe die prophetische deuttung / Ich will meyn Munchkalb meinem stand zu dienst deutten / Das pfaffenkalb findet auch wol seinen deutter.

---

[13] *geramen* with gen., variant of ENHG *ramen* 'to take as aim / target' (MHG *râm*).

[14] A *nit*, BCG *nu*, later editions: *nur*.

[15] ENHG compounds are frequently spelled as two words.

[16] *A stands* (which is the normal strong gen. form of the noun, rather than the weak form *standen*).

[17] CE *vermessen*. I take the *und allerlei* to stand for the Latin etcetera and construct in NHG = *sich vermessen hoch zu steigen etc.*

[18] *die* refers back to the monks.

[19] The edition writes *denn* instead of A *den*. The doubling of the *n* seems to be a typographical error or a line-filler.

I will just aim to show as clearly as possible why God has chosen a monk-calf as such a sign, desecrating the holy garment in such a perverse and repulsive way, when He could just as well have warned of such a future calamity by a miracle not involving a monk's habit and, what is more, at Landsberg He has now also created a priest-calf: this year He wants to proceed only with miraculous signs that are spiritual and holy, to make clear in each case that He is paying particular attention to the clergy, and that He has something in mind for them.

He did the same in former times when, in Daniel 8,[20] He had Alexander the Great signified by a billy-goat to show, in addition to the prophetic interpretation of the future fall,[21] what kind of nation the Greeks were, namely lascivious and impudent people like the goats are, and who, with their reason and other such approaches, presumed to rise high.

Likewise, in the case of the monk-calf, He has also shown, in addition to the prophetic vision, what kind of people monks are, and perhaps also this: that such a misfortune will befall the world because of the iniquities of the clergy who, because of their doctrine of the flesh,[22] (2r) have destroyed faith and turned the world to calf-flesh. Let somebody else give the prophetic interpretation. I will interpret my monk-calf as a service to my own order.[23] I am sure the priest-calf will find its interpreter too.

---

[20] This refers to Daniel's vision of a ram and a goat which the angel Gabriel interprets for him, with the goat standing for the king of Greece (Daniel 8:21).

[21] Referring to the fall of the Hellenistic empire.

[22] Literally: carnal doctrine, referencing the contrast between those 'carnally minded' and 'spiritually minded' in Romans 8, a key chapter for Luther's argument for living by faith alone.

[23] Luther refers to the fact that he himself had been a member of a monastic order; it is thus his own former *Stand* (class or order) he is discussing when interpreting the monster as referring to monks.

Dise deuttung stelle ich so vil deste lieber / das ich weiß / wie sie nur hertter verstocken wirt die ienigen / so sie betrifft / weyl sie alles verachten vnd fur ketzerey halten / was ich sage. Darumb sollen sie mir hierin auch nicht gleuben / sondern sich ye mehr vnd mer dran stossen vnd verstocken / auff das sie ia nicht tzu rechter erkentnis komen / vnd ir vnglewbigeß leben bessern. Wie tzu Isaias .vi. gesagt wart. Uerstocke das hertz dises volckß vnd verblende yr augen vnd verschlemme[24] yr oren / das sie nichs hoͤren / sehen noch mercken / damit sie sich bekerten vnd selig wurden:

Wie nu der Balaam / da er Gottis worttenn nichtt gehorchet[25] tzu letzt auch von seiner eselin gestrafft must werden vnd sich doch nicht dran keret / also sollen auch vnsere geystlichen Uetter[26]. nach dem sie bißher / fur der hellenn warheitt deß Euangeli ir oren / wie die otter / verstopffen / itzt auch an dem kalb vnd kuhe fur yren augen / alß im spiegel sehen / wer sie sind fur got / vnd was man ym hymel von inen helt. wye wol[27] sie die augen dennoch sollen fest tzu schliessenn / das sie ya des keins sehen / sie mochten sonst sich bekeren / vnd dem grewlichen vrteil Gottis entrynnen. Denn den verstocktenn pharao bewegen wedder wort noch tzeychenn

[24] = NHG *verschlämmen, mit Schlamm anfüllen, verstopfen* (fill with mud).

[25] This edition has *gehorehet*. A etc. *gehorchet.* Typographical error of this edition.

[26] = NHG *Väter*; the MHG short syllable is lengthened in ENHG, but Luther uses double consonant in his early writings, only later settling on *vater* (sg.) / *veter* (pl.). The plural of NHG *Vetter* = cousin would be *Vettern.*

[27] = NHG *obwohl.*

I am putting forward this interpretation all the more readily as I know how it will only further harden those who are targeted by it because they despise what I say and consider it heresy. For that reason they should not believe what I am saying here either, but rather rail and harden themselves against it all the more, so that they do not, in fact, come to the right conclusion and improve their infidel lives. As was said in Isaiah 6, Harden the heart of this people and blind their eyes and stop their ears, so that they do not hear, see, or feel anything, in order that they may convert and be saved.[28]

Now just as Balaam,[29] when he did not listen to God's words, in the end had to be castigated even by his own donkey and still did not pay attention to her, so also our spiritual fathers, having up to now stopped their ears like adders against the bright truth of the Gospel,[30] in the calf and the cow now before their eyes, see as in a mirror who they are in the sight of God, and how they are thought of in heaven – although despite this they should shut their eyes tight to avoid actually seeing any of this at all, as otherwise they might be converted, and escape God's terrible judgement: stubborn Pharaoh is moved by neither words nor signs.[31]

---

[28] Is 6:10 (KJV): *Make the heart of this people fat, and make their ears heavy, and shut their eyes; lest they see with their eyes, and hear with their ears, and understand with their heart, and convert, and be healed.* In his Bible translation (1545 edition), Luther rendered the verse as: *Verstocke das hertz dieses Volcks | vnd las jre Ohren dicke sein | vnd blende jre augen | Das sie nicht sehen mit jren Augen | noch hören mit jren Ohren | noch verstehen mit jrem Hertzen | vnd sich bekeren vnd genesen.*

[29] When the prophet Balaam (Numeri 22–24) refuses to do God's bidding and tries to force his donkey to advance, God gives her a voice and she scolds him.

[30] Ps 58:4 (KJV): *they are like the deaf adder that stops her ear*; in Luther's translation of Ps 58:5 (L45): *Wie eine taub Otter | die jr ohr zustopfft.*

[31] Referencing the story of the exodus from Egypt when Pharaoh does not let the Israelites go despite Moses' words and signs such as Aaron turning Moses' staff into a snake (Exodus 7:8-13) and the Egyptian plagues.

Auffs erst vnd tzursumma[32] dises tzeychens / las dir das keinn schimpff sein. Das Got eim kalb das geystlich kleyd. die heilige kutten hat angetzogen. Damit hat er on tzweyffel auf eim hauffen[33] bedeut. das eß bald offenbar werden muß. wie die gantze Muncherey vnd Nonnerey[34] nichtß anderß sei. den ein falscher lugenhafftiger schein / vnd euserlich gleyssen eins geystlichen gotlichen lebens. Den wir armen leut haben bißher gemeynet der heilig geist were vnter der kutten / vnnd das ein solch kleidt nichtz den eyttel[35] geist deckte. So tzeygte Gott hie an / das es nur ein kalb deckt / als solt er sagen. Es ist (2v) ein schalcks hutlin[36]. Den was ein kalb bedeutte / lernet vnnß altzu wol / das gulden kalb Aaron / das in der wusten vom volck Israel fur ein Got auff geworffenn[37] wart. Exo[dus] .xxxiij. vnd p[salmu]s[38] .lxxvij.

---

[32] = (E)NHG *zur Summa*, 'in sum'; the running together of these two words, which should also be two words in ENHG, shows how closely the typesetter of this Erfurt edition a copied the first edition A since they even copied the typographical error.

[33] Literally: 'in a heap', in the sense of making it overly obvious by piling up the signs.

[34] = NHG (obsolete) *Möncherei & Nonnerei*, 'life and state of being a monk or a nun'. Word formations via MHG *-íe*, ENHG *-ei* ending tend to have a derogatory undertone and both terms are mainly used in a polemical context such as here.

[35] *eitel* here in the obsolete meaning of 'thorough', preserved in modern German only in mock phrases such as *eitel Sonnenschein* (total sunshine).

[36] A *schalcks hůtlin* = diminutive of NHG (obsolete) *Schalkshaut*, literally the skin of a villain, in the sense of using a camouflage for fraud, related to medieval fable motifs such as the wolf in sheepskin or the fox preaching to the geese whilst dressed as a clergyman only to poach them and carry them away in the hood of his gown. The diminutive form emphasizes the absurdity of this cover.

[37] = NHG *aufwerfen* in the sense of *erhöhen* (DW[1], s.v. 12).

[38] Latin abbreviation for *psalm(us)*; biblical books and chapters were normally numbered with Roman numerals.

First of all, and to come to the point of this sign, do not treat it as a joke that God dressed up a calf in the ecclesiastical garb of a holy habit. He was doubtless doing this to make it abundantly clear what must soon be revealed, that all monkery and nunnery are nothing but a fake, fraudulent sham and the showy exterior of a spiritual, godly life. For we poor folk have been imagining that it was the Holy Spirit under the habit and that what this garment was covering up was purely spiritual. But what God has shown us here is that it is just covering up a calf, as if He were saying, 'This is (2v) the disguise of a fraudster'. What a calf signifies is taught to us only too clearly by the golden calf of Aaron, which was elevated to the status of asto god by the people of Israel in the desert (Exodus 33[39] and Psalm 77[40])

[39] Ex 32:4 (KJV): *And [Aaron] received [the golden earrings] at their hand, and fashioned it with a graving tool, after he had made it a molten calf: and they said, These be your gods, O Israel, which brought you up out of the land of Egypt*; (L45): *Vnd er nam sie von jren henden | vnd entwarffs mit eim griffel | Vnd machte ein gegossen Kalb | vnd sie sprachen | Das sind deine Götter Jsrael | die dich aus Egyptenlande gefüret haben.* Luther often quotes biblical material and chapter numbers from memory, and this is rarely corrected in later editions.

[40] Ps 106:20 (KJV): *Thus they changed their glory into the similitude of an ox that eats grass*; (L45): *Vnd verwandelten jre Ehre | Jn ein gleichnis eines Ochsen der gras isset.* (with a gloss on *Ehre*: *Das ist Gott*). Luther's quotations from the Psalms are even more prone to misnumbering since, around this time, he changes from using the Vulgate numbering system (which follows the Septuagint) to using the numbering of the Hebrew Bible. But, in this case, the number given (77) is nowhere near the actual quotation from Psalm 106 (which is 105 in the Vulgate).

Sie wandelten yr herligkeit in ein bild einß kalbß das graß frisset. vnd die kelber Ieroboam[41] zu Bethel vnd dan iij. Re[gum][42] xij. Da widder die propheten so hefftig schreyen.
Also sihe du nun dis munchkalb auch an / das die kutte sey das gantz geystlich wesen mit alle yrem gottis dienst[43]. den sie gros achten / mit beten / messenn / singen / fastenn etc.[44] Aber wem thun sie solchen gottis dienst. wer wirt da mit geehret. An wem hanget er. Am kalbe. Den die kutten zieret vnd kleidett das kalb wie du sihest. Was ist den das kalb. Es ist ir falscher[45] abgot in irem lugenhafftigen hertzen. Wie geht daß tzu. Also gehet es tzu. Sie haben ein meinung vnd gewissen. das sie dem rechten waren Got dienen mit yrem geistlichenn wesen / vnnd wollen den himel mit iren wercken verdienenn. und stellen auch yren gotts diennst auff lautter[46] menschlich werck. nicht auff den glauben

---

[41] The edition has a space before the name ending *-am*, which shows again how closely the typesetter of edition 'a' follows edition A, where the (much smaller) space between *Jerobo* and *am* might have been due to a slightly wider type *o* or *a*.
[42] Abbreviation *Re.* for *regum*, short for *liber regum*, the Latin name for the Book of Kings. Luther follows the old practice of counting the two books of Samuel as the first two books of Kings, hence ending up with 3 Kings.
[43] The genitive construction *Dienst Gottes* is written from the 14th century occasionally as a compound *Gottesdienst*, but, in Luther's texts, retains the earlier wider sense of worshipping God, not as in the NHG meaning of a formal religious service.
[44] The edition uses the seven-shaped traditional abbreviation, a so-called Tironian note, named after Cicero's scribe Tiro who was credited with inventing this form of shorthand, for the Latin *et* in *etcetera*.
[45] This edition has *falcher*; B rightly corrects this to *falscher*. The same typographical error with the missing *s* is also in edition A which again shows how closely the Erfurt typesetter follows the Wittenberg model.
[46] In this edition *aufflautter* is one word. A has *auff lautter*, but since the ligature *ff* has a fairly wide type, it looked to the typesetter of the Erfurt edition as if this was one word.

They transformed their glory into the likeness of a calf munching grass; and there are also the calves of Jeroboam at Bethel and Dan (3 Kings 12),[47] against which the prophets cry out so vociferously.
In the same way, just look at this monk-calf, how the habit is the entire clergy with all their religious observance, which they take very seriously with praying, masses, singing, fasting, etc. But who do they do such religious service for? Who is honoured by it? Who is it because of? The calf. For, as you can see, the habit adorns and clothes the calf. So what is the calf? It is the false idol in their mendacious hearts. How does this work? This is how it works: they are of the opinion and conviction that they, in their spiritual estate, are serving the right and true God and they claim to deserve heaven by their deeds, and so they base their divine service on purely human works and not on faith.

[47] 1 Kings 12:28f (KJV): *Whereupon the king took counsel, and made two calves of gold, and said unto them, It is too much for you to go up to Jerusalem: behold your gods, O Israel, which brought you up out of the land of Egypt. And he set the one in Bethel, and the other put he in Dan*; (L45): *Vnd der König hielt einen Rat | vnd macht zwey güldene Kelber | vnd sprach zu jnen | Es ist euch zu viel hin auff gen Jerusalem zu gehen | Sihe | Da sind deine Götter Jsrael | die dich aus Egyptenlande gefürt haben. Vnd setzet eins zu BethEl | vnd das ander thet er gen Dan* |. The following chapter tells of the prophet preaching against the worship of the calf.

Nu ist kein Gott in hymel vnd erden. der sich damit eren last. es sey dan der Teuffel odder ein abgot. Den dem rechten waren Got / kan man nicht anderß den ym geist vnd warheit dienen. Iohan[ni][48] iiij. das ist im glauben vnd vber menschlichen wercken[49]. die der geist Christi in vnß thut. Iohan[ni] vi vnd Isa[ia][50] lv. Darumb kunden solch falsche geistliche iren gottiß dienst. vnter dem namen gottis / niemant anders thun den yrem eigen falschen dunckel[51] / der in furgibt / Gotte sey da mitt gedienet / Der selb dunckel ist die lugen[52] / vnd der abgot in irem hertzen / gleich wie den Iuden auch war yn iren abgöttereyenn: Sihe das ist das kalb / vnnd die falsch fleischliche meinung[53] des geistlichen wesens / daran sie hangen / vnd den sie schmucken mit irem schonen gleyssen vnd glatten kutten

So frist nu das kalb nur gras / Den solch heiligen haben nichts von tzukunfftigen guttern / sondern mastenn sich hie auff erden / wie wir sehen / das die besten gutter die meysten wollust / die hohiste ehre die grossist gewalt (3r) bey den geistlichenn ist / Solch gras / muß solch kalb essenn / vnd so wurt an in auch war / daß sie yr herlickeit verwandeln ynn ein bild eins kalbs / daß graß frisset / Den Christus ist vnser herlickeyt / des wyr vns rhumen vnd frewen sollten / so richten sie an sein stat an / ein ander rhum im hertzen / daß sie sich verlassen vnd rhumen yrer eigen werck vnd verdienst / da steht daß kalb yn Christus[54] statt vnd furet Christus namen

---

[48] *Johanni* (of John) or *Evangelium secundum Johannem* (Gospel according to John).

[49] Typographical error *wertken* for *wercken* = NHG *Werken*, correct in A.

[50] Either *Isaias* (the Latin form) or *Jesaia* (the German form).

[51] = NHG *Dünkel*, 'hubris / arrogance / deceit'; the MHG *duncelîn* means 'weak, wrong assumption' or in compounds 'something that is made up or unsubstantiated' whilst *dunc* is neutral in meaning.

[52] = NHG *Lüge*; MHG, *lüge* and *lügen(e)* continue into ENHG until the 18th century; it is also used without umlaut until the 17th century, DW1 s.v.

[53] In this edition typographical error *meiuung* (*u* instead of *n*; this is not an upside-down *n* since the *n* in this font looks slightly different) instead for *meinung*, correct in A.

[54] The nine-shaped Latin *-us* abbreviation, spelled out as *Christus* in edition A, points to the use of the German genitive for *Christus* which is also *Christus*, rather than, as was usual in earlier pamphlets by Luther, the Latin genitive *Christi*.

Now there is not a god in heaven or on earth who allows himself to be honoured like that, except the devil or an idol. For the right and true God can be served only in the spirit and in truth (John 4),[55] that is, in faith and beyond human works, which the spirit of Christ performs in us (John 6 and Isaiah 55)[56]. So when these false men of the spirit do divine service in the name of God, it can only be for their own false conceit, which deceives them into believing that God is thereby being served. This same conceit is the lie and the idol in their hearts, just as it was for the Jews with their idolatries. Look, that is what the calf is, the false, fleshly beliefs of the spiritual estate, which they cling to and trick out with a flashy outward appearance and the sleek cloth of their habits.

Now, the calf only eats grass, and these holy men care nothing for good things in the future, but fatten themselves up here on earth; as we can see, the best things, the finest pleasures, the highest honours, the greatest power (3r) lie with the clergy. The calf cannot help eating the grass and so it becomes true of them, too, that they transform their own glory into the likeness of a calf munching grass. Christ is our glory, whom we should praise and in whom we should rejoice. But in His stead they set up in their hearts another prize, trusting and praising their own works and their own merit; there we have the calf standing in place of Christ and bearing Christ's name.

---

[55] Jo 4:24 (KJV): *God is a Spirit: and they that worship him must worship him in spirit and in truth*; (L45): *Gott ist ein Geist | vnd die jn anbeten | die müssen jn im Geist vnd in der Warheit anbeten.*

[56] Jo 6:63 (KJV): *It is the spirit that quickens; the flesh profits nothing: the words that I speak unto you, they are spirit, and they are life*; (L45): *Der Geist ists | der da lebendig macht | Das fleisch ist kein nütze. Die wort die ich rede | die sind Geist vnd sind Leben.* Is 55:7 (KJV): *Let the wicked forsake his way, and the unrighteous man his thoughts: and let him return unto the LORD, and he will have mercy upon him; and to our God, for he will abundantly pardon*; (L45): *Der Gottlose lasse von seinem wege | vnd der Vbeltheter seine gedancken | vnd bekere sich zum HERRN | So wird er sich sein erbarmen | vnd zu vnserm Gotte | Denn bey jm ist viel vergebung.*

Auffs ander[57] / das die kutten[58] am hyndersten vnd an beynen vnd fornen entgentzet[59] vnd zurissen ist / bedeut das in solchem geistlichen wesen vnd gots dienst keinn einickeit ist / so doch nichts hoherß in der schrifft gefodert wirt / den das die Christen sollen gleich gesinnet sein. wie p[salmu]s[60]. lxvij·[61] Gott machtt im haußе wonen / die einerley gesynnet sind. Und p[salmu]s. c.xxxij. O wie feyn ists vnnd lieblich / wenn bruder eyns mit eynander wonen / Aber disze vnchristliche vngeystliche geyster / haben so mancherley syn vnd weise / alß farben / Die barffsen dunckt yhr regel die beste / die prediger widderumb achtenn ir regel die beste / Augustiner hienaus / die Carthuser dort hinaus / keine dunckt daß gut sein / das den andern gut dunckt / Also ist dye kutten am hyntern des kalbs tzwryssen[62] vnd an denn beynen / ob sie gleich wol alle darynnen eynß sind / daß sie eynerley kalb schmucken / daß ist / gleichen vnglawben vnd meynung durch die werck den hymel tzu erlangen

[57] In ENHG, *ander* is normally used instead of *zweitens*; Luther likes piling up arguments in bullet-point style; here, the list starts on 2r with *Auffs erst* and continues on 3v with *Auffs dritte* and on 4r with *Auffs letzst*.

[58] *kutten* is a rare form of weak declension of *kutte*, the habit worn by monks and nuns.

[59] = NHG (obsolete) *entgänzen*, 'to break a whole (*ganz*) into pieces', the opposite of *ergänzen*, i.e. *zerstücken*.

[60] The Latin term for 'psalms' is abbreviated as 'p̄s.' with both an abbreviation marker for the contraction above the 'p' and an abbreviation dot following.

[61] The dot above the line is an older form of punctuation mark, used by the printer interchangeably with a full stop.

[62] A *zu rissen* = NHG *zerrissen*.

Secondly, the fact that the habit has come apart and is torn on the backside and on the legs and the front signifies that in the spiritual estate and in divine service there is no unity, even though the highest requirement in scripture is that Christians should be like-minded, as in Psalm 67;[63] God makes those that are of one mind live in the same house. And Psalm 132:[64] Oh how fine and pleasant it is when brothers live together with one another. But these unchristian, unspiritual spirits have as many opinions and practices as colours:[65] the Discalced[66] think their rule is best, the Predicants[67] on the other hand regard their rule as the best, the Augustinians go this way, the Carthusians that; nobody thinks that what the other considers good is actually good. This is why the habit is shredded on the calf's backside and legs, although they are in full agreement about one thing, which is that they should adorn the calf in the same way, that is, the same infidel opinion that they can reach heaven through works.

---

[63] Ps 68:7 (= Vulgate Ps 67:7) (KJV Ps 68:6): *God sets the solitary in families: he brings out those which are bound with chains: but the rebellious dwell in a dry land.*; (L45): *Ein Gott der den Einsamen das haus vol Kinder gibt | Der die Gefangen ausfüret zu rechter zeit | Vnd lesst die Abtrinnigen bleiben in der dürre.*

[64] Ps 133:1 (= Vulgate Ps 133) (KJV): *Behold, how good and how pleasant it is for brethren to dwell together in unity!*; (L45): *Sihe | wie fein vnd lieblich ists | Das Brüder eintrechtig bey einander wonen.* A gloss explains this as: *Das ist | Wenn die reichen grossen | heiligen | weisen sich der armen kleinen sünderthören annemen.* (That means when the rich, great, holy, wise ones take care of the poor, little sinful fools).

[65] Meaning the differently coloured habits of the different orders. Of the orders mentioned in the following list, the Franciscans are known as Greyfriars for their habit, the Dominicans as Blackfriars, etc.

[66] Branch of the Franciscans which walks barefoot or in sandals.

[67] Dominicans.

Und sonderlich ist das tzu mercken / das der hynderst / bedeut das ende / vnd die beyne / bedeutt die / auff welchen das kalb (das ist solche falsche meinung) bestehtt Denn es noch nie so vil secten / orden / vnterscheid vnd namen der geistlichen gewesen sind / als ytzt ein tzeyt her / nach dem eß anß[68] end komen ist / vnd ir buberey da hin fellet vnd aufhoren muß. Und die beine / sind die frechen bruder vnd lerer. Magistri nostri eximij. vnd ir gelertisten hin vnd her in den orden / die solch geistlich wesen mit yrem schreyben / predigen / lesen vnnd leren vnter yn / vnd in der welt / erhalten / Und doch keiner mitt dem andern eines ist. So vil kopffe / so mancherley opinion sind da

(3v)

Auffß dritte / furet das kalb aller dinge[69] / die geperde einß predigerß / eß streckt die hinderbein alß stunde[70] / vnd reckt auß die rechte pfotte / wie ein prediger sein rechte hand / vnd zeucht die lincke zu sich / wirfft den kopff auff / vnd hat die zunge im maul / vnd ist alleß gestalt / als stund eß vnd prediget / Darumb wie der Bapstesel das Bapstum abmalltt / So malet eygentlich diß Munchkalb / die Apostel vnd schuler deß Bapsts / das alle welt sehe / was sie bißher fur prediger vnd lerer gehortt vnd noch hören / Den was solt ein eselskopff billicher tzu Apostel haben / den ein kalbs kopff[?][71] fleyschlich regiment hatt auch fleyschliche lere / Darumb hats auch noch nichtt augen / das es die ienigen deutte / da Christuß von sagt Mat[thei][72] xxiij. Wee euch schrifftgelertenn yr verblendte blind leytter. Und Isaie lvi. Yhr verseher[73] sind alle blind vnd wissen nichts

[68] Typographical error *auß* for *ans* (correctly in A).

[69] = NHG (obsolete) *allerdinge,* 'at all, overall'; DW s.v. points to Latin *omnino* as a parallel.

[70] A *stunds*; the Erfurt typesetter seems to have misread the final *s* as an *e*.

[71] In A, a question mark follows this, which the Erfurt typesetter missed out.

[72] *Matthei* or *Evangelium secundum Mattheum* (Gospel according to Matthew).

[73] = NHG *Aufseher*, 'custodians, stewards, or deputies'.

And it should be noted in particular that the backside signifies the end, and the legs signify the things (that is, this wrongheaded opinion) on which the calf stands. For there have never been so many sects, orders, distinctions, and names for the spiritual estate as there have been for a while now, after which it will have come to an end and their knavery will collapse and have to cease. And the legs are the impertinent friars and teachers, 'our distinguished teachers',[74] including the most learned of them here and there amongst the orders, who maintain this spiritual estate through their writing, preaching, reading, and teaching between themselves and in the world. And yet none of them agree with each other. Take a headcount amongst them, and that's the number of different opinions there are. (3v)

Thirdly, the calf has the overall posture of a preacher: it is stretching out its hind legs as if standing up and is lifting its right paw as a preacher raises his right hand, and is pulling its left one towards itself, throwing up its head, its tongue showing in its mouth, and it is fashioned in every respect as if it were standing and preaching. So just as the pope-donkey portrays the papacy, so this monk-calf in fact portrays the apostles and disciples of the pope, so that the whole world can see what kind of preachers and teachers it has been listening to and still is. For what could a donkey-head have more fittingly as its apostle than a calf-head? Those who rule by the flesh teach by the flesh. The reason why it does not yet have eyes is that that signifies those of whom Christ says (Matthew 23):[75] Woe to you scribes and you blinded, unseeing guides. And Isaiah 56: Their watchmen are all blind and know nothing.[76]

---

[74] Ironic use of Latin to refer to the clergy with an established honorific formula.

[75] Mt 23:16 (KJV): *Woe unto you, you blind guides*; (L45): *WEh euch verblente Leiter.*

[76] Is 56:10 (KJV): *His watchmen are blind: they are all ignorant, they are all dumb dogs, they cannot bark; sleeping, lying down, loving to slumber*; (L45): *Alle jre Wechter sind blind | sie wissen alle nichts | stumme Hunde sind sie | die nicht straffen können | sind faul | liegen vnd schlaffen gerne.* (with a gloss: *Das sind falsche Lerer*).

Uil anders mehr mag man wol an dem kalbe auff die munch vnd lerer deutten / Als das / daß ore an der kutten / die vntregliche Tiranney der beicht bedeutte / damit sie die weltt marteren vnd zum teuffel furen / Die Zunge ym maul / daß yre lere nichts den tzunge / das ist / eyttel vnnutz geschwetze ist / Die tzw wartzen yn der platten[77] auff dem kopff / sollten hörner worden sein / Hörner aber bedeutten die predigtt des Ewangeli[78] / daß vom creutz prediget vnd tzu stosset[79] den alten menschen / Michee[80] .iij. Ich wil deyn horrn eysern machenn das du vil volcks tzustossist etc.[81] Aber dißkalb hat nicht hörner / sondern nur malzeichen[82] vnd schein daruon / Den sie haben woll den namen / das sie das Euangelion predigen / aber sie habens gefangen vnd auff yre menschen lere gezwungen / vnd stehn die wartzen yn der platten / den was der platten gefelt / das mus Euangelion heyssen / vnd das Euangelion mus auch nicht auser diszer plattenn faren / sondern sich reymen vnd fugen auff yhr platten heiligkeit / Sonderlich was yr heubt / den Bapst betrifft

---

[77] ENHG *Platte* (literally 'blank plate') is the German term for the tonsure of the Catholic clergy or a bald patch.

[78] This should be *evangelii*, with a double i, the Latin genitive form of the Latin and German word for Gospel, *evangelium*.

[79] = NHG *zerstößt*, also found in the following quotation from Micah: *tzuſtoſſiſt* = *zerstößest*. The preposition can be separated from the stem in ENHG typesetting.

[80] The medieval Latin genitive form of Micah: *Prophetia Michææ* (Prophecy of Micah).

[81] The edition uses the composite mark '7c̄' which consists of a 7-shaped sign as the antique shorthand form for 'et', together with the c with a bar as abbreviation marker above it. The following dot in the original edition is above the line '·', an older form of the punctuation or abbreviation mark.

[82] In the edition, the space between *nur* and *malzeichen* missing; the typesetter probably did not understand the word *malzeichen*; *mal* means 'mark'; the compound in NHG is replaced by *Kenn-* or *Denkzeichen*.

There is certainly a lot more about the calf that can be applied to monks and teachers, such as the fact that the ear on the habit[83] signifies the intolerable tyranny of confession with which they torment the world and lead it to the devil. The tongue in its mouth signifies that their teaching is nothing but tongue, that is, nothing but totally idle chatter. The two warts within the tonsured bald patch on its head should have become horns, but horns stand for the preaching of the Gospel, which preaches about the cross and crushes the old man.[84] Micah 3:[85] I will make your horns iron so you may crush many people etc. But this calf does not have horns, only marks and the illusion of horns. For they do preach the Gospel in name, but they have taken it captive and forced it onto their human teachings. The warts are inside the bald patch, for what goes well with a tonsured bald patch can only be the Gospel, and the Gospel must not venture outside this bald patch, but has to chime in with and conform to its pure sanctity, especially when it comes to their head, the pope.

---

[83] Referring to the position of the calf's right ear on the woodcut directly above the cowl-like neck-fold.

[84] Meant in the sense of Col 3:9 (KJV): *put off the old man with his deeds*; (L45): *Ziehet den alten Menschen mit seinen wercken aus*. Similarly, Rom 6:6 (KJV): our old man is crucified with him and Eph 4:22 (KJV): *put off concerning the former conversation the old man, which is corrupt according to the deceitful lusts*.

[85] Mi 4:13 (KJV): *Arise and thresh, O daughter of Zion: for I will make your horn iron, and I will make your hoofs brass: and you shall beat in pieces many people*; (L45): *Darumb mache dich auff vnd dressche du tochter Zion | Denn ich wil dir eisern Hörner | vnd eherne Klawen machen | vnd solt viel Völcker zurschmeissen*. (with a gloss: *Du wirst Babylon vnd alles dresschen in aller Welt | ob du schon jtzt must leiden | Das beide Babel vnd Rom | deine Richter vnd dein Reich verstören*).

Das die kutten vmb den hals szo hart gewunden ist / tzeygt yhren hallstarrigen vorstockten syn yn yrer muncherey vnd heiligem weszen / das ihr gewissen so tieff darynnenn (4r) verpunden vnd verstrickt synd / das sie durch keine macht der aller hellisten warheit er aus komen mugen. Und daß die kutten auff dem rucken gantz vnnd fornen offen ist / bedeutt das sie fur der welt nur geystlich sind / die sie hinder sich mussen lassen / Aber fur got vnd gegen dem tzukunfftigen leben / sind es yn der warheit blosse beuche vnd nur eittel freßlinge[86] / vnd was durch vnd an dem bauch mehr sunden geschehenn fur got / der ich schweige.

Das aber das vntermaul menschen maul gleich / vnd das vbermaul mit der nasen dem kalbmaul gleich ist. bedeut. das ir prediget wol etwan von den wercken gotlichs gesetzß leren. Aber es reucht alles kelbisch / vnd wirt gewandtt auff eygen gerechtikeit vnd frumkeit. Denn dye tzwo lippen des munds. bedeutten / die tzwo predigt / die vnterst deß gesetzs predigt / die vberst / des Euangeli odder verheyssung gottis. Aber an stat deß Ewangeli vnd gotlicher verheyssung / predigen sie das kalbmaul / das ist aureolas[87] vnd grossen verdienst ym himel fur yr eigen werck / die sie on glauben mit grosser muhe thun.

Auffs letzst / ist das kalb glat allenthalben / widder dye natur der kelber / daß bedeut / die hubsche feyne zarte gleissenerey vnd heuchley / damit sie bis her yederman gefallen vnd betrogen haben / das wir sie fur heilige geistliche vetter gehalten haben / die seel morder vnd teuffelß vorleuffer· Das ist nun alleß an den tag komen / das kalb ist erauß / auß der kue Sie konnen sich nicht mer bergen in der welt. man weiß nu wer sie sind

---

[86] = NHG (obsolete) *Fräßling*, somebody given to *Fraß* 'gluttony', with a nomen agentis ending, cf. *Schwächling* 'weakling', *Liebling* 'darling'.

[87] Typographical error *anreolas* for *aureolas* (correct in A and the other editions), accusative plural of medieval Latin *aureola*, derived from *aureolus* (gold coloured, beautiful), which is used in MHG and ENHG for the crown of the virgin martyrs and, as it is a loan word, it retains Latin endings, DW2 s.v.

The fact that the habit is wound so tightly around the neck shows the stiff-necked, stubborn attitude of their holy estate of monkery, that their consciences are so deeply (4r) bound and tangled up in it, that they cannot break free of them even through the power of the brightest truth. And the fact that the habit covers the whole back and is open at the front means that they are spiritual only for the world which they must leave behind them, but towards God and the life to come they are in fact just bellies and complete and utter gluttons, and as for the other sins which are done before God because of the belly and in the belly, I will pass over them in silence.

But the fact that the lower mouth resembles a human mouth and the upper mouth and nose resemble a calf's means that their sermons do sometimes teach about the works of divine law, but it all reeks of calf and is directed towards their own righteousness and piety. For the two lips of the mouth signify the two sermons, the lower one being the sermon of the law, the upper that of the Gospel or God's promise. But instead of the gospel and divine promise, they preach the calf's mouth, that is, aureolae and great reward in heaven for their own works which, without faith, they take great pains to perform.

Finally, the calf is smooth all over, against the nature of calves, which signifies the nice, fine, delicate fakery and hypocrisy with which they have been attracting and deceiving everyone, so that we have been considering these murderers of souls and harbingers of the devil as holy men of spirit. All of this has come to light now that the calf is out, out of the cow. They can no longer hide in the world: people know who they are.

Dise deuttung / gebe ich tzu richten yderman / den ob die deuttung gleich sich nicht reymette[88] / so ist sie doch an ihr selb vnd in der schrifft vor hin gnugsam gegrund / das der Munch stand der artt sey / wie gesagtt ist. Weyl den daß kalb drein[89] so eben stimmet / so sehe yderman tzw / waß er verachte / wen er mein deuttug veracht. Es ist vns gnugsam an disem (4v) kalb gesagt / das got der muncherey feynd ist / wo er yr hold were / het er die kutten einem erlicher bild an gezogen / So mag solch wunder / nicht einen man odder person / sondernn muß eyn gantzen hauffen ein regiment viler person bedeutten wye aller wunder vnd gesicht art ist / yn der schrifft. dan[iel]. viij.

Hutt euch Munch vnd Nonnen / Es gilt euch warlich mit ernst / vnd last euch gottis vermanung nichtt ein schertz seyn / Werdet ander munch vnnd nonnen / odder last kloster vnd kutten ligen / vnd werdet widderumb Christen / ehe euch die tzeit vbereylet[90] / vnd darnach nicht kundet / wenn yr gern wolltet / die ir ytzt nicht wolttet / weil yr wol kundt.

Und ynn sonderheit bitte ich euch demutigklich yhr lieben herren vom Adel / helfft ewern freunden vnd kindern aus dem grewlichen ferlichen stand / Denckt / das sie auch menschen sind eben als yr / vnd ia so hartt verpunden sind / dem natturlichen orden alß alle ander / vnd nicht müglich ist / das ein solch grosse mengen / solten keusche odder willigklich Iunckfrawen seyn. Ich wil das meine than vnnd euch alle gewarnet habenn.

---

[88] = NHG *reimte*, literally ‘to be put into rhyme, versified’, in ENHG = ‘to be coherent’; in NHG, still used as *sich etwas zusammenreimen* or *sich einen Reim auf etwas machen* = ‘to make something coherent, to make sense of something’.

[89] = NHG *darein, darin*.

[90] = NHG *ereilt*, ‘catch somebody whilst running’.

I offer this interpretation for everyone to judge because, although the interpretation might not be coherent, it still is solid enough in itself and sufficiently based on scripture, that the status of monks is of the nature that has been stated. For since the calf in the picture is such a close match, let everyone see what they are despising when they despise my interpretation. Through this calf we are being clearly told (4v) that God is the enemy of monkery; if He were favourable to it, He would have put the habit on a more respectable likeness. So such a miracle cannot signify one man or one person, but must signify a whole collection, a multitude of people, as is the way with all miracles and visions in scripture (Daniel 8).[91]

Take heed, monks and nuns, this really and truly applies to you, and do not treat God's admonition as a joke. Become different monks and nuns, or leave monastic houses and habits behind, and become Christians again before time catches up with you: you could not possibly do so later even if you wanted to, you who do not do so now when you actually can.

And, in particular, I humbly ask you, dear lords of the nobility, to help your friends and children out of this awful, dangerous state. Remember that they too are human, just like you, and just as closely linked to the natural order as everybody else, and it is not possible that such a large a group should all be chaste and willing virgins. I want to make sure I have done what I can and warned you all.

---

[91] Probably refers to the fact that each of the animals in the Book of Daniel signifies a whole kingdom or people, like, for example, the ram and the goat in chapter 8. WA 11 points specifically to Dan 8:7 (KJV): *And I saw him* [i.e. the goat] *come close unto the ram, and he was moved with choler against him, and smote the ram, and brake his two horns: and there was no power in the ram to stand before him, but he cast him down to the ground, and stamped upon him: and there was none that could deliver the ram out of his hand*; (L45): *Vnd ich sahe jm zu | das er hart an den Widder kam | vnd ergrimmet vber jn | vnd sties den Widder | vnd zubrach jm seine zwey Hörner. Vnd der Widder hatte keine Krafft | das er fur jm hette mügen bestehen | Sondern er warff jn zu boden | vnd zutrat jn | vnd niemand kund den Widder von seiner hand erretten.*

Quadrilingual Edition of the 'Mönchkalb'

A comparison of the Erfurt 1523 edition of the 'Mönchkalb' with the Latin, French, and English translations.

Titlepage of the Erfurt edition, 1523[1]

(a1r) DEUTTUNG DER GREWLICHEN FIGUR DES MUNCHKALBS TZU FREYBERG IN Meyssen gfunden D[octor] MARTIN. LUTHER.

Heading in the French version, 1557[2]

(p. 1) De deux monstres prodigieux, à savoir d'un asne-pape qui fut trouvé à Rome en la rivière du Tibre l'an 1496, et d'un veau-moine nay à Friberg en Misne l'an 1528, qui sont vrais présages de l'ire de Dieu attestez et declarez, l'un par P. Melancthon et l'autre par M. Luther, avec quelques exemples des jugemens de Dieu en la mort espouvantable et désespoir de plusieurs, pour avoir abandonné la vérité de l'Évangile

(p. 28)[3] SENSVIT LE POVRTRAIT DE L'AVTRE: A SAVOIR, D'VN Veau-Moine nay en ceste façon en la ville de Friberg au pays de Misne, l'an M.D.XXVIII.

---

[1] See Introduction 2.1.1.3. Erfurt: Wolfgang Stürmer, 1523. Taylor Inst. Library, ARCH.8°.G.1523(8).

[2] See Introduction 2.1.3. Geneva: Jean Crespin 1557. New College Library BT1.17.6(1). The first title is for the full volume. It is not clear how the mistake of dating the calf to 1528 came about. The French version is based on the extended 1535 edition which does not give a date for either of the two monsters.

[3] Subtitle for the second part. The reference to the monk-calf which is depicted on the following page as 'the portrait of the other' refers to the fact that Melanchthon's explanation of the pope-donkey precedes this text. It sits at the bottom of the page with the first three lines centred and in capitals, followed by two indented lines.

Titlepage in the Latin edition, 1546/1551/1562/1572[4]

(f. 395r) INTERPRETATIO DVorum horribilium Monstrorum Papaselli Romæ in Tyberi Anno 1496. inuenti, & Monachouituli, Fribergæ in Misnia, Anno 1523. editi, Per Philippium Melanthonem & Martinum Lutherum.

(p. 399r) INTERPRETATIO MOnachouituli Monstri Fribergæ editi: Per Martinum Lutherum.

Heading in the English translation, 1579

(a1r) Of two VVoonderful Popish Monsters, to wyt, Of a Popish Asse which was found at Rome in the riuer of Tyber, and of a Moonkish Calfe, calued at Friberge in Misne.
¶Which are the very foreshewings and tokens of Gods wrath, against blinde, obstinate, and monstrous Papistes. Witnessed and declared, the one by Philip Melancthon, the other by Martyn Luther.

(d4r) HEERE FOLLOWETH THE PORtrayture or Figure of the other, that is to wit, of a Moonkish Calfe, calued after this fashion in the Citie of Friberge in the countrey of Misne. Anno. 1528.[5]

---

[4] See Introduction 2.1.2. The layout of the page has the woodcut and above the title centred in five lines, the first (up to MO, followed by a hyphen) in capitals. The calf is looking to the right as in all editions except the first Wittenberg edition. The woodcut is adjusted to fit the different page ratio of the larger format.

[5] The layout of the page (cf. illustration) has the woodcut and above the title centred in five lines, the first in capitals, the second in the Roman font, the third (starting with *Moonkish*) in black letter, the final two (after 'fashion') in italics.

Erfurt edition, 1523, a1v

DEUTTUNG DES MUNCHKALBS Zu Freyberg Martin Luthers Die Prophetische deuttung dises Munchkalbs wil ich dem geist lassen / den ich kein prophet bin / on daß gewiß ist / der gemeinen deuttung nach / yn allen wunderzeichen / daß dadurch ein gros vnfall vnd verenderung zukunfftig / Got tzu verstehen gibtt / der sich auch gewiszlich deutschland versehen mag / Welche aber die selben sei / vnd wie eß zu gehen werde / gepurt den propheten tzu sagen /

French version, 1557, p. 30

INTERPRETATION DE MARTIN LVTHER DV MONstre en figure de Veau-Moine, pourtrait en la page precedente.
QVANT à l'interpretation Prophetique de ce Veau-Moine, ie la lerray à l'Esprit: car ie ne suis pas Prophete. Toutesfois on peut bien affermer cecy en general de plusieurs telles merueilles, que Dieu les enuoye comme presages de tristes aduentures, d'esmotions, bruits, troubles, esbranslemens à venir. Et i'exhorte la Germanie de se promettre hardiment, & d'attendre pour certain de telles venues. Mais de determiner les euenemens, & predire combien de temps ils dureront, ou en quel temps aduiendra la deliurance, cela est à faire à Prophetes.

Translation in the Latin edition, 399v

INTERPRET. MONACHOVITVLI
PROpheticam interpretationem huius Monachouituli relinquam spiritui, non enim sum Propheta. Illud tamen in genere de plerisque miraculis talibus adfirmari potest, Deum per ea funestos casus, motus et quassationes futuras quodammodo prænunciare, quales Germaniam certò sibi polliceri & expectare iubeo. Sed qui nominatim euentus propendantur[6], quamque durabiles, ac tempus liberationis præfinire, Prophetarum est.

English translation of the French version, 1579, 12r

THE INTERpretacion of Martin Luther, of the Monster, in the figure and lykenesse of a Moonkish Calfe, drawen out in the leafe before.
AS touching the Propheticall interpretacion of this Moonkish Calfe, I will leaue it to the spirit: for I am no prophet. Yet neuertheles one may well affirme this generally of many such meruayles, that God doth send them as presages and forewarnings of sorrowfull aduentures, motions, brutes, troubles and commotions to come. And I doe exhort Germany to assure themselues boldly and to attende certeinely such commings. But to determine of chaunces and to foreshew how long time they shall continue, or in what time the delyueraunce shall come, the same belongeth to the Prophets.

---

[6] 1546 *portendantur*.

Erfurt edition, 1523, a1v

Mein wundsch vnd hoffnung ist / daß der Iunst tag sei. Den der zeichen biß her vil auff ein ander fallen / vnd gleich alle welt in einer grossen woge steht / Die on grossen wandel nicht kan abgehn / Dartzu daß Euangelische liecht so helle auffgangen / welchem alle mall / gros verenderung / vmb der vngleubygen willen / erfolget hatt

French version, 1557, p. 30/31

De moy, ie desireroye volontiers que le dernier iour fust prochain: ce que ie pense außi, que les iours ou nous sommes sont comme auant-coureurs de ce iour bien-heureux, lequel ne tardera gueres apres: & me semble bien que la cause que i'ay de l'esperer ainsi, n'est pas friuole ne legere. Et de fait, par cy deuant il y a eu presque vne continuation de quelques siecles, ausquels on a tousiours veu des choses prodigieuses & dignes de grande admiration: & auiourdhuy tout le monde bruslant d'vne ardeur terrible, conçoit des esmotions fort pernicieuses, lesquelles coustumierement (p. 31) ne s'appaisent point sans grans changemens & alienations notables des royaumes. Ioint que la lumiere de l'Euangile est maintenant resplendisante d'vne façon excellente, laquelle a accoustumé d'apporter ordinairement auec soy des mutations, troubles & orages, à cause de l'obstination endurcie, & des rages furieuses des meschans.

Translation in the Latin edition, 399v

Ego sane optarim, quod sperare profecto non leui de causa uideor, extremi iudicij diem nos[7] non longo interuallo ceu præcursores consequi. Etenim continuis fere seculis mirifica uelut ostentorum series extitit, ac nunc totius orbis uelut æstu quodam fluctuans ingentes motus parturit, qui sine magnis conuersionibus[8] insignique regnorum distractione non abire solent. Adde quòd Euangelij lux splendere[9] tanto rursus inclaruit, quæ perpetuo commutationes tempestatesque turbulentas, ob impiorum contumaciam & furores attulit.

English translation of the French version, 1579, 12r/12v

As for me, I will desire willingly that the latter day were at hande: the which I also doe thinke, that the dayes wherein we are, are as forerunners of that blessed day, the which will not tary long after. And me thinketh that the cause that I haue to hope so, is not friuolous nor vaine. And in very déede, before time ther hath ben almost a continuation of certeine worlds, in which men haue séene dayly monstrous things, and worthy of great admiration: And at this day all the worlde burning with a terrible heat, bringeth forth motions very pernicious, who commonly are not appeased without great chaunges & alterations of kingdoms. To conclude, that the lyght of the Gospell, shineth (12v) now wonderfully, the which commonly was wont to bring with it alterations, troubles and tempests, bicause of the hard obstination, and furious ragings of the wicked.

---

7 1546 *hos.*

8 1546 *conuersionibua.*

9 1546 *splendore.*

Erfurt edition, 1523, 1v

Ich wil nur des gewissesten geram / vnd mit antzeigen / warumb Got zu solchem zeichen ein munch kalb genomen hat / vnd daß heilige kleid so verkerlich vnd grewlich schendet / so er doch eben so wol solch kunfftig vngluck hette durch ein wunder on munchkutten mugen angeben / Datzu nu auch zu landßberg ein pfaffenkalb hat geschaffen / vnd wil dyß iar nur mit geistlichen / heiligen wundertzeichen faren / damitt er yhe sich mercken lest / daz er deß geistlichen standen sonderlich acht hat / vnd etwas ym syn hat auff die selben

French version, 1557, p. 31

Et certes ie ne parleray que des choses qui sont bien certaines: & monstreray pourquoy Dieu a proposé vn tel signe en ce Veau-Moine, & pour quelle raison il a souillé l'habit religieux d'vne si vilaine macule: veu que sans vn habit de Moine il pouuoit se signifier & denoncer les maux à venir außi proprement par quelque autre prodige. Ainsi donc il n'y a pas fort long temps que par sa volonté, nasquit à Langdsberg vn certain Chanoine-Veau, ou Moine-Veau. Il declare bien par cela, que tous religieux & Moins doyuent auoir les yeux là fichez, & que luy á l'œil sur eux, &qu'il a deliberé de les punir: car ceste année-cy il n'a voulu vser d'autres miracles, que de ceux qui s'addressent à telles gens sacrez & spirituels.

Translation in the Latin edition, 399v

Equidem certissima tantum persequar, & ostendam, quare Deus in Monachouitulo huiusmodi signum proposuerit, religioseque uestitam[10] peruersam atque turpem asperserit maculam, cum non minus commode uentura mala prodigio aliquo sine habitu monastico potuerit innuere. Itaque nuper Landsbergæ Canonico uitulum condidit, uultque sacris & spiritualibus hoc anno miraculis duntaxat uti, quo certe declarat, se religiosorum[11] ordinem ceu defixis oculis intueri, deque cohercendis illis cogitare.

English translation of the French version, 1579, 12v

And truly I will not speake but of things which are true: and will shew wherefore God hath set foorth such a signe in that Moonkish Calfe, and for what cause hée hath defiled the religious habite or apparayle with one so vyle a spotte: Forasmuch as without the habite of a Moonke hée might signifie and declare the euills to come as properly and well by any other shew or token. Euen so then it is not long sithence that by his prouidence was calued at Langdesberge a certeine Canon Calfe, or a Moonkish Calfe. It declareth thereby, that all religious men and Moonkes ought to haue their eyes thereon still fixed, and that he beholdeth them, and that he hath determined to punish them: For this same yeare he will vse none other miracles, then those which haue respecte vnto such holy and spirituall people.

---

[10] Should be *vestita*.

[11] 1546 *Religiosorum*.

Erfurt edition, 1523, 1v

Also thet er vortzeitten auch / Da er Danielis .viij. den grossen konig Alexander durch ein zigen bock ließ bedeutten. damit er anzeigt / vber die prophetische deuttung deß zukunfftigen fals / was die kriechen fur ein volck weren / nemlich / geylle vnd furwitzige leut / wie die geissen sind / die sich mit irer vernunfft hoch tzusteigen vnd allerley vermassen.

French version, 1557, p. 31

Or depeignant iadis ce monarque excellent Alexandre Roy des Macedoniens sous la figure d'vn Bouc, Daniel VIII, outre l'interpretation Prophetique de la desconfiture à venir: il a außi voulu figurer ou representer la nature des Grecs, qui sont safres & lubriques conme les Boucs. Et tout ce qu'ils auoyent basty ou conceu en leur esprit, tant haut & difficile fust, ils esperoyent en venir à bout, & y paruenir par bons conseils, par grande viuacité d'esprit.

Translation in the Latin edition, 399v

Quid, quod olim cum præstantissimum Monarcham Alexandrum Macedonem Dan. 8. in forma hirci caprarum depingeret, præter interpretationem propheticam futuræ uastationis, naturam simul indolemque Græcæ[1] Nationis adumbrauit, uidelicet, salacitatem petulantiamque similem hœdis, quod nihil tam arduum, sublime, præruptum animo conciperent, quo se non ingenij acrimonia, rationis excellentia, consilij prudentia euadere, penetrare, ascendere posse confiderent.

English translation of the French version, 1579, 12v

For god paynting out of late that excellent Monarch[2] of Alexander king of Macedonia vnder the figure and lykenesse of a Goate, besides the Propheticall interpretacion of the discomfiture and vanquishing to come: he hath also set foorth and represented the nature of the Grecians, which are wanton as the Goates. And all that that they haue conceiued in their minde how high and harde that it be, they hope to bring it to passe, and to atteine vnto it through good councells, through great viuacitie and stoutnesse of the minde.

---

[1] 1546 *græcæ*.

[2] Marginalia: *Daniel 8.d.*

Erfurt edition, 1523, 1v/2r

Also hat er auch hie im Munchkalb vber die prophetische deuttung an tzeigt / was die Munche fur leut sind / Unnd villeicht auch: das solch vnfall vber die welt komen werde / vmb der geystlichen missethat willenn / die durch yhr fleyschliche lere den (2r) glauben vertilget vnd die welt zu kalb fleisch gemacht haben / Ein annder gebe die prophetische deuttung / Ich will meyn Munchkalb meinem stand zu dienst deutten / Das pfaffenkalb findet auch wol seinen deutter.

French version, 1557, p. 32

Semblablement en ceste figure de ce Veau-Moine, outre la declaration Prophetique, il y a außi vne image ou figure de la vie, de la doctrine, des seruices & obseruations des Moines: & poßible est qu'auec cela il y a vn aduertissement de la cause des calamitez bien prochaines. A sauoir, que les superstitions, les fallaces & meschancetez des Moines font croistre les punitions,[3] d'autant que par la doctrine Pharisaique des œuures, ils abolißent la foy qui est en nostre Seigneur Iesus Christ, & transforment en chair de Veau le cœur humain, qui deuoit estre le temple du sainct Esprit. Au reste, qu'vn autre tire le sens Prophetique: de moy, pour faire plaisir à mon ordre, i'ay entrepris d'interpreter mon Moine-Veau: le Chanoine-Veau aura vn autre pour son expositeur.

---

[3] Marginalia: *Les superstitions des Moines font croistre les punitions Diuines.*

Translation in the Latin edition, 399v

Ita hic quoque præter explicationem propheticam[4] monasticæ uitæ, doctrinæ, cultuumque imago proponitur, ac interim fortassis de causa impendentium calamitatum erudimur, uidelicet, Monachorum superstitione, imposturis, flagitijs cumulari pœnas, quòd per pharisaicam carnalemque operum doctrinam, fidem in Christum aboleant, & cor humanum, quod Spiritus sancti debuit esse templum, in uitulinam carnem transforment. Cæterum alius eruat intellectum propheticum, Ego meum Monachouitulum in gratiam Ordinis mei interpretandum suscepi, Canonico uitulo suus erit ἐξηγητής[5]

English translation of the French version, 1579, 12v/13r

In lyke manner in this figure of this Moonkish Calfe, besides the Propheticall declaration, there is also an Image or figure of the lyfe, of the doctrine of the seruices and obseruations of the Moonkes: And it is possible that thereby there is an aduertisement of the (13r) cause of the calamities nighe at hande. That is to saye, that the superstitions, the deceites and wickednesse of the Moonkes, doe cause the punishment to increase, for as much as by the Pharisaycall doctrine of woorkes, they doe abolish the fayth which is in our Lorde Iesus Christ, and doe transforme and chaunge into the flesh of a Calfe mans heart, which ought to bée the Temple of the holy Ghost. Furthermore, let an other drawe the propheticall sence: as for mée for to please my order, I haue taken vpon me to interpret my Moonkish Calfe: The Canon Calfe shall haue an other for his expositer.

---

[4] 1546 has a comma after *propheticam*.

[5] Transliteration: *exegetes*, Greek term for those who do exegesis, interpret.

Erfurt edition, 1523, 2r

Dise deuttung stelle ich so vil deste lieber / das ich weiß / wie sie nur hertter verstocken wirt die ienigen / so sie betrifft / weyl sie alles verachten vnd fur ketzerey halten / was ich sage. Darumb sollen sie mir hierin auch nicht gleuben / sondern sich ye mehr vnd mer dran stossen vnd verstocken / auff das sie ia nicht tzu rechter erkentnis komen / vnd ir vnglewbigeß leben bessern. Wie tzu Isaias .vi. gesagt wart. Uerstocke das hertz dises volckß vnd verblende yr augen vnd verschlemme yr oren / das sie nichs hören / sehen noch mercken / damit sie sich bekerten vnd selig wurden:

French version, 1557, p. 32/33

Or tant plus volontiers pren-ie la charge de faire ceste declaration, que ie voy bien que les courages obstinez & plus durs que rochiers de ceux qui seront taxez ou piquez de ceste mienne explication, en seront tant plus naurez, & en deuiendront plus aigres. Comme de fait ils desprisent arrogamment tout ce qui sort de ma bouche, & babillent par tout que toutes mes paroles sont autant de crachats de heretiques. Pour ceste raison ils ne doyuent point außi maintenant adiouster foy à mes aduertissemens,[6] mais s'endurcir & se rendre obstinez de plus en plus, s'aheurter & se tempester plus que iamais, à ce qu'ils ne paruiennent point à la cognoissance de verité, & ne delaissent leur vie orde & meschante. comme il est dit en Isaye chapitre sixieme, (p. 33) Aueugle le cœur de ce peuple, appesanty ses oreilles, ferme ses yeux: afin que parauenture il ne voye de ses yeux, & qu'il n'oye de ses oreilles, & entende de son cœur, & qu'il se conuertisse, & que ie le guerisse.

---

[6] Marginalia: *Interpretation faite pour endurcir dauantage ceux qui n'adioustent foy aux aduertissemens des fideles.*

Translation in the Latin edition, 399v/400r

Hanc autem enarrationem eo libentius aggredior, quòd futurum uideo, ut illorum pertinaces animi, ipsisque Caucasi rupibus asperiores, qui explicatione nostra perstringentur, tanto magis exulcerentur, & acerbiores fiant. Quandoquidem arroganter despiciunt[7] hæreticorumque saliua conspersum dictitant, quidquid à me profertur. Quamobrem nec iam adhibere fidem præmonitionibus meis debent, sed magis ma(400r)gisque obdurari, offendere, perturbari, ne ad agnitionem ueritatis perueniant, aut ab impia uita deficiant, Sicut Esa. 6. dicitur: Excæca cor populi huius, & aures eius aggraua, & oculos eius claude, ne forte uideat oculis suis, & auribus suis audiat, corde suo intelligat, & conuertatur, & sanem eum.

English translation of the French version, 1579, 13r

For so much the more willingly doe I take the charge to make this declaration, for that I doe sée that the obstinate courages and more harder then the rockes, of those which shall bée grieued with this my explication, shall bée so much the more wounded and shall bée come more eger. As in very déede they doe arrogantlye despise all that whiche commeth out of my mouth, and doe babble euery where, that all my woordes are as much to bée estéemed as the spittinges of heretickes. For that cause they ought not also now to giue any credite vnto mine aduertisement, but doe waxe more harde harted, and doe make themselues more and more obstinate, hurting and molesting themselues more then euer any did, and forsake not their filthy and wicked lyfe, as it is sayde in Esay the sixte Chapter,[8] harden the heart of this people, stoppe their eares, and shutte their eyes, that they sée not with their eyes, heare not with their eares, and vnderstande not with their heartes, and conuerte and bée healed.

---

[7] Komma after this in 1546 edition.

[8] Marginalia: *The interpretation made for to harden the heartes of those vvhich do giue no credit vnto the aduertisments of the faithfull. Esa 6.c.10.*

Erfurt edition, 1523, 2r

Wie nu der Balaam / da er Gottis worttenn nichtt gehorchet tzu letzt auch von seiner eselin gestrafft must werden vnd sich doch nicht dran keret / also sollen auch vnsere geystlichen Uetter. nach dem sie bißher / fur der hellenn warheitt deß Euangeli ir oren / wie die otter / verstopffen / itzt auch an dem kalb vnd kuhe fur yren augen / alß im spiegel sehen / wer sie sind fur got / vnd was man ym hymel von inen helt. wye wol sie die augen dennoch sollen fest tzu schliessenn / das sie ya des keins sehen / sie mochten sonst sich bekeren / vnd dem grewlichen vrteil Gottis entrynnen. Denn den verstocktenn pharao bewegen wedder wort noch tzeychenn

French version, 1557, p. 33

Tout ainsi donc que Balaam n'a peu nullement obtemperer à la parole de Dieu,[9] & combien qu'il fust redargué par son Anesse parlante en voix humaine, neantmoins n'a peu estre amendé: außi on peut dire le semblable de ces Peres venerables, qui ont iusques à present estoupé leurs oreilles à la voix tresclaire de la verité Euangelique. Maintenant ils se doyuent contempler eux-mesmes en ce Veau & en la vache, comme en vn miroir, & considerer quels ils sont deuant Dieu, & quelle reputation & quelle voix ils ont au ciel. & toutesfois ils doyuent fermer les yeux à ce qu'ils ne voyent rien de tout cecy, dont ils puissent auoir quelque repentance, pour fuir ou euiter le iugement horrible de Dieu. Car il n'y auoit ne remonstrance, ne parole, ne signe qui peust esmouuoir ou flechir l'endurcissement de Pharaon.[10]

---

[9] Marginalia: *Papistes endurcis à lexemple de Balaam.*

[10] Marginalia: *Endurcis a l'exemple de Pharaon.*

Translation in the Latin edition, 400r

Sicut igitur Balaam, cum uerbo Dei, non obtemperaret, tandemque asina loquente redargueretur, nihil tamen emendabatur, Ita quoque nostri Patres, postquam hactenus ad charissimam[11] uocem veritatis euangelicę aures uiperarum more obstruxerunt, iam in uitulo & uacca tanquam in speculo seipsos debent contemplari, qui sint coram Deo, & quam in cœlo existimationem, qualia suffragia obtineant, Nihilominus uero claudere debent oculos, ne quid horum uideant, unde resipiscentes, horribile iudicium Dei effugiant, Nam obstinatum Pharaonem nec uerba nec signa mouebant.

English translation of the French version, 1579, 13r/13v

Euen as then Balaam coulde by no meanes obey the woorde of God,[12] and although hée was rebuked by his Asse speaking vnto him in a mans voice, yet (13v) neuerthelesse hée could not amende it: so one may say the lyke of those holy Fathers, which haue hetherto stopped their eares at the cléere voyce of the veritie of the Gospell. Nowe they ought to beholde themselues in this Calfe and in the Cowe, as in a glasse, and to consider what they are before God, and what reputacion and what voice they haue in heauen. And yet neuerthelesse they ought to shut their eyes that they doe sée nothing of all this, whereoff they may repent themselues, for to auoid the horrible iudgement of God. For there is neither forewarning, word nor signe that could moue or bend the hard heart of Pharao.[13]

---

[11] 1546: *clarissimam*. This shows that the French translation was done from the 1546 edition.

[12] Marginalia: *The Papistes hearts hardened after the example of Balaam.*

[13] Marginalia: *The hearts hardened after the example of Pharao.*

Erfurt edition, 1523, 2r

Auffs erst vnd tzursumma dises tzeychens / las dir das keinn schimpff sein. Das Got eim kalb das geystlich kleyd. die heilige kutten hat angetzogen. Damit hat er on tzweyffel auf eim hauffen bedeut. das eß bald offenbar werden muß. wie die gantze Muncherey vnd Nonnerey nichtß anderß sei. den ein falscher lugenhafftiger schein / vnd euserlich gleyssen eins geystlichen gotlichen lebens. Den wir armen leut haben bißher gemeynet der heilig geist were vnter der kutten / vnnd das ein solch kleidt nichtz den eyttel geist deckte.

French version, 1557, p. 33/34

En premier lieu, afin que ie dise tout en vn mot, ne pensez point que ce soit vne moquerie ou quelque fable controuuée à plaisir, que Dieu a vestu vn Veau d'vn habit religieux, & d'vn capuchon de Moine. Il ne faut point douter qu'il n'ait voulu par vne telle image ou figure denoter quelque assemblée, de laquelle on puisse bien tost & clairement cognoistre, que la moinerie n'est rien qu'vne vaine apparence & vn fard de pieté,[14] & vne hypocrisie externe (p. 34) d'vne vie saincte & approuuée de Dieu. Car iusques à present nous autres poures & miserables hommes auons eu ceste opinion, que le S. Esprit habitoit sous le froc, & que cest habit ne couuroit rien que l'Esprit.

[14] Marginalia: *La moynerie est vne vaine apparence.*

Translation in the Latin edition, 400r

PRincipio, ut summatim uniuerseque complectar, Noli iocum ludumue putare, quod uitulo Deus religiosam uestem, nempe sacrosanctum cucullum induit, qua imagine proculdubio cœtum aliquem demonstrauit, unde quam primum innotescere manifestarique oportet, Monachatum nihil esse quam fucatam inanemque speciem pietatis, & externam hypocrisin sanctæ atque diuinitus approbatæ uitæ, Nos enim infelicissimi homines constanter hactenus opinati fuimus habitare sub cucullo Spiritum sanctum, uestemque illam nihil præter spiritum operire.

English translation of the French version, 1579, 13v

First, that I may speak briefly, thinke not, that the same is a mockery or a fable, that God hath clothed a Calfe with a religious habite, & with a Moonkes coole. Wée must not doubt, but that he noteth by that Image or figure, a certeine assemble of people, of whiche one may cléerely knowe, that the Moonkery is nothing els but a vaine appearaunce and shewe of godlynesse, and outward hipocrisie of a holy lyfe allowed of God.[15] For euen vntil this times we poore and miserable men haue had this opinion and haue beléeued, that the holy Ghost dwelleth vnder the frocke, and that the same habit doth couer nothing but the holy Ghost.

[15] Marginalia: *The Moonkery is but a vaine appearaunce.*

Erfurt edition, 1523, 2r/2v

So tzeygte Gott hie an / das es nur ein kalb deckt / als solt er sagen. Es ist (2v) ein schalcks hutlin. Den was ein kalb bedeutte / lernet vnnß altzu wol / das gulden kalb Aaron / das in der wusten vom volck Israel fur ein Got auff geworffenn wart. Exo[dus] .xxxiij. vnd p[salmu]s .lxxvij. Sie wandelten yr herligkeit in ein bild einß kalbß das graß frisset. vnd die kelber Ieroboam zu Bethel vnd dan[ielis] iij. Re[gum] xij. Da widder die propheten so hefftig schreyen.

French version, 1557, p. 34

Mais Dieu reuele icy, qu'il n'y a rien sous cest habit qu'vn Veau. Comme s'il vouloit monstrer qu'il y a vn serpent caché sous l'herbe. Car le Veau d'or d'Aaron,[16] fondu au desert, auquel le peuple d'Israel presentoit des honneurs appartenans à Dieu, Exode chapitre trentetroisieme, enseigne ouuertement ce que le Veau peut signifier. Il est dit au Pseau. cent sixieme, Ils ont mué leur gloire en similitude d'vn Veau mangeant l'herbe. Il est parlé außi des veaux de Ioroboam, faits en Bethel & Dan, I. Rois chapitre douzieme, contre lesquels les Prophetes ont crié si aspremement.

[16] Marginalia: *Le Veau d'or d'Aaron.*

Translation in the Latin edition, 400r

At hic reuelat Deus, quod solummodo uitulum tegat[17], Quasi dicat: Latet anguis in herba.[18] Nam quid uitulus significet perspicuè docet aureus uitulus Aaronis in deserto. Cui populus lsraël diuinos honores tribuebat, Exod. 33. Psal. 106. Et mutauerunt gloriam suam in similitudinem uituli, comedentes[19] fœnum, Et uituli Ieroboam in Bethel & Dan. 1. Reg. 12. In quos Prophetæ tantis clamoribus inuehuntur.[20]

English translation of the French version, 1579, 13v/14r

But God hath reuealed héere, that there is nothing vnder that habite but a Calfe. As if he would shewe that there is a Serpent hid vnder the grasse. For the golden calfe of Aaron,[21] lifted vp in the wildernesse, vnto whom the children of Israel did represent & giue the honour that apperteined and belonged vnto God, Exodus Chapter. 32. teacheth playnelye what the Calfe may signifie. It is sayde in the 106. Psalme. They haue turned their glory into ẏ similitude of a Calfe, that eateth hay. It is spoken also of ẏ Calues of Iereboam, made in Bethell and Dan. 1. Reg. Chapter. 12.[22] (14r) against whome the Prophets haue cryed very sharply.

---

[17] 1551 *degat.*

[18] Marginalia: *Monachacci fucata & Inanis species pietatis.*

[19] 1546 *commedentis.*

[20] Marginalia: *Aureus uitulus Aaronis.*

[21] Marginalia: *The golden Calfe of Aaron.*

[22] Three marginalia: *Exo.32. Psa.106.c.28. 1.Reg.12.*

Erfurt edition, 1523, 2v

Also sihe du nun dis munchkalb auch an / das die kutte sey das gantz geystlich wesen mit alle yrem gottis dienst. den sie gros achten / mit beten / messenn / singen / fastenn etc. Aber wem thun sie solchen gottis dienst. wer wirt da mit geehret. An wem hanget er. Am kalbe. Den die kutten zieret vnd kleidett das kalb wie du sihest. Was ist den das kalb. Es ist ir falscher abgot in irem lugenhafftigen hertzen.

French version, 1557, p. 34

En ceste mesme façon qu'on iette vn peu les yeux sur ce Veau-Moine, comme son capuchon represente ici vne figure de tout l'ordre des Moines, auec tous leurs seruices diuins & obseruations, desquelles ils font si grand cas: comme de leurs pate-nostres tant de fois repetées, de la foire de leurs Messes, de leurs beaux chants & iusnes, & autres choses semblables. Mais à qui est presenté tout ce beau seruice? qui en est honnoré? de qui depend-il? à qui est-il attache? Au Veau. Car le Veau est vestu & paré du froc, comme on le voit icy. Est quest-ce que ce Veau? C'est vne idole forgée & controuuée, residente en leurs esprits pleins de fallaces.[23]

---

[23] Marginalia: *Le Veau est l'idole forgée aux esprits des Moines.*

Translation in the Latin edition, 400r

Eodem modo aspice hunc Monachouitulum, ut cucullus typum gerat totius ordinis Religiosorum cum uniuersis cultibus, quos maximi faciunt, ut βαττολογίαι precum, nondinatio Missarum, cantilenæ & ieiunia &c.[24] Sed cui præstatur, quem honore affecit, à quo pendet, cui adhæret iste cultus? Vitulo, Nam cucullus uestit & ornat uitulum, quemadmodum uides, Quid porro est Vitulus? est commenticium idolum insidens fallacissimis mentibus eorum.

English translation of the French version, 1579, 14r

In lyke manner let vs beholde a little that same Moonkish Calfe, howe that his coole doth represent there a figure of all the order of Moonkes, with al their seruices and diuine obseruations, of which they do make so great accompt: as of their Pater noster, so oftentimes repeted, of ye faire of their Masses, of their goodly songs, and fastings, and other lyke. But vnto whom is that goodly seruice represented? who is honoured? of whome doth it depende? vnto whom is it tyed and fastened? vnto the Calfe. For the Calfe is clothed with a frock, as we may sée heere. And what is that Calfe?[25] It is an Idoll forged and made, abiding and dwelling in their spirites full of deceites.

---

[24] Marginalia: *Vitulus*.

[25] Marginalia: *The Calfe is an Idoll forged in the spirites of Moonkes.*

Erfurt edition, 1523, 2v

Wie geht daß tzu. Also gehet es tzu. Sie haben ein meinung vnd gewissen. das sie dem rechten waren Got dienen mit yrem geistlichenn wesen / vnnd wollen den himel mit iren wercken verdienenn. und stellen auch yren gotts diennst auff lautter menschlich werck. nicht auff den glauben

French version, 1557, p. 34/35

Comme est-ce que ces choses se font? Elles se font ainsi, Ces venerables ont vne persua(p. 35)sion ou vne opinion imprimée en leur entendement, qu'en leur religion monachale & solitaire ils seruent & rendent obeissance au seul vray Dieu, laquelle religion ils ont constituée en ceremonies & obseruations de quelques œuures externes,[26] pour lesquelles ils pensent qu'ils ont bien merité le ciel: & non point en la certitude & fiance qui embrasse le benefice de Iesus Christ.

---

[26] Marginalia: *La religion des Moines bastie sur ceremonies & œuures externes.*

Translation in the Latin edition, 400r

Quomodo fiunt hæc? Ita fiunt, Habent impressam animo opinionem seu persuasionem, quod uniuero Deo seruiant in religione solitaria, quam in cæremonijs externorum operum, propter quæ cœlum sibi deberi existimant, non in fiducia amplectente Christi beneficium ponunt.

English translation of the French version, 1579, 14r

What is that that these things doo? They do after this sorte. These holy Masters haue an opinion imprinted in their vnderstanding, that in their Moonkish and solitary religion, they doe serue and render obedience vnto the true God, the whiche religion they haue constituted in Ceremonies & obseruations of certeine outward woorkes,[27] by which they doe thinke that they haue well deserued heauen: and not in the certeinty & trust which embraceth the benefit of Iesus Christ.

---

[27] Marginalia: *The religion of the Moonkes builded vpon ceremonies and outvvard works.*

Erfurt edition, 1523, 2v

Nu ist kein Gott in hymel vnd erden. der sich damit eren last. es sey dan der Teuffel odder ein abgot. Den dem rechten waren Got / kan man nicht anderß den ym geist vnd warheit dienen. Iohan[ni] iiij. das ist im glauben vnd vber menschlichen wercken. die der geist Christi in vnß thut. Iohan[ni] vi vnd Isa[ia] lv. Darumb kunden solch falsche geistliche iren gottiß dienst. vnter dem namen gottis / niemant anders thun den yrem eigen falschen dunckel / der in furgibt / Gotte sey da mitt gedienet /

French version, 1557, p. 35

Or est-il ainsi qu'il n'y a aucun Dieu, soit au ciel ou en la terre, qui veuille estre ainsi serui & adoré, sinon le diable & les idoles. Car nul ne peut seruir ny obeir au vray Dieu, sinon en esprit & verité, Iean quatrieme: c'est à dire, en foy & vrais & spirituels mouuemens de l'esprit, les quels le S. Esprit crée, suscite & viuifie en nous, Esa. chapitre L V. Parquoy ces faux religieux ne peuuent offrir à nul leurs seruices, les quels ils couurent du nom de Dieu cependant se destournans de toutes les ordonnances & manifestations Diuines,[28] & ne les peuuent rapporter ny adresser, sinon en applaudissant & flattant leur vaine imagition, laquelle ils ont forgée en leur cerueau, songeant que tels seruices & obseruations sont agreables à Dieu.

[28] Marginalia: *Le service des Moines ne peut profiter à nul.*

Translation in the Latin edition, 400r

Iam nullus est Deus uel in cœlo uel in terra, qui sic coli se uelit, præter Diabolum & idola. Nam uero Deo nemo seruire potest nisi spiritu & ueritate, Iohan. 4. hoc est, in fide, animique ueris & spiritualibus motibus, quos creat, exuscitat, uiuificat in nobis spiritus sanctus, Esa. 55. Itaque hi falso religiosi cultus suos, quibus nomen Dei prætexunt, discedentes interim à mandato & patefactione diuina reipsa nemini præstare nusquam referre ac dirigere Possunt, quàm ut blandiantur à se confictæ imaginationi, quæ somniat hæc officia placere Deo[29].

English translation of the French version, 1579, 14r/14v

For it is euen thus, that there is no God, either in heauen or earth which would be so serued & worshipped but ẙ diuel & the Idols. For none can serue nor obey the true God, but in spirit & truth, Iohn ẙ 4. Chapter[30]: That is to say, in faith and true & spirituall mouinges of the spirit, the which the holy Ghost doth create, stirre vp, & quicken in vs. Esa. Chapter. lv.[31] Wherfore these false religious people cannot offer vnto any their seruices, ẙ which they do cloak & hide vnder the name of God, & in the meane time turning themselues from all the ordinances & heauenly manifestations,[32] & cannot bring them back againe, nor set them vp, but in reioysing & flattering (14v) their vaine imaginations, the which they haue forged of their own braine, dreaming that such seruices & obseruations are agréeable vnto God.

---

[29] 1551 conversion *Deo placere.*

[30] Marginalia: *Iohn.4.c.24.*

[31] Marginalia: *Esa.55.*

[32] Marginalia: *The seruice of the Monks can not profit any man.*

Erfurt edition, 1523, 2v/3r

Der selb dunckel ist die lugen / vnd der abgot in irem hertzen / gleich wie den Iuden auch war yn iren abgoͤttereyenn: Sihe das ist das kalb / vnnd die falsch fleischliche meinung des geistlichen wesens / daran sie hangen / vnd den sie schmucken mit irem schonen gleyssen vnd glatten kutten / So frist nu das kalb nur gras / Den solch heiligen haben nichts von tzukunfftigen guttern / sondern mastenn sich hie auff erden / wie wir sehen / das die besten gutter die meysten wollust / die hohiste ehre die grossist gewalt (3r) bey den geistlichenn ist

French version, 1557, p. 35/36

Vne telle folle imagination n'est que mensonge & vne idole forgée en leurs cœurs, ny plus ny moins que les Payens ou les Iuifs se forgeoyent des dieux estranges. Voici, c'est-ci le Veau: c'est-ci l'impieté: c'est-ci la charnelle opinion couuerte d'habit religieux: c'est-ci l'idole à laquelle ils sont attachez, laquelle ils embrassent & ornent de la beauté des ceremonies & contenances, & d'vne forme notable de paremens. (p. 36) Or le Veau ne vit que d'herbes.[33] cartels hypocrites n'ont nulle cognoissance des biens eternels, ains s'engraissent des delices de la vie presente: comme on void manifestement que les puissances les plus florissantes, les plus amples richesses, les plus grandes voluptez, & les plus hautes dignitez & honneurs sont pardeuers les gens d'eglise, comme on les appelle.

---

[33] Marginalia: *Que c'est d'estre nourri d'herbe.*

Translation in the Latin edition, 400r/400v

Hæc imaginatio est mendacium & commentitium idolum in cordibus eorum, prorsus ut Ethnici aut Iudæi fingebant sibi numina. Ecce hic est uitulus, hæc impietas, opinioque carnalis, operta religioso habitu, hoc idolum, cui adhærent, quod amplectuntur, exornant cæremoniarum gestuumque decoro, atque notabili indumentorum forma. POrro, uitulus solo gramine uescitur, Tales enim hypocritæ nullis futuris & æternis bonis fruuntur, sed præsentis uitæ delicijs pinguescunt,[34] (400v) sicut apparet florentissimam potentiam, preciosissimas opes, maximas uoluptates, amplissimos honores penes Ecclesiasticos, ut uocantur, esse,

English translation of the French version, 1579, 14v

Such foolish and fonde imagination is nothing but lyings and an Idoll inuented and forged of their owne braine, neither more nor lesse, but euen as the Panims or Iewes doe forge straunge Gods. Beholde, this is the Calfe, this is the impietie: this is the carnal opinion couered and hid with the religious habite: this is the Idoll to the which they are bounde and tyed, the which they dooe garnish and beautifie with Ceremonies and with a goodly kinde of shewes. The Calfe doth not liue but of hearbes and grasse. For such hipocrites haue no knowledge of the eternall goodnesse, but doe fat themselues with the pleasures of this present lyfe: As one may playnly sée that the most puissantest and ample riches,[35] and the most greatest pleasures, and the most highest dignities and honours are belonging vnto the people of the Church, as one calleth them.

---

[34] Marginalia: *Hypocritæ præsentis uitæ delicijs dediti sunt.*

[35] Marginalia: *VVhat it is to be nourished & fed vvith grasse.*

Erfurt edition, 1523, 3r

Solch gras / muß solch kalb essenn / vnd so wurt an in auch war / daß sie yr herlickeit verwandeln ynn ein bild eins kalbs / daß graß frisset / Den Christus ist vnser herlickeyt / des wyr vns rhumen vnd frewen sollten / so richten sie an sein stat an / ein ander rhum im hertzen / daß sie sich verlassen vnd rhumen yrer eigen werck vnd verdienst / da steht daß kalb yn Christus statt vnd furet Christus namen

French version, 1557, p. 36

& ainsi ces veaux ont trouué des herbes selon leur goust. Et ceci leur est aduenu, qu'ils ont changé leur gloire en vne similitude de veau mangeant le foin. Car Christ est nostre vraye gloire, en qui il nous faudroit triompher, glorifier & resiouir. ceux-ci au rebours cerchent vne autre gloire en leurs cœurs, & se vantent orgueilleusement de la confiance de leurs merites & œuures. Vn tel veau est succedé au lieu de Iesus Christ: & en vsurpant le nom d'iceluy, il le blaspheme & deshonnore.

Translation in the Latin edition, 400v

Ita suas habent lactuacas labra uitulina.[36] Et sic contingit illis, ut mutent gloriam suam in similitudinem uituli comedentis fœnum. Christus enim uere est gloria nostra, in quo triumphari gloriari, lætarique deberemus. Hi ècontra loco eius aliam parant gloriam in cordibus uidelicet, qua iactant fiduciam suorum operum & meritorum, Talis uitulus in Christi locum successit, & nomen eius usurpando dedecorat.

English translation of the French version, 1579, 14v

And euen so these Calues haue found grasse for their owne tooth. And this is happened vnto them, that they haue turned their glory into the similitude of a Calfe that eateth Haye.[37] For Christ is our true glory, in whom wée must triumph, glory, and reioyce. These héere cleane contrarye, doe séeke an other glorye in their heartes, and doe aduaunce and bragge themselues verye proudly of the trust of their merites and woorkes. Such a Calfe is come in the stéed of Iesus Christ, & in vsurping the name of him, he doth blaspheme and dishonour it.

---

[36] Marginalia: *Hypocritæ præsentis uitæ delitijs deditis sunt.*

[37] Marginalia: *Psa.106.c.10.* Additional reference added by the English translation.

Erfurt edition, 1523, 3r

Auffs ander / das die kutten am hyndersten vnd an beynen vnd fornen entgentzet vnd zurissen ist / bedeut das in solchem geistlichen wesen vnd gots dienst keinn einickeit ist / so doch nichts hoherß in der schrifft gefodert wirt / den das die Christen sollen gleich gesinnet sein. wie p[salmu]s. lxvij· Gott machtt im haußе wonen / die einerley gesynnet sind. Und p[salmu]s. c.xxxij. O wie feyn ists vnnd lieblich / wenn bruder eyns mit eynander wonen / Aber disze vnchristliche vngeystliche geyster / haben so mancherley syn vnd weise / alß farben /

French version, 1557, p. 36/37

Secondement,[38] l'habit monachal deschiré par taillades à l'entour des cuisses, & és pieds & au ventre, signifie que en ceste religion solitaire & en ces ceremonies & obseruations pleines de fallaces, il n'y a rien d'accord, ou qui s'entretienne, ou qui soit entier: & toutesfois la saincte Escriture requiert ceci singulierement & auant toutes choses, que les Chrestiens & fideles soyent bien vnis. Comme il est dit au Pseaume cent treizieme, O que c'est chose bonne & bien delectable, que les freres soyent de bon acord habitans ensemble! Mais ces esprits frenetiques, superstitieux & irreligieux ont bien seu forger & controuuer autant de differences de sectes & opinions, qu'il y a eu de diuers (p. 37) Vestemens & habits entre eux.

---

[38] Marginalia: *Qui signisie la peau de ce Veau deschiquettée.*

Translation in the Latin edition, 400v

SEcundo Monastica uestis circa coxas in pedibus, & uentre diloricata significat in hac solitaria religione nugatorijsque cæremonijs, nihil concors, cohærens, integrum existere, cum tamen in primis & ante omnia postulet Scriptrura, ut Christiani sint ὁμοφρονοῦντες, ut Psal. 133.[39] Ecce quàm bonum & quàm iucundum habitare Fratres in unum, Verum hi superstitiosi irreligiosique spiritus tot inuenerunt opinionum sectarumque discrimina, quot distinctos colore uestitus.

English translation of the French version, 1579, 14v/15r

Secondly, the Moonkish apparaile rent full of holes[40] about the thighes, féete, and belly, doe signifie that in that solytarie religion and in those Ceremonies and obseruations ful of deceits, there is no agréeing that is perfect or whole: And yet the holye Scripture re(15r)quireth chiefely and before all things, that the Christians and faythfull be of one felowshippe and vnitie. As it is sayde in the 133. Psalme, O how good and ioyfull a thing it is:[41] bretheren to dwell together in vnitie. But these madde braynes, supersticious and too holy Moonkes knew very well to forge, inuent & finde out so many differences of sectes and opinions, as there is of diuers apparayle among them.

---

[39] Marginalia: *Vestis uituli laceræ significatio.*

[40] Marginalia: *VVhat doth signifie the skinne of this Calfe, being torne or rent.*

[41] Marginalia: *Psa.133.2.2.8.*

Erfurt edition, 1523, 3r

Die barffsen dunckt yhr regel die beste / die prediger widderumb achtenn ir regel die beste / Augustiner hienaus / die Carthuser dort hinaus / keine dunckt daß gut sein / das den andern gut dunckt / Also ist dye kutten am hyntern des kalbs tzwryssen vnd an denn beynen / ob sie gleich wol alle darynnen eynß sind / daß sie eynerley kalb schmucken / daß ist / gleichen vnglawben vnd meynung durch die werck den hymel tzu erlangen

French version, 1557, p. 37

Les Cordeliers magnifient leur ordre: les Iacopins maintiennent leur reigle:[42] les Benedictins ne veulent nullement perdre leur honneur: les Augustins tirent du costé droict, les Chartreux du gauche: les Celestins tiennent leur reng: brief, il n'y en a pas vn à qui son froc ne semble estre beau. Ainsi voyons-nous que le froc est deschiré par bribes à l'endroict des cuisses & és pieds de ce Veau: combine que tous soyent d'vne mesme volonté & s'accordent bien, entant que touche l'accoustrement & parement du Veau: c'est à dire, combien que tous nourrissent ceste opinion obstinée en leurs cœurs: à sauoir, qu'ils doutent ou se defient de la misericorde de de Dieu: & au contraire s'appuyent sur la fiance & asseurance charnelle de leurs œuures, selon leurs obseruations.

---

[42] Marginalia: *Le froc diuise en plusiers sectes.*

Translation in the Latin edition, 400v

Inde Franciscani suam iactant regulam, Prædicatorum ordo suam effert. Augustiniani ad dextram, Carthusiani ad sinistram deflectunt, denique suum cuique pulchrum. Ita uides, circa coxas & in pedibus Vituli lacerum cucullum, etiam si omnes unanimes consentientesque sint, quod ad Vituli cultum & ornatum attinet, id est, etiamsi omnes dubitationem seu diffidentiam de misericordia Dei, contra uero fiduciam operum & securitatem carnalem suis obseruationibus confirment alantque.

English translation of the French version, 1579, 15r

The Cordeliers, that is of the order of Sainct Fraunces, doe magnifie their order:[43] The Iacopins, that is of the order of saint Dominicke, their rule: The Benedictines will in no case loose their honour: The Augustines do goe on the right side: The Charterhouse Moonkes on the lefte: The Celestines doe keepe their company: To conclude, there is not one but that he thinketh himselfe very fine and trimme in his apparel. so we seing that the frocke is rent and torne about the thighes and féete of that Calfe: Although that all were of one will and did agrée well, as much as concerneth the apparell of the Calfe: that is to say, although that all did nourish that obstinate opinion in their hearts: to wit that they did doubt or distrust of the mercie of God: and on the contrary did leane and stay vppon the affiaunce and carnall assurance of their woorkes, according to their obseruations.

---

[43] Marginalia: *The frocke deuided into many sects.*

Erfurt edition, 1523, 3r

Und sonderlich ist das tzu mercken / das der hynderst / bedeut das ende / vnd die beyne / bedeutt die / auff welchen das kalb (das ist solche falsche meinung) bestehtt Denn es noch nie so vil secten / orden / vnterscheid vnd namen der geistlichen gewesen sind / als ytzt ein tzeyt her / nach dem eß anß end komen ist / vnd ir buberey da hin fellet vnd aufhoren muß. Und die beine / sind die frechen bruder vnd lerer. Magistri nostri eximij.

French version, 1557, p. 37/38

On cognoistra ceci encore plus clairement, si on entend la fin &[44] extremité par les cuisses, & si on veut des pieds en faire des porte-faix, desquels ce Veau, c'est à dire ceste fausse masque, est soustenue. Car iamais il n'y eut tant de sectes, tant de familles, tant de differences, tant de noms, tant d'ordres, ou plustost desordres introduits, qu'on en a veu de nostre temps, quand la fin en est prochaine, & que ceste bosse doit creuer : puis que la vanité & les fallaces sont descouuertes, außi verrons-nous tomber bas toute ceste infection. Les pieds donc signifient ces hardis freres &[45] autres, ces Sophistes, & nos maistres venerables qui ont préeminence par dessus les autres: & qui sont les plus audacieux (p. 38) & les plus sauans cloistriers, lesquels sauent bien conseruer, amplifier & establir la dignité

---

[44] Marginalia: *Le cuisses signifient l'extremité.*

[45] Marginalia: *Que signifient les pieds de ce Veau.*

Translation in the Latin edition, 400v

Hæc magis erunt illustria, si coxæ intelligantur finis & extremum, pedes uero baiuli, à quibus hic Vitulus, hoc est, falsa talis opinio fulcitur ac sustentatur.[46] Nunquam enim tot sectæ, familiæ, discrimina, nomina Religiosorum prodire quàm nostra memoria cœperunt, cum finis instat, deprehensaque uanitate labes illa intercidit ac elanguescit. Pedes igitur significant audaculos Fratres & Sophistas Magistros nostros eximios,

English translation of the French version, 1579, 15r/15v

We shall know this more cléerely, if wée doe vnderstande the ende and extremitie by the thighes,[47] and if we will make of the féete proppes by the which this Calfe, that is to say, this false Maske, is holden vp and maynteined. For there was neuer so many sects, so many housholds, so many differences, so many names, so many orders, or rather disorders brought in, as haue bene séene in our time, when the ende is nigh, and that that byle should breake: séeing that the vani(15v)tie and the deceits are vncouered and made knowen, so shall wee see all this infection to fall downe. The féete doe signifie those bolde bretheren and others,[48]

---

[46] Marginalia: *Coxæ. Pedes.*

[47] Marginalia: *The thighes do signifie extremitie.*

[48] Marginalia: *What the feet of this Calfe do signifie.*

Erfurt edition, 1523, 3r/3v

vnd ir gelertisten hin vnd her in den orden / die solch geistlich wesen mit yrem schreyben / predigen / lesen vnnd leren vnter yn / vnd in der welt / erhalten / Und doch keiner mitt dem andern eines ist. So vil kopffe / so mancherley opinion sind da (3v) Aufffß dritte / furet das kalb aller dinge / die geperde einß predigerß / eß streckt die hinderbein alß stunde / vnd reckt auß die rechte pfotte / wie ein prediger sein rechte hand / vnd zeucht die lincke zu sich

French version, 1557, p. 38

& grande autorité de ceste religion monachale, ou par escrits, ou par predications, ou par lectures, ou par disputations, ou par doctrine: & employent toutes leurs forces à cela, & l'impriment dedens les cœurs de leurs gens par tous les lieux du monde. Quelque chose qu'il y ait, si est-ce qu'ils discordent entre eux: & autant qu'il y a de testes entre eux, autant y a il de diuerses opinions.[49] Tiercement, ce Veau represente de tous costez les gestes & contenances d'vn prescheur. Car il est leué & se tient sur ses pieds de derriere: & des deux pieds de deuant il iette le droit à la façon d'vn prescheur, &[50] retire le gauche:

[49] Marginalia: *Les moines discordans en opinions.*
[50] Marginalia: *Le Veau contrefait le Moi ne prechant.*

Translation in the Latin edition, 400v

item eruditiores cœnobiorum incolas, qui dignitatem autoritaremque huius solitariæ religionis concionando, scribendo, legendo, disputando, docendo, quo ad possunt in suorum animis ac ubique gentium conseruant, amplificant, stabiliunt. Omnes, tamen inter se discrepantes, ac labyrinthos opinionum nectentes. Quot capita, tot sententiæ. TErtio, repræsentat Vitulus unde quaque gestum concionantis, Postremis enim pedibus innititur, quasi stans erectus, ex prioribus autem dextram proijcit ungulam uelut Concionator retrahens sinistram,

English translation of the French version, 1579, 15v

those Sophisters, and our worshipfull masters which haue the preheminence aboue other: & which are the most boldest, and the most skilfull or cunningest Cloysterers, who do know full well to kéepe, amplifie and establish the dignitie and great authoritie of that Moonkish religion, eyther by writings, preachings, lectures, disputacions or doctrines: and doe endeauour themselues with all their strength thereto, and doe imprint it into the heartes of the people throughout the whole world. For euery trifling thing they fall out and disagrée among themselues: and as many as there be of heads among them, so many opinions there be.[51] Thirdly, this Calfe representeth the gesture and countenaunce of a Preacher. For he standeth vpright vppon his hinder féete: and of the two fore féete, he casteth the right after the manner of a Preacher, and holdeth backe the lefte,

[51] Marginalia: *The Moonkes disagreeing in opinions. The Calde doth counterfait the Moonkish Preachers.*

Erfurt edition, 1523, 3v

wirfft den kopff auff / vnd hat die zunge im maul / vnd ist alleß gestalt / als stund eß vnd prediget / Darumb wie der Bapstesel das Bapstum abmalltt / So malet eygentlich diß Munchkalb / die Apostel vnd schuler deß Bapsts / das alle welt sehe / was sie bißher fur prediger vnd lerer gehortt vnd noch hoͤren / Den was solt ein eselskopff billicher tzu Apostel haben / den ein kalbs kopff? fleyschlich regiment hatt auch fleyschliche lere / Darumb hats auch noch nichtt augen / das es die ienigen deutte / da Christuß von sagt Mat[thei] xxiij. Wee euch schrifftgelertenn yr verblendte blind leytter.

French version, 1557, p. 38

il a la teste leuée: il tire la langue hors: il n'y a rien en luy qui ne represente ces grans criars en chaire. Tout ainsi donc que l'Asne-Pape[52] a esté vne image & figure du royaume Papistique, außi ce Veau-Moine represente au vif les apostres & disciples du Pape, en sorte que tout le monde voit bien quels docteurs ou prescheurs il a ouy iusques à present, & quels il oyt encores auiourdhuy. Car pourroit-on trouuer vn apostre plus propre pour le cerueau d'vn Asne, que la teste d'vn Veau? C'est vn couuerde propre pour le pot. Le gouuernement charnel porte par tout vne doctrine charnelle. Et pourtant le veau est encore sans yeux, pour figurer ceux desquels Iesus Christ dit en S. Matthieu chapitre vingttroisieme, Malheur sur vous Scribes & Pharisiens, conducteur aueugles.

---

[52] Marginalia: *Les Moines, apostres du Pape.*

Translation in the Latin edition, 400v

caput sursum fert, linguam exerit, ac omnia referunt e suggesto uociferantem ad populum.[53] Ideo sicut Papasellus fuit imago regni Pontificij, Ita proprie Monachiuitulus exprimit Apostolos Discipulosque Papæ, ut totus uideat orbis, quos audierit hactenus Prædicatores & Doctores, hodiesque audeat. Quis enim magis appositus foret, ad asininum cerebrum Apostolus uituli capite? Dignum patella operculum.[54] Carnale regimen, carnalem docrtinam circumfert, Itaque uitulus adhuc oculis caret, ut adumbret illos, de quibus inquit Christus Matth. 23. Væ uobis Scribæ & Pharisæi, duces cæci.

English translation of the French version, 1579, 15v/16r

hée hath his heade lyfted vp: he putteth out his tongue: there is nothing in him, which doth not represent those greate Cryers in the flesh. Euen then as the Popish Asse hath bene an Image or figure of the Papisticall kingdome,[55] so this Moonkish Calfe doth represent the Apostles and Disciples of the Pope, in such sort that all the world doth well sée what Doctors or Preachers they haue heard vntil this present time, and what they doe heare at this day. For can any man finde an Apostle more fit for the braine of an Asse, then the head of a Calfe: This is a fit couer for the pot. The carnall gouernment hath alwayes a carnall doctrine. And therefore the Calfe is yet without eyes, or blinde, for to figure those of whome Iesus Christ (16r) speaketh off in Saint Mathew the 23. chapter, saying.[56] Wo be vnto you Scribes and Pharisies, blinde guydes.

---

[53] Marginalia: *Vitulus representat gestum concionantis.*

[54] Marginalia: *Papasellus. Monacho uitulus.*

[55] Marginalia: *The Moonkes the Apostles of the Pope.*

[56] Marginalia: *Mat.23.b.16.*

Erfurt edition, 1523, 3v

Und Isaie lvi. Yhr verseher sind alle blind vnd wissen nichts / Uil anders mehr mag man wol an dem kalbe auff die munch vnd lerer deutten / Als das / daß ore an der kutten / die vntregliche Tiranney der beicht bedeutte / damit sie die weltt marteren vnd zum teuffel furen /

French version, 1557, p. 38/39

Et Esaie (p.39) chapitre cinquantesixieme, Ses gardes ont esté aueugles, tous ont esté ignorans: les pasteurs mesmes n'ont seu que c'estoit d'intelligence. On pourroit bien proprement accommoder beaucoup d'autres choses en ce monstre aux Moines & Sophistes. Comme ceci, L'oreille attachée au froc, signifie la tyrannie insupportable des confeßions, par laquelle ils iettent les poures consciences en la geule du diable, & les mettent en vne terrible torture.[57]

---

[57] Marginalia: *L'aureille denote les confeßions.*

Translation in the Latin edition, 400v

Et Esa. 56. Speculatores eius cæci omnes, nescierunt uniuersi, Ipsi Pastores ignorauerunt intelligentiam.[58] LOnge plura in hoc Monstro ad Monachos Sophistasque concinne accommodari possunt, uerbi causa, ut auris inserta cucullo, significet intolerandam confessionum tyrannidem, qua conscientias acerbissime cruciatas Diaboli faucibus obijciunt:

English translation of the French version, 1579, 16r

And Esay in his. 56. chapter sayth. All his watchmen are all blinde,[59] they haue altogether no vnderstanding, they are all dumme Dogges, not being able to barke, they are slippery: sluggish are they, and lye sweating: they are shamelesse Dogges that be neuer satisfied. The shepheards also in lyke manner haue no vnderstanding. We might very properly or fitly apply many other things in that Monster, vnto the Moonkes and Sophisters. As this: The eare tyed to the frocke, signifieth the insupportable tyranny of confessions,[60] by the which they doe cast and throw the poore consciences into the diuells throate, and doe put them in a terrible bondage.

---

[58] Marginalia: *Auris*.

[59] Marginalia: *Esa.56.c.10*.

[60] Marginalia: *The eare noteth the confessions*.

Erfurt edition, 1523, 3v

Die Zunge ym maul / daß yre lere nichts den tzunge / das ist / eyttel vnnutz geschwetze ist / Die tzw wartzen yn der platten auff dem kopff / sollten hoͤrner worden sein / Hoͤrner aber bedeutten die predigtt des Ewangeli / daß vom creutz prediget vnd tzu stosset den alten menschen / Michee .iij. Ich wil deyn horrn eysern machenn das du vil volcks tzustossist etc. Aber dißkalb hat nicht hoͤrner / sondern nur malzeichen vnd schein daruon

French version, 1557, p. 39

La langue sortant dehors, signifie que toute leur doctrine n'est autre chose que l'angue: c'est a dire, vn babil affetté, & parolles friuoles.[61] Les deux petis pois se monstrans sur le test deuoyent estre deux cornes.[62] Et les cornes signifient la predication de l'Euangile, lequel nous assuiettissant à la croix, brise le vieil homme: Michée chapitre quatrieme, Ie mettray la corne de fer, & tu briseras beaucoup de peuples. Or toutefois ce Veau-ci n'a point de cornes, mais seulement quelques apparences qui n'apparoissent gueres.[63]

---

[61] Marginalia: *La langue.*

[62] Marginalia: *Les deux grains de pois.*

[63] Marginalia: *Les Moines destournent la predication de l'Euangile aux traditions humaines.*

Translation in the Latin edition, 400v/401r

Lingua exerta, significat doctrinam eorum nihil esse quàm linguam, id est, uolubilitatem uerborum futilemque loquaciatem.[64] Duæ Cicerculæ in caluitie capitis prominentes debebant in cornua surgere, Cornua uero significant prædicationem Euangelij, quod cruci nos subijciens confringit ueterem hominem, Mich. 4. Cornu tuum ponam ferreum, & comminues populos multos.[65] (401r) Hic autem uitulus non habet cornua. Sed obscura quædam uestigia, & speciem qualemcunque,

English translation of the French version, 1579, 16r

The putting out of the tongue, doth signifie that all their doctrine is no other thing but the tongue.[66] That is to saye, a bablyng and full of vayne words. The two lyttle warts or knobbes which appeare vppon the head, should haue bene two hornes. And the hornes doe signifie the Preaching of the Gospell,[67] the which make vs obedient vnto death or to the crosse, destroying the olde manne: as it is sayde by the Prophet Micheah the fourth Chapter. I will make thy horne yron and thy clawes shall bée of brasse,[68] that thou mayst grinde and crush in péeces many people. Yet neuerthelesse this Calfe hath no hornes, but onely certeyne appearaunce or tokens of hornes, which doe not much appeare.[69]

---

[64] Marginalia: *Lingua.*

[65] Marginalia: *Cicerculæ. 2.*

[66] Marginalia: *The tongue.*

[67] Marginalia: *The two warts or knobs lyke peason.*

[68] Marginalia: *Micheah.4.d.13.*

[69] Marginalia: *The Moonkes doe turne the preaching of ẏͤ Gospell vnto mens tradtions.*

Erfurt edition, 1523, 3v/4r

Den sie haben woll den namen / das sie das Euangelion predigen / aber sie habens gefangen vnd auff yre menschen lere gezwungen / vnd stehn die wartzen yn der platten / den was der platten gefelt / das mus Euangelion heyssen / vnd das Euangelion mus auch nicht auser diszer plattenn faren / sondern sich reymen vnd fugen auff yhr platten heiligkeit / Sonderlich was yr heubt / den Bapst betrifft / Das die kutten vmb den hals szo hart gewunden ist / tzeygt yhren hallstarrigen vorstockten syn yn yrer muncherey vnd heiligem weszen / das ihr gewissen so tieff darynnenn (4r) verpunden vnd verstrickt synd / das sie durch keine macht der aller hellisten warheit er aus komen mugen.

French version, 1557, p. 39/40

Car combien que ceux-ci se vantent de ce tiltre, qu'ils sont docteurs de l'Euangile: toutesfois ils le retreignent & le destournent sottement aux traditions humaines. Ainsi donc du sommet de la teste, qui est chauue, sortent deux petis pois. Car il couure du tiltre de l'Euangile tout ce qu'il luy plaist & ne peut souffrir que l'Euangile sorte hors de ceste pelure: mais il faut qu'il conuienne & s'accorde à la sainctеté de ceste teste rase: & principalement quant au Pape, (p. 40) qui est le chef de toutes ces testes pelées. Quant à ce que le capuchon tient si ferme à l'entour du col, cela demonstre l'obstination incroyable de la superstition & des erreurs de ces cagots, touchant les observations & ceremonies monastiques.[70] Comme de fait ils sont plongez & fichez si profondement dedans telles ordures, que il n'y a ne vertu ne force, ne splendeur de la verité Chrestienne, tant grande soit elle, qui les en puisse tirer hors pour regarder la lumiere.

---

[70] Marginalia: *Le capuchon attaché au col.*

Translation in the Latin edition, 401r

Quamuis enim titulo Doctorum Euangelij se uenditent, tamen id constringunt, & ad humanas traditiones insulse detorquent, Prominent igitur è glabro uertice duæ cicerculæ, Nam quidquid illi arridet, huic nomen Euangelij prætendit, nec sinit Euangelium extra hanc glabriciem progredi, Sed oportet ipsum quadrare & congruere ad tonsi uerticis huius sactimoniam, præfertim quod ad Caput illorum Pontificem spectat. Quod cucullus adeo tenaciter circundat collum, monstrat pertinaciam incredibilem superstitionis atque erroris illorum de cultibus Monasticis, quibus usque eo fordibus immersi infixique sunt, ut nulla ui, nullo splendore Christianæ ueritatis inde reuocari ad aspiciendam lucem possint.

English translation of the French version, 1579, 16r/16v

For although that those dooe bragge and boaste themselues of that title, that they are Doctours of the Gospell: Yet neuerthelesse they doe tourne (16v) it foolyshly vnto the traditions of men. So then from the crowne of the head, which is shauen, doe appeare two lyttle knobbes lyke vnto pease. For vnder the title of the Gospell, he hydeth and couereth what him lysteth, and cannot suffer or abide, that the Gospell shoulde come foorth of that hull or shell: But it must agree to the sanctitie of that shauen crowne: And chiefly as touching the Pope which is the head, of all those shauen heads. And for that that the Coole is so fast behinde the necke,[71] the same declareth the incredible obstination of the supersticion and of the errours of these doltishe Moonkes, concerning the obseruations and Monasticall ceremonyes. As in very déede they are plunged and fastened so déepe within such filthinesse, that there is neyther vertue nor force, nor the lyght of the Christian veritie, how great soeuer that it bée, which canne in any wise draw them foorth for to beholde the lyght.

---

[71] Marginalia: *The Moonkes coole or hood tyed to ẙ neck.*

Erfurt edition, 1523, 4r

Und daß die kutten auff dem rucken gantz vnnd fornen offen ist / bedeutt das sie fur der welt nur geystlich sind / die sie hinder sich mussen lassen / Aber fur got vnd gegen dem tzukunfftigen leben / sind es yn der warheit blosse beuche vnd nur eittel freßlinge / vnd was durch vnd an dem bauch mehr sunden geschehenn fur got / der ich schweige. / Das aber das vntermaul menschen maul gleich / vnd das vbermaul mit der nasen dem kalbmaul gleich ist. bedeut. das ir prediget wol etwan von den wercken gotlichs gesetzß leren.

French version, 1557, p. 41

Or que le capuchon soit attaché au dos, & que vers le ventre il apparoist descousu, signifie que ceux-cy donnent semblant de pieté en habits exterieurs:[72] & est sous ombre qu'ils quittent & laissent tous biens transitoires. mais s'il faut venir à Dieu, & si on les confere à la vie eternelle, on trouuera que ce sont des ventres nuds, & des fardeaux inutiles, pour consumer le bien de la terre, voire conmettans toutes enormitez: dont i'aime mieux me taire. Quant à ce que les machoeres de dessous semblent aux machoeres d'vn homme, & celles de dessus auec les nareaux à celles d'vn veau, cela signifie qu'en leur doctrine on parlera bien assez souuent des œuures ciuiles de la loy Diuine:

[72] Marginalia: *Les moines retiennent le capuchon, & laissent biens transitoires.*

Translation in the Latin edition, 401r

Et quod cucullus in tergo coniungitur, sed in uentre dissutus apparet, significat, quod habitu externo pietatem simulent, quam umbram cum alijs fugacibus uitæ bonis deponunt.[73] Verum coram Deo & ad futuram collati uitam, reuera sunt nudi uentres, & ignaua terræ pondera, fruges consumere nata, aut si quæ præterea fœdiora uenter admittit coram Deo, quæ reticere malim. Quod autem pars oris inferior humana, superior cum naribus uitulina uidetur, significat doctrinam eorum utcunque ciuilia diuinæ legis opera inculcare.

English translation of the French version, 1579, 16v

Now for that the Coole was tyed and close behinde at the backe,[74] and that towards the belly or before it appeared to be open or vnsewed, doth signifie ẏͤ those doe shew in their outward apparayle a certeine godlynesse: and it is vnder the coulour that they doe forsake and renounce all transitory goodes. But if they must come vnto God, or if one would bring them to the eternall lyfe, one shal finde that those are naked bellyes, and vnprofitable burthens for to consume the goods of ẏͤ earth, yea committing all enormities: of which I loue rather to holde my peace. And whereas that the Iawes below are lyke vnto the Iawes of a man, and those aboue with the nostrels lyke vnto those of a Calfe, the same signifieth that in their doctrine they speake very oft of the ciuile workes of the heauenly law:

---

[73] Marginalia: *Cucullus in tergo coniunctus.*

[74] Marginalia: *The Moonkes do keepe and hold fast the hood & forsake & let go transi tory goods.*

Erfurt edition, 1523, 4r/4v

Aber es reucht alles kelbisch / vnd wirt gewandtt auff eygen gerechtikeit vnd frumkeit. Denn dye tzwo lippen des munds. bedeutten / die tzwo predigt / die vnterst deß gesetzs predigt / die vberst / des Euangeli odder verheyssung gottis. Aber an stat deß Ewangeli vnd gotlicher verheyssung / predigen sie das kalbmaul / das ist aureolas vnd grossen verdienst ym himel fur yr eigen werck / die sie on glauben mit grosser muhe thun. Auffs letzst / ist das kalb glat allenthalben / widder dye natur der kelber / daß bedeut / die hubsche feyne zarte gleissenerey vnd heuchley

French version, 1557, p. 41/42

mais ce pendant il n'y a rien qui ne sente le veau: c'est à dire, que la discipline, iustice & les vertus philosophales y sont exceßiument louées. Car les deux leures de la bouche signifient deux sortes de doctrines. La leure basse signifie l'explication de la Loy: celle de dessus la predication de l'Euangile & des (p. 41) promesses Diuines. Mais au lieu de l'Euangile & de la promesse touchant la reconciliation faite par Iesus Christ, ils preschent la bouche du Veau: c'est à dire, ils preschent les grandes & belles recompenses qui sont données au ciel pour les œuures humaines faites diligemment, mais sans foy.[75] Finalement ce Veau n'est point velu en quelque part que ce soit, & n'a point de poil comme les autres Veaux ont accoustumé d'auoir.[76] Cela signifie la belle & reluisante hypocrisie,

[75] Marginalia: *Prescher la bouche du Veau.*

[76] Marginalia: *Le Veau sans poil.*

Translation in the Latin edition, 401r

Sed olent omnia uitulum, id est, immodice exaggerantur laudes honestæ disciplinæ, iusticiæ, & uirtutum Pilosophicarum. Nam duo labia oris duo genera doctrinarum significant, inferius legis enarrationem, superius Euangelij & promissionum diuinarum prædicationem. Sed loco Euangelij & promissionis de reconciliatione os uituli prædicant, hoc est, aureolas & magnas compensationes in cœlo pro humanis operibus magno conatu sed sine fide factis.[77] POstremo, Vitulus hic undique leuis nec hirsutus est, ut solent uituli, id significat splendidam speciosamque hypocrisin,

English translation of the French version, 1579, 16v/17r

But in the meane season there is (17r) nothing but that it smelleth and sauoreth of the Calfe: that is to say, that the discipline, righteousnesse and the Philosophicall vertues are there too much praysed. For the two lips of the mouth, do signifie two sorts and kindes of doctrines: the nether lip signifieth the explycation of the Law: and the vpper lyp the preaching of the Gospell and of the heauenly promises. But in stéede of the Gospell, and of the promises touching the reconcilyation made by Iesus Christ, they doe preach the mouth of a Calfe: That is to say, they doe preach the great recompences and rewards which are giuen in heauen for mans workes dilygently done, but without faith.[78] Finally this Calfe is not hairy in any part, or hath no haire as other Calues haue,[79] the same doth signifie the goodly and shining hipocrisie by the which these doltifh Moonkes haue deceiued all the world.

---

[77] Marginalia: *Duo labis quid significent &c.*

[78] Marginalia: *To preach the mouth of a calfe.*

[79] Marginalia: *The calfe vvithout haire.*

Erfurt edition, 1523, 4v

damit sie bis her yederman gefallen vnd betrogen haben / das wir sie fur heilige geistliche vetter gehalten haben / die seel morder vnd teuffelß vorleuffer. Das ist nun alleß an den tag komen / das kalb ist erauß / auß der kue Sie konnen sich nicht mer bergen in der welt. man weiß nu wer sie sind Dise deuttung / gebe ich tzu richten yderman / den ob die deuttung gleich sich nicht reymette / so ist sie doch an ihr selb vnd in der schrifft vor hin gnugsam gegrund / das der Munch stand der artt sey / wie gesagtt ist.

French version, 1557, p. 41

par laquelle ces cagots ont deceu tout le monde: tellement qu'eux, qui sont cruels homicides des ames, & supposts enragez du diable, ont toutesfois esté estimez Peres saincts & spirituels. Or toutes ces choses sont maintenant manifestées ouuertement par vne claire lumiere: ce Veau est sorty hors des cachettes du ventre de sa mere.[80] Ils ne se pourront plus retirer en vn lieu caché & secret de deuant les yeux des hommes, ne si bien faire qu'on ne les apperçoiue. Ils se boucheront tant qu'ils voudront, mais cela ne fera point que le masque ne leur soit arraché, & qu'ils ne soyent tirez en lumiere, & leur turpitude ne soit descouuerte, afin que tous les monstrent au doigt. Or ie laisse en la liberté d'vn chacun de iuger de ceste interpretation.[81] Car encore que l'exposition ne fust assez propre, neantmoins elle est de soy assez ferme & tresbien fondée sur tesmoignages de la saincte Escriture, que la moinerie est telle à la verité que nous l'auons descrite.

---

[80] Marginalia: *Le Veau hors du ventre de sa mere.*

[81] Marginalia: *L'exposition du Veau, ferme & fondée sur les Escritures.*

Translation in the Latin edition, 401r

qua placuerunt & imposuerunt omnibus, ut sancti spiritualesque Patres haberentur immanes animarum parricidæ, Diabolique satellites. Hæc omnia iam luce manifesta patefacta sunt, uitulus hic emersit ex alui maternæ latebris, non poterunt deinceps ab oculis & animaduersionibus hominum se in occultum & abditum recipere, nulla ualebit obstructio, quin detracta larua producti in publicum sibilis omnium conscindantur. HAnc interpretationem cuilibet relinquo iudicandam, Nam etiamsi expositio non satis apposita uel concinna uideretur, Tamen per sese firma & in Scripturæ testimonijs preclare fundata est, quod Monachatus talis reuera sit, qualem descripsimus.

English translation of the French version, 1579, 17r/17v

Insomuch that they which are the cruell homicides of soules, and the madde vpholders of the diuell haue bene notwithstanding estéemed and counted holy and spirituall fathers. All these things are now openly knowen by a cléere lyght: This Calfe is come foorth from the hidde secrets of the belly of his mother.[82] They can no longer be kept in a secret place and hid from the sight of men, nor cannot chuse but that they must be perceiued. Lette them cloke or hide it asmuch as they will, but that shall not lette that the maske or disguising be not taken from them, and that they be not brought foorth in the lyght, and their turpitude and filthinesse bée not knowen or vncouered, that all men may shew or poynt at them with their finger. For I will leaue to euery mans lybertie to iudge of this interpretation. For although that the exposition [?] fit inough, yet neuerthelesse it is (17v) of it selfe sound inough and very well buylded and grounded vppon the witneses of the holy Scripture,[83] that the Moonkery is such in very deede as we haue described.

---

[82] Marginalia: *The Calfe coming out of the belly of his mother.*

[83] Marginalia: *The exposition of the calfe builded vppon the Scriptures.*

Erfurt edition, 1523, 4r/4v

Weyl den daß kalb dreinso eben stimmet / so sehe yderman tzw / waß er verachte / wen er mein deuttug veracht. Es ist vns gnugsam an disem (4v) kalb gesagt / das got der muncherey feynd ist / wo er yr hold were / het er die kutten einem erlicher bild an gezogen / So mag solch wunder / nicht einen man odder person / sondernn muß eyn gantzen hauffen ein regiment viler person bedeutten wye aller wunder vnd gesicht art ist / yn der schrifft. dan[iel]. viij. / Hutt euch Munch vnd Nonnen / Es gilt euch warlich mit ernst / vnd last euch gottis vermanung nichtt ein schertz seyn

French version, 1557, p. 41/42

Comme (p. 42) ainsi soit donc que ce Veau s'accorde & conuienne proprement auec les oracles Diuins, qu'vn chacun regarde diligemment & aduise bien que c'est qu'il mesprisera, quand il mesprisera & reiettera ceste mienne interpretation. En ce monstre il y a vn aduertissement assez & plus que suffisant, pour nous faire entendre que Dieu est courroucé contre les obseruations monachales.[84] Car s'il les aimoit, il est bien certain qu'il eust reuestu le froc d'vne plus honneste figure. Et il faut bien dire que par vne telle figure monstrueuse n'est point denoté quelque homme seul:[85] mais vne association, ou vn conuent, ou vne frairie, ou vn gouuernement de plusieurs, selon la nature & condition de toutes les visions, desquelles est faite mention en la saincte Escriture, Daniel chapitre huitieme. O vous Moines & Nonnains, donnez-vous garde, vostre affaire est icy traité à bon escient: & ne reputez point qu'vn tel aduertissement de Dieu soit vn ieu de batelerie ou enchantement.

[84] Marginalia: *Dieu courroucé contre les obseruations des moynes.*

[85] Marginalia: *Que denote la figure du Veau.*

Translation in the Latin edition, 401r

Cum igitur uitulus apte congruat & consentiat cum diuinis oraculis, circumspiciat unusquisque, & diligenter consideret, quid contemnat, quando meam Interpretationemcontemnit. Satis superque in hoc monstro admonemur, Deum infensum esse cultibus monasticis, si enim amaret, certe honestiori imagini cucullum induisset. Et consentaneum est tali miraculo non unum aliquem, sed consotiationem, cœtum, administrationemque plurimum personarum significari, iuxta naturam omnium prodigiorum uisionumque in Scriptura Daniel. 8. Cauete uobis, Monachi & Nonnæ, uestra profecto serio res agitur, nec præmonitionem diuinam inanes ludos & præstigias putatote,

English translation of the French version, 1579, 17v

Forasmuch then as this Calfe agreeth properly with ẏͤ diuine Oracles, let euery one diligently take héede or be wel aduised what & is ẏͤ he shal dispise when he shal dispise & reiect this my interpretation. In this Monster ther is more then a sufficient warning, for to make vs to vnderstand ẏͤ god is offended & angry with those Moonkish obseruations. For if he loued them, it is most certeine he would haue cloathed it with a frock of a more honester figure.[86] And we must very well say that by such a monstrous figure is not signified or ment any man alone: But a sociation, a couent, a brotherhood, or a gouernment of many, according to the nature and condition of all the visions, of which is made mention in the holy Scripture,[87] Daniel chapter. 8. O you Moonkes and Nunnes, take you héede, your dooings are héere intreated of earnestly: and thinke not that such aduertisement of God is a play to iest at, or an enchauntment.

---

[86] Marginalia: *God is angry vvith the obser-uations of the Moonkes.*

[87] Marginalia: *What the figure of the calfe doth signifie.*

Erfurt edition, 1523, 4v

Werdet ander munch vnnd nonnen / odder last kloster vnd kutten ligen / vnd werdet widderumb Christen / ehe euch die tzeit vbereylet / vnd darnach nicht kundet / wenn yr gern wolltet / die ir ytzt nicht wolttet / weil yr wol kundt. Und ynn sonderheit bitte ich euch demutigklich yhr lieben herren vom Adel / helfft ewern freunden vnd kindern aus dem grewlichen ferlichen stand

French version, 1557, p. 42/43

Appaisez Dieu d'autres oblations & sacrifices que ceux que vous auez: ou bien abandonnez vos conuents, & iettez moy vos frocs, & retournez à ce pourquoy vous estes naiz, & ou vous estes appelez de Dieu, auant que ceste occasion que Dieu vous presente se esuanouisse. Car apres cela, quand vous voudrez vous ne pourrez : maintenant que vous le pouuez bien faire, vous ne le voulez pas. Or sur tous ie supplie affectueusement les nobles familles, & tous gentils-hommes, qu'ils veuillent deliurer (p. 43) leurs enfans & cousins & autres parens, ou ceux desquels ils aiment le salut, d'vne telle vie si horrible & si perilleuse, comme d'vne prison fort fascheuse.

Translation in the Latin edition, 401v

Aut alijs sacrificationibus, quam illis quas uos habetis. Deum placetis aut Cœnobia cucullosque deseratis, & eo redeatis, ad quod nati à Deoque uocati estis antequam elapso tempore diuinitus oblata pereat occasio, Postea enim, cum uoletis non poteritis, nunc cum potestis non uultis. In primis autem nobiles Familias obtestor, ut cognatos liberosque suos aut eos, quorum salus ipsis cara est, ex tàm horribili periculosoque genere uitæ, tanquam ex ergasculo quopiam, eripere uelint.

English translation of the French version, 1579, 17v

Appease God with other oblations and sacrifices then those which you haue: Forsake your Couents, and cast away your frockes, and retourne vnto that wherefore you were borne, and wherevnto you are called by God, before that this occasion that God sheweth vnto you doe vanish away. For afterwards, when you would ye cannot: Now when you may doe well, ye will not. Aboue all I do earnestly beséech the noble families and all gentlemen that they wil delyuer their children and cousins, or those whose soules health they do loue, from such so horrible and perillous lyfe, as from a most filthy prison.

Erfurt edition, 1523, 4v

Denckt / das sie auch menschen sind eben als yr / vnd ia so hartt verpunden sind / dem natturlichen orden alß alle ander / vnd nicht müglich ist / das ein solch grosse mengen / solten keusche odder willigklich Iunckfrawen seyn. Ich wil das meine than vnnd euch alle gewarnet habenn.

French version, 1557, p. 43

Pensez qu'ils ne sont point encore hors des liens du corps humain: & qu'ils sont obligez à la communion des hommes, & à la loy de nature außi bien que les autres hommes. Car ceci n'est point ottroyé à la nature, qu'vne si grande multitude de gens non mariez se puisse contenir, & viure honnestement & chastement: ou qu'ils se puissent de leur bon gré & volontiers passer du mariage.[88] De moy, i'ay bien voulu faire ce qui estoit en moy & de mon office, & vous aduetir außi de bonne heure.

---

[88] Marginalia: *Le don de continence n'est point ottroyé à tous.*

Translation in the Latin edition, 401v

Cogitate illos nondum euolasse ex corporis humani uinculis, tamque communioni hominum inter se & legi naturæ deuinctos, quàm cæteros homines. Non est enim in re atque natura positum, ut cœlibatum[89] tanta multitudo, aut caste continenterque uiuat, aut coniugio libenter & iucunde careat. Ego meo saticfactum officio, uosque præmonitos à me uolui. M. D. XXIII.

English translation of the French version, 1579, 17v/19r

Thinke that they are not yet out of the bondes of mans body: and but that they are bound to (19r[90]) the communion of men, and to the law of Nature as well as other men. For this is not graunted to Nature, that so great multitude of vnmaried people can lyue honestly and chastly:[91] or that they can of their own free wil liue witho[u]t mariage. As for me I would gladly do that which lay in mée, and which apperteineth to mine office, and to warne you in time. FINIS. ¶ Imprinted at London by Thomas East, dwelling by Paules Wharfe. 1579.

---

[89] 1551 *cœlibum*.

[90] Folio 18 was accidentally left out.

[91] Marginalia: *The gift of continencio is not graunted vnto all men.*

Edition of 'Ursache und Antwort'

Like the edition of the 'Munchkalb', this is a semi-diplomatic transcription of the pamphlet in the Taylor Institution Library, here ARCH.8°.G.1523(34) *Vrsach. vnd anttwortt. das iungkfrawe(n). kloster. gotlich. v(er)lassen muge(n).* Wittenberg: [Lukas Cranach und Christian Döring] 1523 (VD 16 L 1888), a copy from the first print-run of the first edition (A1) of the text (see Introduction 2). Typographical corrections made in A2 are adopted in the text with references in the footnotes, corrections in later editions are noted in the footnotes with the sigla from WA 11, p. 389.

The commentary to the edition consists of two sets of footnotes. Those on the edition side (left hand pages) are not a full linguistic analysis but are designed to help readers understand Luther's German and typographical features, comparing Early New High German (ENHG) forms with modern (NHG) usage and English parallels. The footnotes to the English translation (right hand side) include biblical references and other background information, to be read in conjunction with the historical introduction.

The transcription, translation and footnotes have been prepared by Timothy Powell in collaboration with Florian Gieseler and with additional editorial work by Henrike Lähnemann.

(a1r) Vrsach.[1] vnd anttwortt. das iungkfrawen. kloster. gotlich verlassen mugen.
Doctor Martinus[2] Luther. Wittemberg. M.D.xxiij.

(a1v) ¶ Dem fursichtigen[3] vnd weyszen[4] Leonhard Koppen[5] Burger zu Torgaw meynem[6] besondern freunde Gnad und frid Martinus Luther.

GNad vnd frid ynn Christo.[7] Es ist freylich also[8] wie die schrifft sagt/ dasz niemant kan frumen odder schaden thun/[9] er sey denn datzu verordenet von Gott/ wie der Prophet sagt/ 4. Reg. 5. von dem Naaman zu Syrien/ das Gott durch den selben gluck vnd heyl gab dem land Syrien. Widderumb[10] vom konige[11] Pharao schreybt Mose/ dasz er nicht aus seynem vermugen die kinder Jsrael bedrenget. Sondern Got verstockt seyn hertz da er spricht zu yhm.

---

[1] A1 *Vrsacb*. Corrected in A2 B.

[2] Latinate form of the name, typeset with abbreviation for the *-us* ending.

[3] A1 *fursiichtigen*; accidental doubling of the 'i' through a combination of a *si* ligature and a single *i*. WA misreads *fursüchtig*. ENHG *für-/vorsichtig* is a loan-translation of Latin *prudens* as 'honorific'. The Nuremberg 'Titelbüchlein' of 1517 recommends using *dem fürsichtigen und weisen* when writing to an officeholder in major towns (*Burgermeyster. Schultheysen oder dapfern eyner ansichtigen Statt*, fol. 25r).

[4] = NHG *weisen*. On the use of y for *i* and *sz* for s see 1.3.3. and 1.3.5.

[5] *Dem … Koppen:* the dedicatee is addressed in the dative form (to Leonhard Koppe, with ENHG dat.m. ending *-n*). The family name is also given as *Koppen* in the nominative case: *Der narr Leonhard Koppen* (a1v).

[6] A1 *meynē*, the only case for a nasal bar in German standing for an *-m*. C, E, F, G give the full form *meynem*.

[7] Latin dative for *Christus* 'in Christ'.

[8] = NHG *genauso* 'just as, exactly as'.

[9] = NHG *tun*. On *th* and *rh*-spelling see 1.3.5.

[10] = NHG *wiederum*, in the obsolete sense of 'in the same way'.

[11] ENHG dat. sg. ending *-e*; on the missing umlaut marking see 1.3.4.

Reason and Justification Why it Pleases God that Nuns[12] May Leave Their Convents Doctor Martin Luther, Wittenberg 1523

(a1v) To the judicious and wise Leonhard Koppe,[13] Freeman of Torgau,[14] my special friend, Grace and peace! Martin Luther.

Grace and peace in Christ. It is indeed just as the Scripture says: that no-one can do good or evil unless they are ordained to do so by God. As the Prophet says in 2 Kings 5 of Naaman of Syria, God brought joy and deliverance to the land of Syria through him.[15] Similarly, Moses writes of King Pharaoh that he did not oppress the children of Israel through his own might, but because God hardened his heart, as He said to Moses:

---

[12] ENHG *Jungfrau* can mean 'young woman', 'virgin' or in the context of monasticism, as indicated here by 'kloster', 'nun'.

[13] On Leonard Koppe (d. 1552) and the city of Torgau see Introduction 1.1.

[14] ENHG *Bürger* was an individual who enjoyed various rights and privileges granted by a municipal corporation (including the right to stand as a candidate and vote in municipal elections) and was required to pay municipal taxes.

[15] See 2 Kings 5:1: "Now Naaman, captain of the host of the King of Syria, was a great man with his master, and honourable, because by him the LORD had given deliverance unto Syria: he was also a mighty man in valour, but he was a leper." (KJV). In this paraphrase, Luther emphasizes the point made in this verse that Naaman was successful in defending Syria from its enemies not because of his own abilities as a military commander, but only because God had chosen him to defend Syria from his enemies.

Darumb hab ich dich erweckt/ das ich meyne macht an dir beweysze/ auff das meyn name verkundigt werde ynn allen landen. Da her trotzt auch Jsaias. 41. allen gotloszen vnd spricht/ Trotz vnd thutt frumen odder schaden/ last sehen. was kundt yhr? Vnd Machab. 5. steht geschrieben. Sie waren nicht des samens der menner durch wilche heyl vnd gluck Jsrael widderfure.[16]

¶ Mocht yhr[17] sagen. Wo will das hynaus? Dahyn aus/ das yhr eyn new werck gethan habt/ dauon land vnd leuth[18] singen vnd sagen werden/ wilchs viel werden fur grossen schaden aus schreyen. Aber die[19] es mit Gott hallten/ werdens fur grossen frumen preyssen/ auff das yhr gewissz seyt/ das es Gott/ alszo verordeneth hatt/ vnd nicht ewer eygens werck nach radt ist/ vnnd gehen lasszet[20] der ienigen geschrey/ die es fur das aller ergist[21] werck thaddeln werden/ vnd von Gott widder[22] verordenet noch befolhen achten/ Pfw/ Pfw/ werden sie sagen/ Der narr Leonhard Koppen hatt sich den verdampten ketzrisschen Monch lassen fangen vnd feret (a2r) tzu vnd furet neun Nonnen[23] auff eyn mal aus dem kloster/ vnd hilfft yhn yhr gelubd vnd klosterlich leben tzu verleucken[24] vnd tzu verlassen.

---

[16] = NHG *widerfuhr* (from *widerfahren*); the *e*-ending is an East Central German dialect feature.

[17] Here, Luther addresses Koppe using *Ihr*, the second-person plural form of address used in formal contexts in ENHG (i. e. where *Sie* would be used in NHG).

[18] Alliterative formula for 'everybody', taken from oral law where such formulas served as mnemonic device.

[19] = NHG *Aber die(jenigen), die es mit Gott halten,…* ENHG *die* can be both nominative and relative pronoun.

[20] = NHG *auf dass ihr gehen lasst.* ENHG subject pronouns were often not repeated.

[21] = NHG *allerärgste.*

[22] = NHG *weder … noch* 'neither … nor'.

[23] On capitalisation for emphasis see Introduction 1.3.8. Also Monch.

[24] = NHG *verleugnen* 'to deny, renounce, renege on'.

"I have raised you up so that I might show My power in you, and that My name might be declared throughout all the earth".[25] Thus, Isaiah 41 defies all the godless and says: "Do good, or do evil, that we may be dismayed and witness it together".[26] And it is written in Maccabees 5: "They were not of the seed of the men through whom deliverance was given to Israel".[27]

Now, you may well ask: What is the point of this? The point is that you have wrought a new work of which both country and people will sing and speak, and which many will denounce as a great wickedness. But those who are on the side of God will praise it as a great and good deed, so that you may be sure that it was ordained by God and that you did not do this deed by design, and so that you ignore the cries and charges of all those who will reproach it as the worst deed of all and neither ordained nor commanded by God. "Fie, fie!", they will say, "that fool Leonhard Koppe has (a2r) been taken in by that damned heretic of a monk and has gone and led nine nuns out of their convent all at once and helped them to renounce and renege on their vows and life in the convent."

---

[25] Actually Romans 9:17: "For the scripture saith unto Pharaoh, Even for this same purpose have I raised thee up, that I might shew my power in thee, and that my name might be declared throughout all the earth" (KJV). Paul uses Exodus to affirm that those who will be saved do not receive God's mercy through merits.

[26] See Isaiah 41.23: "yea, do good, or do evil, that we may be dismayed, and behold it together." (KJV).

[27] See 1 Maccabees 5:62: "…these men came not of the seed of those, by whose hand deliverance was given unto Israel." (KJV). Luther's argument is that Judas and Simon's attacks succeeded because God had chosen them to rescue the Israelites from Galaad and Galilee. Joseph and Azarias' expedition failed because God did not choose them to attack the enemies of Israel; instead, they did so on their own initiative in a spirit of pride and in defiance of Judas Maccabaeus' orders.

¶ Hie werdet yhr aber mal sagen/ Das ist warlich heymlich gehallten vnd wol verporgen/[28] ia verrhaten[29] vnd̄ verkaufft/ das auff mich erhetzet werde das gantze kloster tzu Nymptzschen/ weyl sie nu[30] horen/ das ich der reuber geweszen byn. Antwortt ich ia freylich eyn seliger reuber/ gleich wie Christus eyn reuber war ynn der wellt/ da er durch seynen todt dem Fursten[31] der wellt/ seynen harnsch vnd haus geredt[32] nam/ vnd furt yhn gefangen/ also habt yhr auch disze armen seelen aus dem gefengnis menschlicher tyranney gefurt eben vmb die rechten tzeyt auff die ostern/ da Christus auch der seynen gefengnis gefangen nam.

¶ Das ich aber solchs aus ruffe/ vnd nicht heymlich hallte/ thu ich aus redlichen vrsachen. Erstlich das es nicht darumb ist durch mich angeregt/ dasz es sollt heymlich bleyben/ denn was wyr thun/ das thun wir in gott vnd schewen vns des nicht/ am liecht/ wollt Gott ich kund[33] auff solche odder andere weysze alle gefangene gewissen erredten vnd alle kloster ledig machen. Jch wollt michs darnach nichts schewen tzu bekennen sampt allen/ die da zu geholffen hetten/ trostlicher zuuersicht Christus der nu widder hatt seyn Euangelion[34] an tag gebracht vnd̄ des Endechrists[35] reich storet/ wurde hye schutz herr seyn/ obs auch das leben kosten muste.

---

[28] = NHG *verborgen.* Initial *p* shows Upper German influence.

[29] = NHG *verraten.* On the Humanist *rh-* spelling cf. Introduction 3.5.

[30] = NHG *nun.*

[31] Luther uses the form *Fürst der Welt* for the devil also in his hymn *Ein feste Burg*. Title capitalised for emphasis.

[32] = NHG *Harnisch und Hausgerät.*

[33] = NHG *ich könnte.*

[34] = NHG *Evangelium.* Luther uses the Greek form εὐαγγέλιον to highlight the etymology of the word (*eu* = good, *angelion* = message, news); *-on* is the Greek ending for nominative and accusative neuter.

[35] = NHG *Antichrist*, originally meaning 'opposite of Christ' or 'in place of Christ' (cf. 1 John 2:18; 2.22; 4:2-3 and 2 John 1.7). The MHG/ENHG form *Endechrist* is the umlauted form and also associates the Antichrist with the end of the world.

Here, again, you may say: "Now, that really is a fine way to keep a secret well-hidden – yes, snitching on me, selling me out and stirring up the entire convent in Nimbschen[36] against me now that they know I was the robber!" My reply: "Yes, certainly, a blessed robber, just as Christ was a robber in the world when He took the armour of the prince of the world,[37] robbed him out of house and home and led him away captive by His death. Like Him, you, too, have led these poor souls out of the captivity of human tyranny at exactly the right time – at Easter, when Christ also took the captivity of His followers captive."[38]

I am announcing this, however, and not keeping it quiet, for honest reasons. Firstly, because I did not instigate it for it to remain a secret, because whatever we do, we do in God, and we are not ashamed of it in the light. Would God that I were able to rescue all captive consciences by these or other means and set all the convents free! I would not for a moment shy away from later confessing, along with all those who had helped me, that our comforter and hope Christ, who has now once more brought his Gospel to light and destroyed the kingdom of the Antichrist,[39] was our protector, even if it cost me my life.

---

[36] Nimbschen, now part of Grimma, is located ca. 30 km south-east of Leipzig and 150 km south of Berlin. A community of Cistercian nuns, originally established by Margrave Henry III of Meissen (reigned 1221–88) in memory of his late wife Constance of Austria in 1243, settled in Nimbschen in the later thirteenth century and remained there until its dissolution in 1536 following the death of the final abbess, Margarethe von Haubitz (reigned 1509–36).

[37] A Biblical reference to Satan which appears in John 12:31; 14:30; 16:11.

[38] See Ephesians 4:7-8: "When he ascended up on high, he led captivity captive, and gave gifts unto men." (KJV).

[39] The *Antichrist* (*Endechrist* in Luther's pamphlet) was closely associated with the end of the world in medieval theology, as an evil counterpart to Jesus who would assume the form of an earthly ruler over all the earth at the end of the world before the Last Judgement. Supporters of the Reformation often associated the *Antichrist* with the Pope as in the *Passional Christi und Antichristi* (Taylor Editions: Reformation Series 4, ed. by Edmund Wareham).

¶ Czum andern[40] thu ichs/ der armen kinder vnd yhrer freundschafft ehre tzu erhallten/[41] denn wie hoch die blinden freuel richter/ solchs auff erden fur ketzerey vnd abtrinnigkeyt schellten (wilchs seyn richter wol[42] finden wirt) so haben wyr doch das verwaret/ das niemant sagen thar/ sie seyen durch losze buben vnredlich ausgefurt/ (a2v) vnd yhrer ehre ynn fahr[43] sich begeben. Die weyl[44] man euch vnd die ewren kan antzeygen. Datzu mus das yder man lassen erbarlich gehandelt seyn/ das sie nicht eyntzelen/ eyne hie hynaus/ die andern dahynaus geloffen sind/ sondern allesampt beyeynander/ mit aller tzucht vnd ehre/ an redliche stett[45] vnd ortte komen/ da mit den lester meulern[46] die vrsach genomen werde/ yhr lugenhafftige tzungen mit frumen kindern tzu wasschen. Denn das sie solchs widder Gott vnd yhr gelubdt gethan schellten/ wollen wyr leyden vnd wagen.

---

[40] = NHG *Zweitens* (*zwei* and *ander* were used interchangeably as ordinal numbers for 'second(ly) ' in ENHG). 'Other' was used in the same way in medieval English where 'second' would be used in modern English.

[41] = NHG would be *um die Ehre der armen Kinder und ihrer Freunde zu erhalten*. An inverted genitive expression; such expressions are uncommon and largely the preserve of literary and poetic language in NHG, e.g. in the titles of Achim von Arnim's *Des Knaben Wunderhorn* (1805/08) or E.T.A. Hoffmann's *Des Vetters Eckfenster* (1822).

[42]= NHG *gewiss, bestimmt.*

[43] = NHG *ihre Ehre in Gefahr bringen* or *ihre Ehre gefährden.*

[44] = NHG *alldieweil* (now archaic/obsolete), *darum.*

[45] = NHG *Stätten*; ENHG *stat* (strong plural *stette*) can be both *Statt* and *Stadt.*

[46] = NHG *Lästermäuler.* As discussed in Introduction 1, this insult is a term of abuse coined by Luther which is first used against the Pope in Luther's pamphlet *Grund und Ursach aller Artikel, so durch die römische Bulle unrechtlich verdammt worden* (1520). Example of an ENHG compound written as two separate words.

Secondly, I am doing this to preserve the honour of these poor children and their family and friends, for however harshly the blind judges of the petty sessions[47] may condemn such worldly deeds as heresy or apostasy (which will, no doubt, find their judge), we have at least made sure that no-one dare say that they have been dishonestly led away by loose young men (a2v) and that their honour has been compromised, whereas people can make remarks about you and yours. Furthermore, everybody must admit that you acted honourably in that they did not run away individually, some this way and some that way, but rather all left together, in all discipline and good order, and have come to good and honest places. This takes away any cause for slanderous mouths to wipe their lying tongues with these pious children. For, if they reproach this as acting against God and their vows: we are willing to suffer and risk this.

---

[47] ENHG *Frevelrichter* is a judge for petty crimes, punishable with a fine. The legal metaphor highlights the minor nature of the misdeed in question and the limited jurisdiction of those condemning it.

¶ Czum dritten tzu warnen die hern vom Adel/ vnd alle frume bider leutte/ so[48] kinder ynn klostern haben/ das sie selbs datzu thun/ vnd sie erausser nemen/ auff das nicht ergers hernach folge. Denn wie wol viel des adels vnd bidder leutte/ der sachen von gottis gnaden verstendig[49] yhre kinder odder freundyn[50] wol gernn eraus hetten vnd doch das exempel schewen/ die ersten[51] ban tzu brechen. Nu aber sie sehen/ das so viel erbarer kinder/ mit verwarter zucht vnd ehre/ die ban gebrochen haben/ vnd des bekentlich sind/[52] werden sie mutiger vnd thurstiger[53] werden. Werden aber ettliche tzorniger/ das mus man lassen geschehen/ vnd sich nicht verwundern. Denn sie dencken es sey vnrecht/ nach dem sie biszher verfurt/ nicht anders geleret sind/ Es wirt mit der zeyt besser werden.

---

[48] = NHG *die. so* can be used as a relative pronoun in ENHG. Here, it refers to the *Herren vom Adel* and *frume bidder leutte* in the previous clause.

[49] The relative clause (= NHG *die der Sache von Gottes Gnaden verständig sind*) is implied here. This might form an extended adjectival phrase preceding the noun in NHG: *obwohl viele der der Sache von Gottes Gnaden verständigen Adlige und Biederleute ihre Kinder und Freundinnen sicher gerne heraus hätten…*

[50] = NHG *Freundinnen* (plural). This word can mean 'female relatives' as well as 'female friends' in ENHG.

[51] This is a strong adjective ending; in NHG, the reader would expect a weak adjective ending following the definite article; *die erste Bahn zu brechen* = (literally) 'to blaze the first trail'.

[52] = NHG *und sich dazu bekannt haben.* In MHG /ENHG *bekennen* + gen.: *des* (= NHG *dessen*) *bekenntlich sind.*

[53] Hendiadys. Derived from the MHG *preterite* present *turren* (obsolete), which is etymologically related to the English verb 'to dare'.

Thirdly, to warn noble men and all pious, upright people who have children in convents to do this for themselves and take them out so that worse things do not happen afterwards. For however many noblemen and upstanding people understand this matter by God's grace and would dearly love to see their daughters or friends out of the convent, they are still reluctant to set an example and be the first to blaze a trail. However, now that they have seen that so many daughters of respectable families have blazed a trail with their discipline and honour intact and are not afraid to admit it, they will become more courageous and daring. If, however, many people are enraged by this, you must simply let that happen and not worry about it. For they think that it is wrong because, until now, led astray, they had not been taught any different. It will get better with time.

¶ Das sey meyn entschuldigunge gegen euch der sunde halben dasz ich solchs ewer werck verraten/ vnd offinbart habe. Auff dasz ich aber auch vnser aller wortt rede/ beyde meyns der ichs geraten vnd gebeten/ vnd ewer mit den ewern die yhrs aus gericht/ vnd der iungfrawen/ die der erlosunge bedurfft haben. Will ich hie mit kurtzlich fur[54] Got vnd aller wellt rechenschafft vnd anttwort geben/ wie wol ichs sonst ynn andern buchlin reichlich gethan habe/ das alle Christliche hertzen mercken sollen/ wie wyr nicht das vnsere/ sondern zuuor gottis ehre vnd des nehisten bestes (a3r) gesucht haben. Aber den vnchristlichen hertzen wollen wyr yhren synn lassen/ bis sie es bas[55] verstehen.

¶ Auffs erst/ das die kinder zuuorn selbs yhr Eldern vnd freundschafft auffs aller demutigst ersucht vnd gebeten haben/ vmb hulff eraus tzu komen/ mit vernunfftigen gnugsamen vrsachen angetzeygt/ das yhnen solch leben/ der seelen selickeyt halben/ nicht lenger zu dulden sey/ sich daneben erbotten zu thun/ vnd zu leyden/ was frum kinder thun vnd leyden sollen. Wilchs yhn[56] alles abgeschlagen vnd versagt ist/ vnd also von yderman verlassen sind/ damit sie recht vnd redlich vrsach gehabt/ ia genottigt vnd gedrungen sind/ yhr gewissen vnd seele zu erredten anderswo wie sie haben kunden/ hulff vnd radt suchen. Vnd die ihenigen so[57] hie haben kunden helffen vnd radten/[58] schuldig geweszen sind/ aus Christlicher liebe pflicht/ die seelen vnd gewissen zu erredten.

---

54 = NHG *vor.*

55 = NHG *besser.*

56 = NHG *ihnen.*

57 = NHG *die* (relative pronoun referring to *diejenigen* immediately before.) Cf. Footnote 37 on *so* as relative pronoun in ENHG.

58 = NHG *die hier haben helfen und raten können.*

Let this be my apology to you for my sins in giving away and revealing your endeavour. So that, however, I can speak for all of us – for myself, who advised and requested this; for you and yours, who carried this out; and for the nuns who were in need of deliverance – I wish to give a brief account and answer before God and the whole world, as I have already done plenty of times in other pamphlets,[59] so that all Christian hearts should remember that we did not do this for our own good, but to the glory of God and the greatest good of our neighbour. (a3r) However, let us leave the un-Christian hearts to their own devices until they can understand this better.

Firstly, these children had themselves previously most humbly asked and pleaded with their parents, family and friends for help to leave and had shown with sensible and compelling reasons that they could no longer tolerate living such a life for the sake of their souls' salvation. Furthermore, they had offered to do and suffer everything that pious children should do and suffer. However, all of this was rejected and ignored, such that they had an honourable and honest cause – that they were pushed and driven to rescue their conscience and soul in whatever way they could and seek help and guidance to do so. And all those who were able to help and guide them were obliged by the duty of Christian love to rescue their souls and consciences.

---

[59] See Introduction 1 for a list of pamphlets to which Luther refers here.

¶ Czum andern[60] ist das eyn hohe wichtige vrsach vnd nott/ das man leyder die kinder/ sonderlich das schwache weyber volck vnd iunge megde ynn die kloster stosset reytzt vnd gehen lest/ da doch keyn teglich vbung ist gotlichs wortts/ ia sellten odder nymer mehr das Euangelion eyn mal recht gehorett wirt. Vnd werden doch ynn den hohisten kampff gestellet. Nemlich vmb die iungfrawschafft zu streytten/ da kaumet vnd gar selten auch die ihenigen bestehen/ die mit gottis wortt allenthalben gerust[61] vnd mit hoher seltzamer wunderbarlicher gnad erhaben sind. Es darff[62] muhe/ die ehliche keuscheyt tzu hallten/ auch mit beystand gottlichs wortts/ vnd dis iunge toriche unerfarne weyber volck/ wirt dahyn gestossen da der streyt am herttisten vnd mechtigisten ist. O der vnbarmhertzigen eldern vnd freunden/ die mit den yhren so grewlich vnd schrecklich faren/[63] O der blinden vnd tollen Bisschoff vnd Ebten die hie nicht[64] sehen noch fulen/ was dye armen seelen leyden/ vnd wie sie verterben.[65] (a3v)

---

[60] = *NHG Zweitens;* cf. above on use of *zwei* and *ander* in ENHG. Many of Luther's works are composed in the style of a bullet-point list (cf. volume 2 in this series, *Sermon von Ablass und Gnade,* written in twenty bullet points, and volume 3 in this series, *Von der Freiheit eines Christenmenschen*, written in thirty). But Luther's lists are not always as systematic as they look. In our pamphlet, Luther uses three separate but related lists: firstly, three reasons why he has chosen to make Koppe's actions public knowledge; secondly, four reasons why he considers it pleasing to God that nuns should leave their convents; and, finally, two potential counterarguments accompanied by his refutation of each.

[61] = NHG *(aus)gerüstet.*

[62] = NHG *Es bedarf der Mühe, ist mühevoll* (MHG *dürfen* + gen.).

[63] = NHG *verfahren.*

[64] = NHG *weder … noch.* Double negatives were frequently used for emphasis in negative statements in ENHG.

[65] E (the Augsburg edition, see Introduction 2) has *O der selben Bischoff und Epten*, referring back to the description of the former nuns' families and friends as 'uncharitable' in the previous sentence, thus softening Luther's criticism of the bishops and abbots as 'blind und toll' in this passage.

Secondly, a very important reason for the urgency of this matter is that, unfortunately, these children, especially vulnerable women and young maidens, are pushed, prompted and permitted to go into the convents, even though the word of God does not go forth daily there; indeed, they hardly ever (or never) even hear the Gospel properly. And yet they are being sent into the highest form of struggle: namely, into the fight for their virginity, in which people rarely – even hardly ever – succeed, even when they are armed with the word of God all around them and are raised up by great, unusual, miraculous grace. The preservation of chastity requires a great deal of effort, even with the help of God's Word, and these young, foolish, inexperienced women are being thrown into the place where the fighting is at its fiercest and mightiest. Oh, what uncharitable parents and friends who treat their own so cruelly and terribly! Oh, what blind and senseless bishops and abbots who cannot see or feel what these poor souls are suffering and how they are perishing. (a3v)

¶ Disze vrsach das man Gottis wort mangeln mus/ ist alleyne gnug/ ob sonst keyn andere were/ vns alle zu entschuldigen/ ia tzu loben vnd tzu preyssen fur Gott vnd der wellt/ das man aus klostern lauffen/ helffen vnd ratten soll/ das die seelen eraus geryssen/ gefurt/ gestolen vnd geraubt werden/ wie man kan/ vnangesehen/[66] ob tausent eyd vnd gelubd geschehen weren/ Denn wissentlich ists/ das ynn klostern/ sonderlich[67] nonnen klostern Gottis wort teglich nicht gehet/ vnd am meysten ortten nymer mehr/ sondern sich nur blewen vnd treyben mit menschen gesetzen vnd wercken. So ists widderumb gewissz/ das man on gottis wort teglich fur gott nicht leben kan. Vnd keyn gelubt fur Gott gellten odder halten kan/ da mit man sich an den ortt verbindet/ da[68] keyn gottis wortt gehet/ vnd den ortt lest[69] da gottis wort gehet/ Denn es ist solch gelubd eben so viel/ als got verleugnen weyl wyr alle tzu gottis wort verpunden sind.

¶ Auffs dritte/ ist das kundlich vnd offinbar/ das eyn mensch mag wol getzwungen werden[70] fur der wellt tzu thun/ das er nicht gerne thut. Aber fur Gott/ vnd ynn Gottis dienst/ soll vnd kan keyn werck noch dienst getzwungen vnd vngerne geschehen/ Denn Gotte[71] gefallen nicht vnd will auch nicht haben getzwungene vnwillige dienste. Wie .S. Paulus. 2. Corin. 9. sagt. Gott hatt lieb ein frolichen geber/ on tzweyffel ist er widderumb feynd eym vnfrolichen vnwilligen geber. Daher auch .S. Paulus die edle iungfrawschafft nicht haben will/ wo sie ertzwungen vnd vnwillig geschicht. 1. Cori. 7. Solche froliche lust aber zu gottis dienst gibt widder kloster noch kappen/ widder gelubd noch werck/ sondern alleyn der heylige geyst.

---

[66] = NHG *ungeachtet*.

[67] = NHG *besonders*.

[68] = NHG *wo*.

[69] = NHG *verlässt*.

[70] = NHG *dass ein Mensch wohl gezwungen werden mag*. The position of the finite verb in ENHG is more flexible.

[71] East Central German retains dative ending more frequently, here *Gotte* as object for *gefallen*; used despite God being also the subject of the following clause where it should be nominative *Gott* (*will auch nicht*).

This reason – that they lack the word of God – is, by itself, enough (as if it were the only reason) to excuse, indeed to praise, us all and to encourage people, in the sight of God and the world, to help them to run away from their convents, and to make sure that these souls are torn out, led away, stolen and robbed from the convents in whatever way they can be, even if they had sworn a thousand oaths or made a thousand vows. For it is common knowledge that in religious houses, especially in nuns' convents, the word of God does not go forth daily, and in most places not at all; instead, they beat and whip themselves with man-made laws and works. Similarly, it is certain that no-one can live in the sight of God without hearing and practising the word of God every day. And that no vow can be valid or endure in the sight of God with which one ties oneself to a place where the word of God does not go forth and leaves a place where the word of God goes forth. For such vows are no different from denying God, because we are all bound to the word of God.

Thirdly, it is clear and evident that a person may well be forced to do things in the world that they do not desire to do. However, before God and in the service of God, no good work or act of service should or can be performed under duress or unwillingly; because acts performed under duress and unwillingly are displeasing to God, and He rejects them. As Saint Paul says in 2 Corinthians 9: "God loves a cheerful giver";[72] likewise, He doubtlessly hates an uncheerful and unwilling giver. Therefore, Saint Paul rejects chastity if it is imposed and unwilling in 1 Corinthians 7.[73] However, it is neither convent nor cowl, neither vows nor good works that give us such a cheerful desire to serve God, but the Holy Ghost alone.

---

[72] 2 Corinthians 9:7: "Every man according as he purposeth in his heart, so let him give; not grudgingly, or of necessity: for God loveth a cheerful giver." (KJV). Luther's argument here is that, if somebody begrudgingly makes a vow, they demonstrate ingratitude for the grace that they have received from God and disobey Jesus' teaching about giving, which leads God to reject their vow.

[73] 1 Corinthians 7:9: "I say therefore to the unmarried and widows, It is good for them if they abide even as I. But if they cannot contain, let them marry: for it is better to marry than to burn." (KJV).

¶ Wie viel meynstu aber das Nonnen[74] ynn klostern sind/ da das teglich gottis wort nicht gehet/ die frolich (a4r) vnd mit lust vngetzwungen yhren gottes dienst thu vnd orden trage?[75] freylich vnter thausent kaum eyne. Was ists denn das[76] du solchs kind lessist also seyn leben vnd[77] alle seyne werck verlieren/ vnd datzu die helle da mit verdienen?[78] Were es nicht besser/ wenn sie ia etwas vngerne/ vnd mit vnlust thun soll/ sie were ehlich vnd thet solche muhe/ vnd vnlust ym ehlichen standt euserlich gegen die menschen/ als[79] yhr man/ kind/ gesind vnd nachbar &c. Weyl denn Gott keyn dienst gefellt es gehe denn willig von hertzen vnd mit lust. So folget das auch keyn gelubd weytter gellten noch geschehen noch gehallten werden soll/ denn so fern die lieb vnd lust da ist/ das ist/ so fern der heylige geyst da ist. Darumb nun solch gelubt/ on lust vnd geist geschicht/ achtets got nicht vnd nympts nicht an. Das also/ dis auch eyn gnugsame vrsach ist/ gelubd vnd kloster tzu lassen vnd yderman eraus tzu helffen ynn einen andern standt.

---

[74] Capitalised for emphasis.

[75] A, C, D, E have singular, probably a typo of A not using the types with nasal bars *thū* and *tragē* for the plural forms *thun* and *tragen*; B, F, G, H correct to plural.

[76] = NHG *Was ist es* [i.e. the reason] *denn, dass*.

[77] A1 *vnv*, corrected A2 and following editions (not mentioned in the WA list of typographical errors).

[78] A1, A2 *derdienen*; corrected in B and following editions; ‘v’ and ‘d’ are similar in this typeface.

[79] = NHG *wie* (*zum Beispiel*).

But how many nuns do you think there are in convents where the word of God does not go forth daily who cheerfully, (a4r) gladly and freely serve God in holy orders? Surely not even one in a thousand. What, then, is the point of you letting these children lose their lives and all their works and, what is more, earn a place in Hell by doing so? Would it not be better, if they had to do anything unwillingly and with no desire to do it, for them to be married and openly show these struggles and this displeasure to other people, such as their husbands, children, servants and neighbours, etc.? For no act of service is pleasing to God unless it is performed willingly from the heart and with pleasure. Thus, it follows that no vows should remain valid or be made or kept, because it is only in as far as love and pleasure are there that the Holy Ghost is also there. Therefore, this is also an adequate reason for abandoning one's vows and convent, and to help all others out of them into a different estate.

¶ Auffs vierde/ Wie wol man sich diszer vrsach schier schemen mus/ so ists doch fast der grossisten eyne/[80] kloster vnd kappen tzu lassen/ Nemlich/ das vnmuglich ist/ die gabe der keuscheyt so gemeyne[81] sey/ als[82] die kloster sind/ Denn eyn weybs bild[83] ist nicht geschaffen iungfraw tzu seyn/ sondern kinder zu tragen/ wie Genesis. 1. Gott sprach nicht alleyne tzu Adam/ sondern auch zu Heua/[84] seyt fruchtbar vnd mehret euch / wie das auch die leyblichen gelidmas weyblichs leybs/ von Gott da tzu eyngesetzt beweyszen.[85] Vnd solchs ist nicht tzu eynem weyb/ noch tzu tzweyen/ sondern tzu allen gesagt/ vnd keyne ausgeschlossen. Got zihe sie denn selber aus/ nicht durch vnser gelubd odder freyen willen/ sondern durch seynen eygen radt vnd willen mechtiglich/ wo er das nicht thutt/ soll ein weybs bild/ eyn weyb bleyben/ frucht tragen/ datzu[86] es gott geschaffen hat/ vnd nicht besser (a4v) machen denn[87] ers gemacht hatt.

---

[80] *fast*, adverb of *fest*, has a much stronger meaning in ENHG than it does in NHG; similarly, ENHG *groß* does not only mean 'great', as in NHG, but also 'frequent'. The practice of placing dependent genitives before a number has become obsolete in NHG. An approximate NHG equivalent of this phrase would be *mit Sicherheit eine der größten*.

[81] = NHG *allgemein, (weit) verbreitet.* The meaning 'universal' for *gemein* survives in NHG as adjective only as 'a common plant / species' and in nouns such as *Gemeinschaft*.

[82] The ENHG comparative particle *als* (from MHG *alsô*) has been replaced by *wie* in NHG.

[83] The suffix *bild* indicates that Luther is referring to the concept of women in general (in the sense of the form of the female body) rather than one specific woman.

[84] Luther uses the spelling of Eve with an initial 'H' to be closer to the Hebrew etymology of the name which is given in Genesis 3:20, which he translates as: *VND Adam hies sein Weib Heua | darumb | das sie eine Mutter ist aller Lebendigen,* and glosses it as follows: *Hai | heisst Leben | Da her kompt Heua oder Haua | leben oder lebendige. Heva* is also the form used in the Latin Vulgate translation of the Bible.

[85] The section from *seyt fruchtbar vnd mehret euch* to *von Gott datzu eyngesetzt beweyszen* has been manually underlined by a reader in the Taylorian copy.

[86] = NHG *wozu.*

[87] The ENHG comparative particle *denn* has been replaced by NHG *als* and only survives in certain set expressions such as *mehr denn je* 'more than ever'.

Fourthly, although one should be ashamed of this reason, it is still one of the most important reasons for leaving convent and cowl: namely, that it is impossible for the gift of chastity to be as widespread as the convents are. For woman was not created to remain a virgin, but to bear children; as it is written in Genesis 1, God said not only to Adam, but also to Eve, "Be fruitful and multiply",[88] which is also shown by the physical proportions of the female body which God designed for this purpose. And this was not said to one woman, or to two women, but to all women with no exceptions, unless God sets them apart, not through our vows or our own free will, but through His own almighty counsel and will. If He does not do this, a woman should remain a woman, bear fruit (which God created her to do) and not try to make things better (a4v) than He created them.

[88] Genesis 1:28: "And God blessed them, and God said unto them, Be fruitful, and multiply, and replenish the earth, and subdue it: and have dominion over the fish of the sea, and over the fowl of the air, and over every living thing that moveth upon the earth." (KJV).

¶ Jtem[89] da er Heua verfluchte/ nam er yhr nicht den weyblichen leyb/ noch weybische gelidmas. Widderrieff auch nicht seynen gesprochen segen vber sie/ das sie sollt fruchtbar seyn/ sondern bestettigt den selben vnd spricht/ Jch will dyr viel muhe schaffen/ wenn du schwanger gehest/ dysze plage ist auch nicht vber eyns odder tzwey weyber gesagt/ sondern vber alle/ das[90] die wortt lautten/ als sey got gewissz/ das alle weyber werden schwanger seyn/ vnd sollen disze plage tragen/ on wilche er selbs aus nympt.[91] Da widder kan yhe keyn gelubt noch bund gelten noch hallten/ Denn es ist gottis wort vnd gemechte.

¶ Hie thun sie denn tzwo[92] eyn rede/ Die erst/ Man solle die gelubd hallten/ Das ist warlich war/ wenn du gottlich gelobist/ das deyn ist/ vnd ynn deyner macht steht. Jch horet hie zu/ eyn gelerten man eyn mal sagen. Meyn mutter hatt gelobt. Jch sollt eyn bischoff werden. Wie soll ichs hallten? Deyn ists aber nicht iungfraw seyn/ widder eyngesetzte natur/ Sondern wie .S. Paulus sagt. 1. Corin. 7. Es ist eyn gottis gabe/ Wie ich nu keyn Gottis gabe kan geloben/ szo kan ich auch keuscheyt nicht geloben. Es mus alles zuuor meyn seyn/ ehe ichs gelobe. Wie auch Samuels mutter yhren son Gott gelobet/ wo er yhr den selben zuuor geben wurde 1. Reg. 1. Also sollt man auch keuscheyt geloben/ szofern sie Gott geben wurde/ wo nichts/ das das gelubde nicht were.

---

89 = *Item* (Latin for 'likewise', 'similarly') is used as a structuring device like a bullet-point, often in combination, like here, with a the paragraph mark.

90 = NHG *so dass.*

91 = NHG *außer denjenigen, die er selbst davon ausnimmt.*

92 A feminine form of *zwei* (same etymology as English *two*), corresponding to the following feminine plural *eyn rede* (= NHG *Einreden, Einsprüche*); masculine form *zween* and neuter form *zwei*, standardized to *zwei* regardless of gender. *Zwo* survives in spoken language in some Austrian and southern German dialects. It is also sometimes used for additional clarity in standard speech to ensure that the listener does not mishear *zwei* as *drei.*

Likewise, when He cursed Eve, He did not take her female body from her, nor her feminine proportions. Neither did He revoke the blessing that He had given her, that she should be fruitful, but instead, He confirmed it and said: "I will greatly multiply your sorrow when you conceive".[93] This plague is not imposed on just one woman or just two women either, but on all women. These words make it sound as though God were certain that all women would conceive and should bear this plague, unless He Himself were to set any apart. No vow or covenant can be valid or last in the face of this, for it is God's word and His creation.

Here, then, they make two objections. The first: that you should honour your pledges. That is indeed true, if you pledge things which are your own and which are in your power. On this matter, I once heard a learned man say: "My mother pledged that I would become a bishop. How am I to keep this?" However, virginity in opposition to inherent nature is not yours to pledge, but rather, as Saint Paul says in 1 Corinthians 7, it is a gift from God.[94] Now, since I cannot pledge any gifts from God, I cannot pledge chastity either. Everything must first be mine before I can pledge it. Just as Samuel's mother only pledged her son to God once He had first given him to her in 1 Samuel 1,[95] one should only pledge chastity in so far as God will grant it: if He will not, let these vows be left unmade.

---

[93] Genesis 3:16: "Unto the woman he said, I will greatly multiply thy sorrow and thy conception; in sorrow thou shalt bring forth children; and thy desire shall be to thy husband, and he shall rule over thee." (KJV). Luther infers from this that it was God's intention that all women should have children, which is obviously impossible if they lead celibate lives as nuns.

[94] 1 Corinthians 7:7: "For I would that all men were even as I myself. But every man hath his proper gift of God, one after this manner, and another after that." (KJV).

[95] 1 Samuel 1:9–11. Luther's argument here is that Hannah recognized that her ability to fulfil this vow was entirely dependent on God granting her the son she had prayed for, because it would have been impossible for her to fulfil this vow if God had decided to grant her a daughter, for example, or indeed no children at all.

¶ Leszen wyr doch auch. 1. Reg. 14. das Saul auch gelobt tzwey mal mit eym[96] eyde/ das niemant des tags essen sollt/ vnd auch seynen son tzu todtenn/ Dennoch must ers lassen/ vnd Gott weret[97] es yhm/ durchs volck vnd seynen son. Da mit yhe Gott gnugsam beweyszet[98] hatt/ das vnchristliche/ vnd schedliche gelubd nichts (b1r) tzu hallten sind/ ob sie gleich auch mir[99] dem leben schaden/ viel mehr wirtt er die gelubd verdamnen/ die der seelen schaden vnd verderben sind. Vnd ist dis exempel woll zu mercken/ das nicht gnug ist gesagt/ ia ich habs gelobt/ ich mus hallten/ lieber/ sihe tzuuor/ obs muglich vnd gotlich ist/ was du gelobest/ sonst wenn vnmuglich gelubd gulde/ mochtestu wol geloben/ eyn mutter gottis werden wie Maria.

¶ So sprechen sie aber mal/ obs gleich vnmuglich sey/ so kan mans mit beten erlangen/ wie .S. Hierony[mus][100] leret. Antwort/ auffs erst. Got gebe myr nur nicht viel der keuscheyt .S. Hieronymi/[101] wilcher selbs bekennet/ dasz er seyns fleysschs wueten vnd brunst mit keyner fasten noch muhe tzemen[102] kund/ Wie vil besser were yhm geweszen/ nach .S. Paulus rad? freyen/ denn also brennen/ Vnd ist hyryn sein exempel nicht gutt nach zu folgen. Denn keuscheyt hat wol anfechtung/ aber solch tegliche brunst vnd wueten ist eyn gewissz tzeichen/ das Gott nicht gegeben hatt noch geben will die edle gabe der keuscheyt/ die da mit willen on nott gehalten werde.

---

[96] = NHG *einem*.

[97] = NHG *(ver)wehrte*.

[98] = NHG *bewiesen* (past participle) here in the sense of *darauf hinweisen*. MHG *wîsen* / ENHG *weisen* is predominately a weak verb and only uses strong forms from the 16th century onwards.

[99] WA reads *nur* here, following G. A1, A2, B, C, E, F *mir*, D *mit*, H *my*.

[100] A1 Hieron. Abbreviated form of 'Hieronymus' for 'Jerome'.

[101] Latin genitive form of 'Hieronymus'.

[102] = NHG *zähmen*.

Yet we also read in 1 Samuel 14 that Saul also swore an oath on two occasions: first, that nobody should eat during the day, and then to kill his son. Nevertheless, he had to abandon them, and God prevented him from fulfilling them through the people and his son.[103] Herewith, God sufficiently proved once and for all that un-Christian and harmful vows are not (b1r) to be kept, even if doing so harms my life more; instead, He will condemn those vows which are harmful and ruinous to the soul. And, from this example, it should be noted that it is not enough simply to say, "Well, I made the vow, so I have to keep it"; but rather, you should consider whether what you have vowed is possible and pleasing to God, because otherwise, if impossible vows counted for anything, you might as well vow to become a Mother of God like Mary.

Once again, they will say: "Even if it is impossible, you can obtain it through prayer, as Saint Jerome teaches." My response: firstly, I pray that God would not give me too much of the chastity of Saint Jerome, who himself confesses that he could not still the raging and burning of his flesh with any amount of fasting or discipline.[104] How much better would it have been for him to follow Saint Paul's advice and marry than to burn in such a way?[105] And, in this respect, the example that he sets is not a good one to follow, because chastity does indeed face its temptations, but such daily burning and raging is a certain sign that God has neither given nor will give you the precious gift of chastity, which you are observing willingly but unnecessarily.

---

[103] In 1 Sam 14, Saul orders the Israelites to fast until the evening before joining his son Jonathan in battle. Jonathan eats some wild honey because he did not know that Saul had ordered the Israelites to fast. Saul declares that Jonathan must die but is stopped by his people and thus breaks his vow.

[104] See, for example, St Jerome's 22nd letter to Eustochium, in which he describes the temptations that he faces whilst doing penance in his cell in the wilderness.

[105] 1 Corinthians 7:8-9: "I say therefore to the unmarried and widows, It is good for them if they abide even as I. But if they cannot contain, let them marry: for it is better to marry than to burn." (KJV).

Auffs ander/ man kan freylich alles von Got erlangen mit beten. Er will aber auch vnuersucht seyn. Christus hette sich wol kunden von der tzynnen[106] des tempels ernydder lassen/[107] wie der teuffel furgab/[108] Er wollts aber nicht thun/ weyl es nicht nott war/ vnd wol auff ander weysze kund erab komen.[109] Jch kund[110] auch wol mit beten erlangen/ das ich nicht esse noch truncke[111] was auff erden wuchsze.[112] Weyl aber das nicht nott ist/ vnnd Gott myr sonst so viel geben hat/ das ich essen sall vnd kan/ soll ich yhn nicht versuchen/ das lassen liegen/ das er gegeben hatt/ vnd eyn anders on nott gewartten/ das er nicht gegeben hatt/ denn da were Gott versucht.

¶ Also auch hie/ weyl er man vnd weyb hat geschaf(b1v)fen/ das sie zu samen sollen/ soll ich myr nicht fur nemen[113] eyn andern stand/ vnd ihenen liegen lassen/ aus eygenem furwitz vnd mutwillen/ Denn da mit gebe ich mich[114] on nott vnd vrsach ynn ferlickeyt/ vnd versuche Gott/ syntemal wol eyn ander gottlich stand da ist/ da ich der ferlickeit vnd versuchung nicht bedarff. Denn wer dringet mich odder berufft/ dasz ich on ehe bleybe? Was ist myr die iungfrawschafft von notten/ weyl ich fule das ich sie nicht habe/ vnd Gott mich sonderlich nicht datzu berufft/ vnd weysz doch/ das er mich tzur ehe geschaffen hatt?

---

106 Weak dat.sg. of ENHG *zinne* = 'battlement'; in NHG the plural *Zinnen* is used.

107 = NHG *hätte sich wohl* (in the sense of 'gewiss') … *herniederlassen können.*

108 ENHG *für-/vorgeben* = 'to suggest'.

109 = NHG *und er wohl* (= *gewiss*) *auf eine andere Weise herunterkommen konnte.* The *er* in the final clause is implied because it would have been deemed obvious from the context that *kund erab komen* is governed by the pronoun *Er* (i.e. 'Christ') which appears two clauses previously.

110 = NHG *Ich könnte* (imperfect subjunctive setting out a hypothetical situation).

111 Double negative for emphasis; subjunctive for describing a hypothetical situation.

112 Imperfect subjunctive form of *wachsen.*

113 = NHG *sich etwas vornehmen* in the sense of 'to set out to', 'to plan to'.

114 = NHG *begebe ich mich.*

Secondly, you can certainly obtain anything from God through prayer. However, He does not wish to be tempted. Christ could well have thrown himself from the pinnacle of the temple, as the Devil claimed. However, he did not wish to do so because it was not necessary, and he could easily come down another way.[115] I might well be able to obtain through prayer that I would have no need to eat or drink anything that grows upon the earth. However, because it is unnecessary, and because God has given me as much to eat as I need to and can anyway, I should not tempt him by rejecting what He has given me and needlessly waiting for something else that He has not given me, because that would be tempting God.

And therefore here, too, since He created man and woman (b1v) to be together, I should not take it upon myself to enter another state and abandon this one out of curiosity or boldness and pride. For thus, I put myself in danger without any cause or reason and I tempt God, since there is another perfectly godly state in which I have no need of such danger or temptation. For who is pushing me or calling me to remain unmarried? What use is celibacy to me, since I feel that I do not have it in myself and that God is not particularly calling me to it, and yet know that He has created me to marry?

---

[115] See Christ's reactions to the three temptations by the devil Matthew 4:5-7 and Luke 4:9-12: Firstly, he refuses to turn the stones into bread on the grounds that people do not just live on earthly food, but also on the word of God. Secondly, He refuses to throw Himself from the pinnacle of the temple in the knowledge that God would send angels to save Him because He knows that this would be tempting God. Finally, the Devil takes Him to the top of a high mountain and promises to give Him everything He can see from the summit if He worships him; Jesus refuses and says that people must only worship and serve God.

Darumb willtu[116] ettwas bitten von Gott/ so bitt das dyr nott ist/ vnd da dich die nott tzu dringet. Jst dyrs aber nicht nott/ so versuchstu yhn gewiszlich mit deynem gepett/ Denn seyn name heyst Adiutor in oportunitatibus in tribulatione. Nothelffer Psalm. 10. Nemlich das er hilfft nur da alleyne/ da sonst keyn hulff vnd mittel durch yhn tzuuor geschaffen ist.

¶ Die Ander eynrede ist/ das es ergerlich sey widder den gemeynen allten brauch vnd lere/ vnd der schwachen gewissen[117] sey tzu schonen. Antwortt/ Ergernis hyn Ergernis her. Nott bricht eyszen/ vnd hatt keyn ergernis. Jch soll der schwachen gewissen schonen/ szo fern es on fahr meyner seelen geschehen mag. Wo nicht/ szo soll ich meyner seelen radten/ es erger sich dran die gantze odder halbe wellt/ Nu ligt hie der seelen fahr ynn allen stucken. darumb soll niemant von vns begeren/ das wyr yhn nicht ergern. Sondern wyr sollen begern/ das sie unser ding billichen/ vnd sich nicht ergern/ das foddert die liebe.

¶ Das will ich auff disz mall meyn gutter freund kurtzlich tzur veranttworttung gegeben haben/ fur euch/ fur mich/ vnd fur disze iungfrawen/ auch fur alle die diszem exempel wollen nach folgen/ byn auch gewissz/ das wyr (b2r) da mit fur Gott vnd der wellt vnuertaddelich bestehen wollen. Aber den widdersachern vnnd verstockten kopffen/ den[118] Gott selber nicht kan gnug thun/ wollen auch wyr vns nicht vermessen[119] gnug tzu thun/ szondern sie lassen toben vnd lestern/ bis sie es mude werden. Wyr haben eynen richter vber vns der wirt recht richten.

[116] = NHG *willst du* (in the sense of *wenn du Gott um etwas bitten willst*).

[117] Inverted genitive expression (= NHG *das Gewissen der Schwachen*).

[118] = NHG *denen.*

[119] = NHG *wollen wir nicht so vermessen sein* (*sich vermessen* is now only used in the sense of 'to get a measurement wrong' in NHG).

Thus, if you wish to ask God for anything, ask Him for what you need and what you are driven to by necessity. However, if you do not need it, then be sure that you are tempting Him with your prayers, for His name is *Adiutor in opportunitatibus in tribulatione*: a help in trouble. Psalm 10.[120] Meaning that He helps us only when He has not provided any help or any other means beforehand.

The other objection is that it is offensive to go against ancient common customs and teachings, and that the consciences of the weak need to be spared. My response: causing offence is neither here nor there. Necessity breaks chains of iron and knows no offence. I should only spare the consciences of the weak in as far as I may do so without endangering my soul. If this is not possible and I should warn my soul that the whole world or even half the world will take offence at it, this is where my soul will be beset by danger upon all sides. Thus, nobody should ask of us that we should not offend them. Instead, we should ask that they approve of our cause and do not take offence; this is what love requires.

Let this be, for now, my good friend, a brief statement in your defence, in mine and in that of these virgins, and of all those who wish to follow their example. I am also certain that we will (b2r) irreproachably stand the test before God and the world. Let us not presume to satisfy the naysayers and stubborn mules, who God Himself cannot satisfy; instead, let them rage and curse until they grow tired of it. We have a Judge above who will judge us justly.[121]

---

[120] See Psalms 9:9: "The LORD also will be a refuge for the oppressed, a refuge in times of trouble." (KJV). The difference in the psalm numbering shows that Luther was quoting from memory since this is part of Psalm 9 in both the Vulgate and the Hebrew tradition.

[121] Referencing 1 Peter 2: 19-24 which praises the unjust suffering of Christ as an example.

¶ Jch will aber auch die iungfrawen hye nennen/ auff das alles ia frey am tage sey/ Vnd sind nemlich dysze. Magdalena Staupitzyn/[122] Elisabeth Canitzyn. Vronica Zesschaw/ Margaretha Zesschaw yhr schwester Laneta von Golis/ Aue Grossyn/ Katherina von Bore/ Aue von Schonfelt/ Margaretha von Schonfeldt yhr schwester. Der almechtig Gott wollt gnediglichen erleuchten alle freunde der ihenygen/ szo[123] mit far[124] vnd vnlust ynn klostern sind/ das sie yhn trewlich eraus helffen[125]/ Wilche aber geyst verstendig sind/ vnd klosterey nutzlich wissen zu brauchen/ vnd gerne drynnen sind/ die lassz man bleyben ym namen Gottis.

¶ Hie mit befelh[126] ich euch Gott/ vnd grust[127] myr ewr liebe Audi[128] vnd alle freunde ynn Christo Gegeben tzu Wittemberg am Freytag ynn der osterwoche. Anno.[129] 1523.

---

[122] The modern, normalised forms of the three women's surnames ending with *-in* are 'Staupitz', 'Canitz' and 'Gross'. The naming convention of adding the High German suffix *-in* (or its equivalent in other German dialects) to women's surnames appears to have developed around the same time as surnames began to be used in the German-speaking world in the twelfth century and persisted into the eighteenth century. As can be seen from this list of names, it was only applied to the surnames of ordinary people, never those of the nobility.

[123] = *die* (relative pronoun).

[124] = NHG *Gefahr*.

[125] = NHG *ihnen treulich heraushelfen*.

[126] = NHG *anempfehle* ('commend'). *Gott befohlen* as phrase of farewell survives in archaic or elevated style into modern times.

[127] = NHG *grüßt* (imperative).

[128] A diminutive form of *Agathe* (indicating friendly endearment).

[129] Abbreviation of Latin *Anno Domini*.

Furthermore, I also wish to name the virgins here so that everything is out in the open – their names are as follows: Magdalena Staupitz;[130] Elisabeth Canitz; Veronica Zesschau and her sister Margaretha Zesschau; Laneta von Golis; Ave Gross; Katharina von Bora; Ave von Schönfeldt and her sister Margaretha von Schönfeldt. May the Almighty God graciously give light to all the friends of those who are in danger in the convents or who are there against their will, so that they may faithfully help them to leave. As for those who are spiritually sage and know how to make good use of life in the convent, and are willing to be there, let them remain there in the name of God.

Herewith, I commend you to God, and give my love to your darling Audi[131] and all friends in Christ. Given at Wittenberg on the Friday of the Easter week, in the year of our Lord 1523.[132]

---

130 On the nuns' biographies see Introduction 1.1.

131 The wife of Leonhard Koppe, mentioned also in Luther's two other surviving letters to Koppe of 17 and 21 June 1525. See WA.B 3, 534 and 538f. The regards to the 'dear wife' underline the point about the blessing of marriage.

132 10 April 1523 (WA 11, 388).

Facsimiles

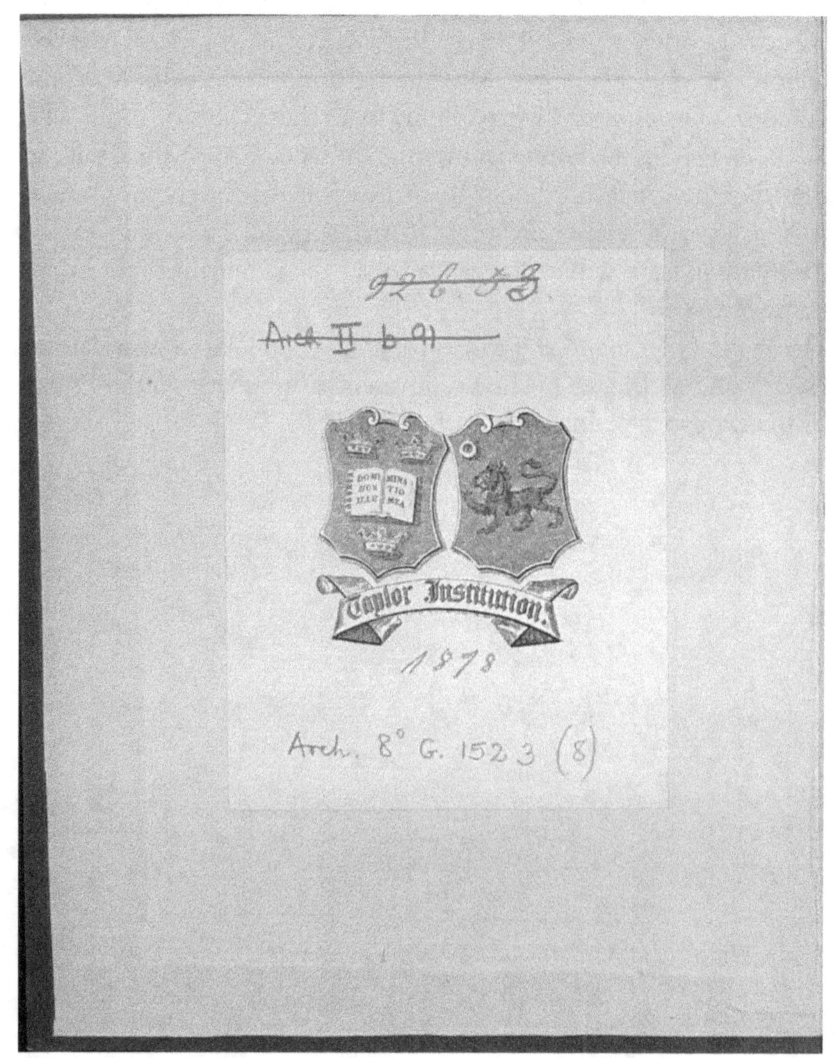

Taylor Institution Library, ARCH.8°.G.1523(8), upper pastedown

Facsimile of the 'Mönchkalb'

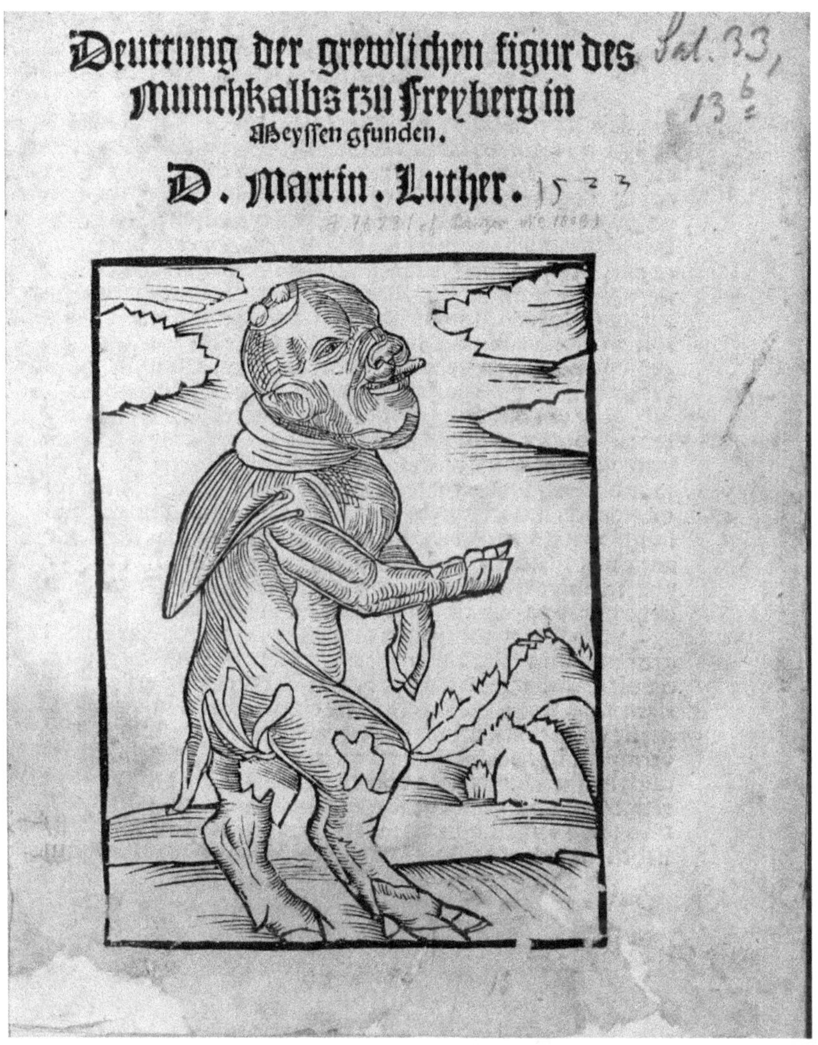

Deuttung der grewlichen figur des Munchkalbs tzu Freyberg in Meyssen gfunden.

D. Martin. Luther.

Taylor Institution Library, ARCH.8°.G.1523(8), a1r

Deuttung des Munchkalbs
Zu Freyberg Martin Luthers

Die Prophetiſche deuttung diſes Munchkalbs wil ich dem geiſt laſſen/den ich kein prophet bin/on daß gewiß iſt/der gemeinen deuttung nach/vñ allen wunderzeichē/daß da durch ein gros vnfall vnd verenderung zukunfftig/ Got tzu verſtehen gibtt/der ſich auch gewiſzlich deutſch land verſehen mag/Welche aber die ſelbē ſei/vñ wie eß zu gehen werde/gepurt den prophetē tzu ſagen/Mein wundſch vñ hoffnūg iſt/daß der Junſt tag ſei. Den der zeichen biß her vil auff ein ander fallen/vñ gleich alle welt in einer groſſen woge ſteht/Die on groſſen wandel nicht kan abgehn/ Dartzu daß Euāgeliſche liecht ſo helle auffgangen/welchem alle mall/gros verenderung/vmb der vngleubygen willen/erfolget hatt

Jch wil nur des gewiſſeſten geram/vñ mit antzeigen/warumb Got zu ſolchem zeichen ein munch kalb genomen hat/vñ daß heilige kleid ſo verkerlich vñ grewlich ſchendet/ſo er doch ebñ ſo wol ſolch kunfftig vngluck hette durch ein wunder on munchkutten mugē angeben/Datzu nu auch zu landßberg ein pfaffenkalb hat geſchaffen/vnd wil dyß iar nur mit geiſtlichen/heilignn wundertzeichen faren/damitt er yhe ſich mercken leſt/daz er deß geiſtlichen ſtanden ſondlich acht hat/vnd etwas ym ſyn hat auff die ſelben

Alſo thet er vortzeitten auch/Da er Danielis .viij. den groſſen konig Alexander durch ein zigen bock ließ bedeuttē. damit er anzeigt/vber die prophetiſche deuttung deß zukūfftigen fals/was die kriechen fur ein volck weren/nemlich/geylle vñ furwitzige leut/wie die geiſſen ſind/die ſich mit irer vernunfft hoch tzuſteigen vñ allerley vermaſſen. Alſo hat er auch hie im Munchkalb vber die prophetiſche deuttung an tzeigt/was die Munche fur leut ſind/Unnd villeicht auch/das ſolch vnfall vber die welt komen werde/vmb der geyſtlichen miſſethat willenn/die durch yhr fleyſchliche lere denn

Taylor Institution Library, ARCH.8°.G.1523(8), a1v

gláubn̄ vertilget vnd die welt zu kalb fleiſch gemácht hábē/
Ein annder gebe die prophetiſche deuttung/Jch will meyn
Munchkalb meinem ſtand zu dienſt deutten/Das pfaffen/
kalb findet auch wol ſeinen deutter:
Diſe deuttung ſtelle ich ſo vil deſte lieber/das ich weiß/
wie ſie nur hertter verſtocken wirt die ienigen/ſo ſie betrifft/
weyl ſie alles verachten vnd fur ketzerey haltē/was ich ſa/
ge. Darumb ſollen ſie mir hierin auch nicht gleuben/ſondern
ſich ye mehr vnd mer dran ſtoſſen vnd verſtocken/auff das
ſie ia nicht tzu rechter erkentnis komen/vnd ir vnglewbiges
leben beſſern. Wie tzu Iſaias.vi.geſagt wart. Verſtocke dz
hertz diſes volckß vnd verblende yr augen vnd verſchlemme
yr oren/das ſie nichs hören/ſehen noch mercken/damit ſie
ſich bekerten vnd ſelig wurden:
Wie nu der Balaam/da er Gottis worttenn nichtt ge/
horehet tzu letzt auch von ſeiner eſelin geſtrafft muſt werden
vnd ſich doch nicht dran keret/alſo ſollen auch vnſere geyſt
lichen Vetter. nach dem ſie bißher/fur der hellenn warheitt
deß Euangeli ir oren/wie die otter/verſtopffen/itzt auch an
dem kalb vnd kuhe fur yren augen/alß im ſpiegel ſehen/wer
ſie ſind fur got/vnd was man ym hymel von inen helt. wye
wol ſie die augen dennoch ſollen feſt tzu ſchlieſſenn/das ſie
ya des keins ſehen/ſie mochten ſonſt ſich bekeren/vnd dem
grewlichen vrteil Gottis entrynnen. Denn den verſtocktenn
pharao bewegen wedder wort noch tzeychenn
Auffs erſt vnd tzur ſumma diſes tzeychens/las dir dz
keinn ſchimpff ſein. Das Got eim kalb das geyſtlich kleyd.
die heilige kutten hat angetzogen. Damit hat er on tzweyffel
auff eim hauffen bedeut. das eß bald offenbar werden muß.
wie die gantze Muncherey vnd Nonnerey nichtß anderß ſei/
den ein falſcher lugenhafftiger ſchein/vnd euſerlich gleyſſen
eins geyſtlichen gotlichen lebens. Den wir armen leut habē
bißher gemeynet der heilig geiſt were vnter der kutten/vnnd
das ein ſolch kleidt nichtz den eyttel geiſt deckte. So tzeygtt
Gott hie an/dz es nur ein kalb deckt/als ſolt er ſagē. Es iſt

Taylor Institution Library, ARCH.8°.G.1523(8), a2r

ein ſchälcks hutlin. Den was ein kälb bedeutte/lernet vnnß
altzu wol/das gulden kalb Aaron/das in der wuſten vom
volck Iſrael fur ein Got auff geworffenn wart. Exo. xxxiij.
vñ ps. lxxvij. Sie wandeltñ yr herligkeit in ein bild einß kalbß
das graß friſſet. vnd die kelber Jerobo am zu Bethel vñ dan
iij. Re. xij. Da widder die propheten ſo hefftig ſchreyen.

Alſo ſihe du nun dis munchkalb auch an/das die kut
te ſey das gantz geyſtlich weſen mit alle yrem gottis dienſt.
den ſie gros achten/mit beten/meſſenn/ſingen/ faſtenn rc.
Aber wem thun ſie ſolchen gottis dienſt. wer wirt da mit ge
ehret. An wem hanget er. Am kalbe. Den die kuttē zieret vñ
kleidett das kalb wie du ſiheſt. Was iſt den das kälb. Es iſt
ir falcher abgot in irem lugenhafftigen hertzen. Wie geht daß
tzu. Alſo gehet es tzu. Sie haben ein meinung vnd gewiſſen.
das ſie dem rechten waren Got dienen mit yrem geiſtlichenn
weſen/vnnd wollen den himel mit iren wercken verdienenn.
vnd ſtellen auch yren gotts diennſt auff lautter menſchlich
werck. nicht auff den glauben

Nu iſt kein Gott in hymel vnd erden. der ſich damit erē
laſt. es ſey dan der Teuffel odder ein abgot. Den dem rechtē
waren Got/kan man nicht anderß den ym geiſt vñ warheit
dienē. Johan. iiij. das iſt im glauben vnd vber menſchlichñ
wertken. die der geiſt Chriſti in vnß thut. Johan. vi vñ Iſa.
lv. Darumb kundē ſolch falſche geiſtliche iren gottiß dienſt.
vnter dem namen gottis/niemant anders thun den yrem ei
gen falſchen dunckel/der in furgibt/Gotte ſey da mitt gedie/
net/Der ſelb dunckel iſt die lugen/vnd der abgot in irem her
tzen/gleich wie den Juden auch war yn iren abgöttereyenn:
Sihe das iſt das kalb/vnnd die falſch fleiſchliche meinung
des geiſtlichen weſens/daran ſie hangen/vñ den ſie ſchmuc
ken mit irem ſchonen gleyſſen vnd glatten kutten

So friſt nu das kalb nur gras/Den ſolch heiligen ha
ben nichts von tzukunfftigen guttern/ſondern maſtenn ſich
hie aufferden/wie wir ſehen/das die beſten gutter die mey/
ſten wolluſt/die hohiſte ehre die groſſiſt gewalt

Taylor Institution Library, ARCH.8°.G.1523(8), a2v

bey den geiſtlichenn iſt/Solch gras/muß ſolch kalb eſſenn/
vñ ſo wurt an in auch war/daß ſie yr herlickeit verwandeln
ynn ein bild eins kalbs/daß graß friſſet/Den Chriſtus iſt
vnſer herlickeyt/des wyr vns rhumen vnd frewen ſollten/
ſo richten ſie an ſein ſtat an/ein ander rhum im hertzen/daß
ſie ſich verlaſſen vnd rhumen yrer eigen werck vñ verdienſt/
da ſteht daß kalb yn Chriſtꝰ ſtatt vñ furet Chriſtꝰ namen
Auffs ander/das die kutten am hynderſten vñ an bey-
nen vñ fornē entgentzet vñ zuriſſen iſt/bedeut dz in ſolchem
geiſtlichen weſen vnd gots dienſt keinn einickeit iſt/ ſo doch
nichts hoherß in der ſchrifft gefodert wirt/den dz die Chri-
ſten ſollen gleich geſinnet ſein. wie p̄s. lxvij· Gott machtt im
hauße wonen/die einerley geſynnet ſind. Und p̄s. c. xxxij. O
wie feyn iſts vnnd lieblich/wenn bruder eyns mit eynander
wonen/Aber diſze vnchriſtliche vngeyſtliche geyſter/haben
ſo mancherley ſyn vñ weiſe/alß farbñ/Die barffſen dunckt
yhr regel die beſte/die prediger widderumb achtenn ir regel
die beſte/Auguſtiner hienaus/die Carthuſer dort hinaus/
keine dunckt daß gut ſein/das den andern gut dunckt/Alſo
iſt dye kutten am hyntern des kalbs tzwryſſen vnd an denn
beynen/ob ſie gleich wol alle darynnen eynß ſind/daß ſie ey-
nerley kalb ſchmucken/daß iſt/gleichen vnglawben vñ mey-
nung durch die werck den hymel tzu erlangen

Und ſonderlich iſt das tzu mercken/das der hynderſt/
bedeut das ende/vnd die beyne/bedeutt die/auff welchen dz
kalb(das iſt ſolche falſche meinung)beſtehtt Denn es noch
nie ſo vil ſecten/orden/vnterſcheid vñ namen der geiſtlichen
geweſen ſind/als ytzt ein tzeyt her/nach dem eß auß end ko-
men iſt/vñ ir buberey da hin fellet vñ auf horen muß. Uñ die
beine/ſind die frechen brud vñ lerer. Magiſtri noſtri eximij.
vnd ir gelertiſten hin vñ her in den orden/die ſolch geiſtlich
weſen mit yrem ſchreyben/predigen/leſen vnnd leren vnter
yn/vnd in der welt/erhalten/Und doch keiner mitt dem an-
dern eines iſt. So vil kopffe/ſo mancherley opinion ſind da

Taylor Institution Library, ARCH.8°.G.1523(8), a3r

Auffß dritte/furet das kalb aller dinge/die geperde einß predigerß/eß ſtreckt die hinderbein alß ſtunde/vnd reckt auß die rechte pfotte/wie ein prediger ſein rechte hand/vnd zeucht die lincke zu ſich/wirfft den kopff auff/vnd hat die zunge im maul/vnd iſt alleß geſtalt/als ſtund eß vn̄ prediget/Darumb wie der Bapſteſel das Bapſtum abmallt/So malet eygentlich diß Munchkalb/die Apoſtel vn̄ ſchuler deß Bapſts/das alle welt ſehe/was ſie biſher fur prediger vnd lerer gehortt vn̄ noch hören/Den was ſolt ein eſels kopff billicher tzu Apoſtel haben/den ein kalbs kopff fleyſchlich regiment hatt auch fleyſchliche lere/Darumb hats auch noch nichtt augen/das es die ienigen deutte/da Chriſtuß von ſagt Mat .xxiij. Wee euch ſchrifftgelertenn yr verblendte blind leytter. Vnd Jſaie lvi. Yhr verſeher ſind alle blind vn̄ wiſſen nichts

Vil anders mehr mag man wol an dem kalbe auff die munch vn̄ lerer deutten/Als das/daß ore an der kutten/die vntregliche Tiranney der beicht bedeutte/damit ſie die weltt marteren vnd zum teuffel furen/ Die Zunge ym maul/daß yre lere nichts den tzunge/das iſt/eyttel vnnutz geſchwetze iſt/ Die tzw wartzen yn der platten auff dem kopff/ ſolten hörner worden ſein/Hörner aber bedeutten die predigtt des Ewangeli/daß vom creutz prediget vnd tzuſtoſſet den alten menſchen/Michee.iij. Jch wil deyn horn eyſern machenn das du vil volcks tzuſtoſſiſt zc̄. Aber diß kalb hat nicht hörner/ſondern nur malzeichen vnd ſchein daruon/Den ſie haben woll den namen/das ſie dz Euangelion predigen/aber ſie habens gefangen vnd auff yre menſchen lere gezwungn̄/vnd ſtehn die wartzen yn der platten/den was der platten gefelt/das mus Euangelion heyſſen/vnd das Euangelion mus auch nicht auſer diſzer platten̄ faren/ſondern ſich reymen vnd fugen auff yhr platten heiligkeit/Sonderlich was yr heubt/den Bapſt betrifft

Das die kutten vmb den hals ſzo hart gewunden iſt/ tzeygt yhren hallſtarrigen vorſtockten ſyn yn yrer muncherey vnd heiligem weſzen/das ihr gewiſſen ſo tieff darynnenn

Taylor Institution Library, ARCH.8°.G.1523(8), a3v

verpunden vnd verſtrickt ſynd/das ſie durch keine macht ð
aller helliſten warheit er aus komen mugen. Und daß die
kutten auff dem rucken gantz vnnd fornen offen iſt/bedeuts
das ſie fur ð welt nur geyſtlich ſind/die ſie hinder ſich muſ-
ſen laſſen/Aber fur got vnd gegen dem tzukunfftigen leben/
ſind es yn der warheit bloſſe beuche vnd nur eittel freßlinge/
vnd was durch vnd an dem bauch mehr ſunden geſchehenn
fur got/der ich ſchweige.

Das aber das vntermaul menſchen maul gleich/vnd
das vbermaul mit ð naſen dem kalbmaul gleich iſt. bedeut.
das ir prediget wol etwan von den wercken gotlichs geſetzß
leren. Aber es reucht alles kelbiſch/vnd wirt gewandtt auff
eygen gerechtikeit vnd frumkeit. Denn dye tzwo lippen des
munds. bedeutten/die tzwo predigt/die vnterſt deß geſetzs
predigt/die vberſt/des Euangeli odder verheyſſung gottis.
Aber an ſtat deß Ewangeli vnd gotlicher verheyſſung/pre-
digen ſie das kalbmaul/das iſt anreolas vnd groſſen verdi-
enſt ym himel fur yr eigen werck/die ſie on glauben mit groſ-
ſer muhe thun.

Auffs letzſt/iſt das kalb glat allenthalben/widder dye
natur ð kelber/daß bedeut/die hubſche feyne zarte gleiſſene-
rey vnd heuchley/damit ſie bis her yederman gefallñ vñ be-
trogen habē/ das wir ſie fur heilige geiſtliche vetter gehaltñ
haben/die ſeel morder vnd teuffelß vorleuffer. Das iſt nū al-
leß an den tag komen/dz kalb iſt erauß/auß der kue Sie kon-
nen ſich nicht mer bergē in der welt. mā weiß nu wer ſie ſind

Diſe deuttung/gebe ich tzu richten yderman/den ob die
deuttung gleich ſich nicht reymette/ſo iſt ſie doch an ihr ſelb
vñ in der ſchrifft vor hin gnugſam gegrund/dz der Munch
ſtand der artt ſey/wie geſagtt iſt. Weyl den daß kalb drein
ſo eben ſtimmet/ſo ſehe yderman tzw/waß er verachte/wen
er mein deuttun verache. Es iſt vns gnugſam an diſem

Taylor Institution Library, ARCH.8°.G.1523(8), a4r

kalb gesagt/das got der muncherey feynd ist/wo er yr hold were/het er die kutten einem erlicher bild an gezogē/So mag solch wunder/nicht einen man odder person/sondernn muß eyn gantzen hauffen ein regiment viler person bedeutten wye aller wunder vnd gesicht art ist/yn der schrifft. dañ. viij.

Hutt euch Munch vnd Nonnen/Es gilt euch warlich mit ernst/vnd last euch gottis vermanung nichtt ein schertz seyn/Werdet ander munch vnnd nonnen/odder last kloster vnd kutten ligen/vnd werdet widderumb Christen/ehe euch die tzeit vbereylet/vnd darnach nicht kundet/wenn yr gern wolltet/die ir ytzt nicht wolttet/weil yr wol kundt.

Vnd ynn sonderheit bitte ich euch demutigklich yhr lieben herren vom Adel/helfft ewern freunden vñ kindern aus dem grewlichen ferlichen stand/Denckt/das sie auch menschen sind eben als yr/vnd ia so hartt verpunden sind/dem natturlichen orden alß alle ander/vnd nicht muglich ist/dz ein solch grosse mengen/soltē keusche oddͤ willigklich Junckfrawen seyn. Jch wil das meine thAn vnnd euch alle gewarnet haben.

Taylor Institution Library, ARCH.8°.G.1523(8), a4v

Facsimile of 'Ursache und Antwort'

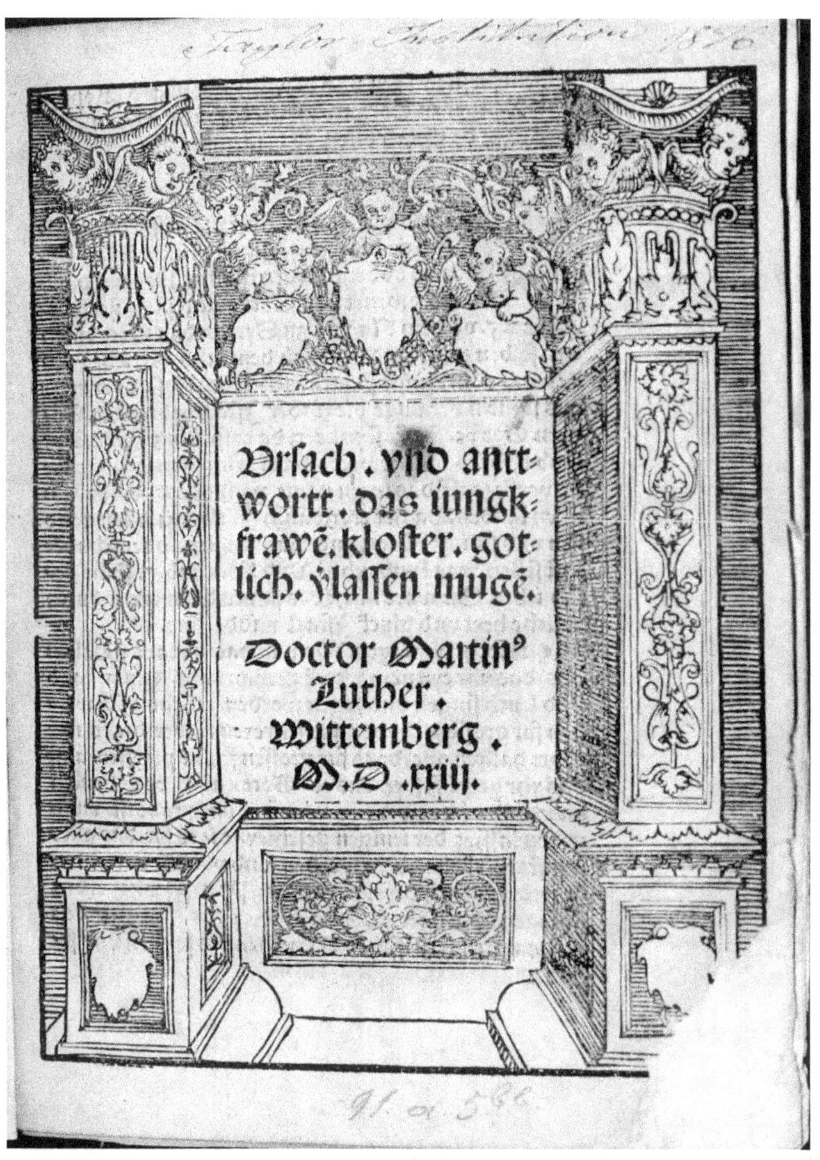

Vrsach. vnd antt=
wortt. das iungk=
frawē. kloster. got=
lich. v̓lassen mugē.

Doctor Martin⁹
Luther.
Wittemberg.
M.D.xxiij.

Taylor Institution Library, ARCH.8°.G.1523(34), a1r

¶ Dem furſichtigen vnd weyſzen Leonhard Koppen
Burger zu Torgaw meynē beſondern freun-
de Gnad vnd frid Martinus Lu-
ther.

GNad vñ frid yñ Chriſto. Es iſt freylich al-
ſo wie die ſchrifft ſagt/ dz niemāt kan fru-
men odder ſchaden thun/ er ſey denn datzu
verordenet von Gott/ wie d̄ Prophet ſagt/
4. Reg. 5. vō dem Naamā zu Syrien/ das Gott durch
den ſelben gluck vnd heyl gab dem land Syrien. Wid
derumb vom konige Pharao ſchreybt Moſe/ dz er nicht
aus ſeynem vermugē die kinder Jſrael bedrenget. Sō-
dern Got verſtockt ſeyn hertz da er ſpricht zu yhm. Dar
umb hab ich dich erweckt/ das ich meyne macht an dir
beweyſze/ auff das meyn name verkundigt werde ynn
allen landen. Da her trotzt auch Jſaias. 41. allen gotlo
ſzen vnd ſpricht/ Trotz vnd thutt frumen odder ſchadē/
laſt ſehen. was kundt yhr? Vnd Machab. 5. ſteht ge-
ſchrieben. Sie warē nicht des ſamēs der menner durch
wilche heyl vnd gluck Jſrael widderfure.

¶ Mocht yhr ſagen. Wo will das hynaus? Dahyn
aus/ das yhr eyn new werck gethan habt/ davon land
vnd leuth ſingen vnd ſagen werden/ wilchs viel wer-
den fur groſſen ſchaden aus ſchreyen. Aber die es mit
Gott hallten/ werdens fur groſſen frumē preyſſen/ auff
das yhr gewiſſz ſeyt/ das es Gott/ alſzo verordeneth
hatt/ vnd nicht ewer eygens werck nach radt iſt/ vnnd
gehen laſſzet der ienigen geſchrey/ die es fur das aller
ergiſt werck thaddeln werden/ vnd von Gott widder
verordenet noch befolhen achten/ Pfw/ Pfw/ werden
ſie ſagen/ Der narr Leonhard Koppen hatt ſich den
verdampten ketzriſſchen Monch laſſen fangen vnd fe-

Taylor Institution Library, ARCH.8°.G.1523(34), a1v

ret tzu vnd furet neun Nonnen auff eyn mal aus dem
kloſter/vnd hilfft yhn yhr gelubd vnd kloſterlich leben
tzu verleucken vnd tzu verlaſſen.
¶ Hie werdet yhr aber mal ſagen/ Das iſt warlich
heymlich gehallten vnd wol verporgen/ ia verrhaten
vñ verkaufft/das auff mich erhetzet werde das gantze
kloſter tzu Nymptzſchen/weyl ſie nu horen/das ich der
reuber geweßen byn. Antwortt ich ia freylich eyn ſe-
liger reuber/gleich wie Chriſtus eyn reuber war vñ der
wellt/da er durch ſeynen todt dem Furſten der wellt/
ſeynen harnſch vnd haus geredt nam/vnd furt yhn ge-
fangen/alſo habt yhr auch diße armen ſeelen aus dem
gefengnis menſchlicher tyranney gefurt eben vmb die
rechten tzeyt auff die oſtern/da Chriſtus auch der ſey-
nen gefengnis gefangen nam.
¶ Das ich aber ſolchs aus ruffe/vnd nicht heymlich
hallte/thu ich aus redlichen vrſachen. Erſtlich das es
nicht darūb iſt durch mich angeregt/dz es ſollt heym-
lich bleyben/denn was wyr thun/das thun wir in gott
vnd ſchewen vns des nicht/ am liecht/ wollt Gott
ich kund auff ſolche odder andere weyße alle gefange-
ne gewiſſen erredten vnd alle kloſter ledig machē. Jch
wollt michs darnach nichts ſchewē tzu bekennē ſampt
allen/die da zu geholffen hetten/troſtlicher zuuerſicht
Chriſtus der nu widder hatt ſeyn Euangelion an tag
gebracht vñ des Endechriſts reich ſtoret/ wurde hye
ſchutz herr ſeyn/obs auch das leben koſten muſte.
¶ Czum andern thu ichs/der armen kinder vñ yhrer
freundſchafft ehre tzu erhallten/deñ wie hoch die blin-
den frevel richter/ſolchs auff erden fur ketzerey vnd ab
trinnigkeyt ſchellten (wilchs ſeyn richter wol finden
wirt) ſo haben wyr doch das verwaret/das niemant
ſagē thar/ſie ſeyen durch loße buben vnredlich ausge-
A ij

furt/ vñ yhrer ehre ynn fahr ſich begebē. Die weyl man
euch vnd die ewren kan antzeygē. Datzu mus das yder
man laſſen erbarlich gehādelt ſeyn/ das ſie nicht eyn-
tzelen/ eyne hie hynaus/ die andern dahynaus gelof-
fen ſind/ ſondern alleſampt beyeynander/ mit aller
tzucht vnd ehre/ an redliche ſtett vnd ortte komen/ da
mit den leſter meulern die vrſach genomen werde/ yhr
lugenhafftige tzungen mit frumen kindern tzu waſſchē.
Denn das ſie ſolchs widder Gott vnd yhr gelubdt ge-
than ſchellten/ wollen wyr leyden vnd wagen.

¶ Czum dritten tzu warnen die hern vom Adel/ vñ
alle frume bidder leutte/ ſo kinder yñ kloſtern habē/ das
ſie ſelbs datzu thū/ vñ ſie erauſſer nemē/ auff das nicht
ergers hernach folge. Deñ wie wol viel des adels vnd
bidder leutte/ der ſachen von gottis gnaden verſtēdig
yhre kinder odder freundyn wol gernn eraus hetten
vnd doch das exempel ſchewen/ die erſten ban tzu bre-
chen. Nu aber ſie ſehen/ das ſo viel erbarer kinder/ mit
verwarter zucht vñ ehre/ die ban gebrochē haben/ vnd
des bekentlich ſind/ werdē ſie mutiger vnd thurſtiger
werdē. Werdē aber ettliche tzorniger/ das mus man
laſſen geſchehē/ vñ ſich nicht verwūdern. Deñ ſie den-
cken es ſey vnrecht/ nach dem ſie biſzher verfurt/ nicht
anders geleret ſind/ Es wirt mit der zeyt beſſer werdē

¶ Dz ſey meyn entſchuldigūge gegē euch d̄ ſunde halbē
dz ich ſolchs ewer werck vͦratē/ vñ offinbart habe. Auff
dz ich aber auch vnſer aller wortt rede/ beyde meyns d̄
ichs geratē vñ gebetē/ vñ ewer mit den ewern die yhrs
aus gericht/ vñ der iungfrawen/ die der erloſunge be-
durfft habē. Will ich hie mit kurtzlich fur Got vñ aller
wellt rechenſchafft vnd antwort geben/ wie wol ichs
ſonſt ynn andern buchlin reichlich gethan habe/ das al
le Chriſtliche hertzen merckē ſollē/ wie wyr nicht das
vnſere/ ſondern zuuor gottis ehre vñ des nehiſtē beſtes

Taylor Institution Library, ARCH.8°.G.1523(34), a2v

geſucht habē. Aber den vnchriſtlichē hertzē wollē wyr
yhren ſynn laſſen/bis ſie es bas verſtehen.

¶ Auffs erſt/das die kind zuuorn ſelbs yhr Eldern
vñ freundſchafft auffs aller demutigſt erſucht vñ gebe
ten habē/vmb hulff eraus tzu komē/mit vernūfftigen
gnugſamē vrſachē angetzeygt/das yhnen ſolch leben/
der ſeelē ſelickeyt halbē/nicht lenger zu duldē ſey/ ſich
danebē erbottē zu thun/vñ zu leyden/was frum kinder
thun vñ leydē ſollē. Wilchs yhn alles abgeſchlagen vñ
verſagt iſt/vñ alſo von yderman verlaſſen ſind/damit
ſie recht vñ redlich vrſach gehabt/ia genottigt vñ ge=
drungen ſind/yhr gewiſſen vñ ſeele zu erredtē/anders=
wo wie ſie haben kundē/hulff vñ radt ſuchen. Vñ die
ihenigē ſo hie habē kūdē helffen vñ radtē/ſchuldig ge
weſzen ſind/aus Chriſtlicher liebe pflicht/die ſeelē vñ
gewiſſen tzu erredten.

¶ Czum andern iſt das eyn hohe wichtige vrſach
vñ nott/das man leyder die kind/ſondlich das ſchwa=
che weyber volck vñ iunge megde yñ die kloſter ſtoſſet
reytzt vñ gehē leſt/da doch keyn teglich vbung iſt got=
lichs wortts/ia ſellten odder nymer mehr das Euāge=
lium eyn mal recht gehorett wirt. Vñ werdē doch ynn
den hohiſten kampff geſtellet. Nemlich vmb die iung=
frawſchafft zu ſtreyttē/da kaumet vñ gar seltē auch die
ihenigē beſtehē/die mit gottis wortt allēthalbē geruſt
vñ mit hoher ſeltzamer wūderbarlicher gnad erhaben
ſind. Es darff muhe/die ehliche keuſcheyt tzuhallten/
auch mit beyſtād gottlichs wortts/vñ dis iunge torich
te vnerfarne weyber volck/wirt dahyn geſtoſſen da d
ſtreyt am herttiſtē vñ mechtigiſten iſt. O der vnbarm=
hertzigē eldern vñ freundē/die mit den yhrē ſo grew=
lich vñ ſchrecklich faren/O der blindē vñ tollen Biſ=
ſchoff vñ Ebten die hie nicht ſehē noch fulē/was dye
armen ſeelen leyden/vnd wie ſie verterben.

A iij

Taylor Institution Library, ARCH.8°.G.1523(34), a3r

¶ Diße vrſach das man Gottis wort mãgeln mus /
iſt alleyne gnug / ob ſonſt keyn andere were / vns alle zu
entſchuldigẽ / ia tzu loben vnd tzu preyſſen fur Gott vñ
der wellt / das man aus kloſtern lauffen / helffen vnd
ratten ſoll / das die ſeelen eraus geryſſen / gefurt / geſto-
len vnd geraubt werden / wie man kan / vnangeſehen /
ob tauſent eyd vnd gelubd geſchehen weren / Deñ wiſ-
ſentlich iſts / das yñ kloſtern / ſonderlich nonnẽ kloſtern
Gottis wort teglich nicht gehet / vnd am meyſten ortẽ
nymer mehr / ſondern ſich nur blewen vnd treyben mit
menſchen geſetzen vnd wercken. So iſts widderumb
gewiſſz / das man on gottis wort teglich fur gott nicht
leben kan. Vnd keyn gelubt fur Gott gellten odd̃ haltẽ
kan / da mit man ſich an den ortt verbindet / da keyn got
tis wortt gehet / vnd den ortt leſt da gottis wort gehet /
Denn es iſt ſolch gelubd eben ſo viel / als got verleugnẽ
weyl wyr alle tzu gottis wort verpunden ſind.

¶ Auffs dritte / iſt das kundlich vnd offinbar / das
eyn menſch mag wol getzwungen werden fur der wellt
tzu thun / das er nicht gerne thut. Aber fur Gott / vñ yñ
Gottis dienſt / ſoll vnd kan keyn werck noch dienſt ge-
tzwungen vnd vngerne geſchehen / Denn Gotte gefal-
len nicht vnd will auch nicht haben getzwungene vn-
willige dienſte. Wie. S. Paulus. 2. Corin. 9. ſagt. Gott
hatt lieb ein frolichen geber / on tzweyffel iſt er widder
umb feynd eym vnfrolichen vnwilligen geber. Daher
auch. S. Paulus die edle iungfrawſchafft nicht haben
will / wo ſie ertzwungen vñ vnwillig geſchicht. 1. Cori.
7. Solche froliche luſt aber zu gottis dienſt gibt widd̃
kloſter noch kappen / widder gelubd noch werck / ſon-
dern alleyn der heylige geyſt.

¶ Wie viel meynſtu aber das Nonnen ym kloſtern
ſind / da das teglich gottis wort nicht gehet / die frolich

Taylor Institution Library, ARCH.8°.G.1523(34), a3v

vnd mit lust vngetzwungen yhren gottes dienst thu vnd orden trage? freylich vnter thausent kaum eyne. Was ists denn das du solchs kind lessist also seyn leben vnd alle seyne werck verlieren/vnd datzu die helle da mit derdienen? Were es nicht besser/weñ sie ia etwas vngerne/vnd mit vnlust thun soll/sie were ehlich vnd thet solche muhe/vnd vnlust ym ehlichen standt euserlich gegen die menschē/als yhr man/kind/gesind vnd nachbar ꝛc. Weyl denn Gott keyn dienst gefellt es gehe denn willig von hertzen vñ mit lust. So folget das auch keyn gelubd weytter gellten noch geschehen noch gehallten werden soll/denn so fern die lieb vñ lust da ist/das ist/so fern der heylige geyst da ist. Darumb nun solch gelubt/on lust vñ geist geschicht/achtets got nicht vnd nympts nicht an. Das also/dis auch eyn gnugsame vrsach ist/gelubd vnd kloster tzu lassen vnd yderman eraus tzu helffen ynn eynen andern standt.

¶ Auffs vierde/Wie wol man sich disser vrsach schier schemen mus/so ists doch fast der grossistē eyne/kloster vnd kappen tzu lassen/Nemlich/das vnmuglich ist/die gabe der keuscheyt so gemeyne sey/als die kloster sind/Denn eyn weybs bild ist nicht geschaffen iungfraw tzu seyn/sondern kinder zu tragen/wie Geñ. 1. Gott sprach nicht alleyne tzu Adam/sondern auch zu Heua/seyt fruchtbar vnd mehret euch/wie das auch die leyblichen gelidmas weyblichs leybs/von Gott da tzu eyngesetzt beweyssen. Vnd solchs ist nicht tzu eynē weyb/noch tzu tzweyen/sondern tzu allen gesagt/vnd keyne ausgeschlossen. Got zihe sie deñ selber aus/nicht durch vnser gelubd odder freyen willē/sondern durch seynen eygen radt vnd willen mechtiglich/wo er das nicht thutt/soll ein weybs bild/ein weyb bleybē/frucht tragen/datzu es gott geschaffen hat/vnd nicht besser

Taylor Institution Library, ARCH.8°.G.1523(34), a4r

machen denn ers gemacht hatt.

¶ Itē da er Heua verfluchte/nam er yhr nicht den weyblichen leyb/noch weybische gelidmas. Widderrieff auch nicht seynen gesprochen segen vber sie/das sie sollt fruchtbar seyn/sondern bestettigt den selbē vñ spricht/Ich will dyr viel muhe schaffen/wē du schwāger gehest/dyße plage ist auch nicht vber eyns odder tzwey weyber gesagt/sondern vber alle/das die wortt lautten/als sey got gewissz/das alle weyber werden schwanger seyn/vnd sollen dißе plage tragen/on wilche er selbs aus nympt. Da widder kan yhe keyn gelubt noch bund gelten noch hallten/Deñ es ist gottis wort vnd gemechte.

¶ Hie thun sie denn tzwo eyn rede/Die erst/Man solle die gelubd hallten/Das ist warlich war/weñ du gottlich gelobist/das deyn ist/vnd ynn deyner macht steht. Ich horet hie zu/eyn gelerten man eyn mal sagē. Meyn mutter hatt gelobt. Ich sollt eyn bischoff werdē Wie soll ichs hallten? Deyn ists aber nicht iungfraw seyn/widder eyngesetzte natur/Sondern wie. S. Paulus sagt. 1. Corin. 7. Es ist eyn gottis gabe/Wie ich nu keyn Gottis gabe kan gelobē/ßo kan ich auch keuscheyt nicht geloben. Es mus alles zuuor meyn seyn/ehe ichs gelobe. Wie auch Samuels mutter yhrē son Gott gelobet/wo er yhr den selbē zuuor gebē wurde 1. Reg. 1. Also sollt man auch keuscheyt geloben/ßofern sie Gott gebē wurde/wo nichts/das das gelubde nicht were.

¶ Leßen wyr doch auch. 1. Reg. 14. das Saul auch gelobt tzwey mal mit eym eyde/das niemant des tags essen sollt/vnd auch seynen son tzu todtenn/Dennoch must ers lassen/vnd Gott weret es yhm/durchs volck vnd seynen son. Da mit yhe Gott gnugsam beweyßet hatt/das vnchristliche/vnd schedliche gelubd nichts

zu hallten

Taylor Institution Library, ARCH.8°.G.1523(34), a4v

gn halltē ſind/ob ſie gleich auch mir dem lebē ſchadē/
viel mehr wirtt er die gelubd verdamnen/die der ſee-
len ſchaden vnd verderben ſind. Vnd iſt dis exempel
woll zu mercken/das nicht gnug iſt geſagt/ia ich habs
gelobt/ich mus halltē/lieber/ſihe tzuuor/ obs muglich
vnd gotlich iſt/was du gelobeſt/ ſonſt wenn vnmug-
lich gelubd gulde/mochteſtu wol geloben/eyn mutter
gottis werden wie Maria.

¶ So ſprechen ſie aber mal/ obs gleich vnmuglich
ſey/ſo kan mans mit beten erlangen/wie. S. Hierony.
leret. Antwort/auffs erſt. Got gebe myr nur nicht viel
der keuſcheyt. S. Hieronymi/wilcher ſelbs bekēnet/ dz
er ſeyns fleyſſchs wueten vnd brunſt mit keyner faſten
noch muhe tzemen kund/Wie vil beſſer were yhm ge-
weßē/nach. S. Paulus rad/freyen/denn alſo brennen/
Vñ iſt hyryn ſein exempel nicht gutt nach zu folgē. Deñ
keuſcheyt hat wol anfechtūg / aber ſolch tegliche brūſt
vñ wuetē iſt eyn gewiſſz tzeichē/das Gott nicht gege-
ben hatt noch geben will die edle gabe der keuſcheyt/
die da mit willen on nott gehalten werde.

Auffs ander/man kan freylich alles von Got erlan-
gen mit betē. Er will aber auch vnuerſucht ſeyn. Chri-
ſtus hette ſich wol kundē von der tzynnen des tempels
ernydd͛ laſſen/wie der teuffel furgab / Er wollts aber
nicht thun/weyl es nicht nott war/vnd wol auff and͛
weyße kund erab komen. Ich kund auch wol mit beten
erlangen/das ich nicht eſſe noch truncke was auff erdē
wuchße. Weyl aber das nicht nott iſt/vnnd Gott myr
ſonſt ſo viel geben hat/das ich eſſen ſall vnd kan / ſoll
ich yhn nicht verſuchen/das laſſen liegen/das er gege-
ben hatt/vnd eyn anders on nott gewartten / das er
nicht gegeben hatt/denn da were Gott verſucht.

¶ Alſo auch hie/weyl er man vnd weyb hat geſchaf

B

Taylor Institution Library, ARCH.8°.G.1523(34), b1r

fen/das sie zu samen sollen/soll ich myr nicht fur nemẽ
eyn andern stand/vnd ihenen liegen lassen/aus eyge-
nem furwitz vnd mutwillen/Deñ da mit gebe ich mich
on nott vnd vrsach ynn ferlickeyt/vnd versuche Gott/
synntemal wol eyn anđ gottlich stand da ist/da ich der
ferlickeit vñ versuchũg nicht bedarff. Deñ wer dringet
mich odđ berufft/dz ich on ehe bleybe? Was ist myr die
iũgfrawschafft võ nottẽ/weyl ich fule das ich sie nicht
habe/vnd Gott mich sonderlich nicht datzu berufft/vñ
weyß doch/das er mich tzur ehe geschaffen hatt? Dar-
umb willtu ettwas bittẽ von Gott/so bitt das dyr nott
ist/vñ da dich die nott tzu dringet. Jst dyrs aber nicht
nott/so versuchstu yhn gewißlich mit deynem gepett/
Deñ seyn name heyst Adiutor in oportunitatibus in tri-
bulatione. Nothelffer Psalm. 10. Nemlich das er hilffe
nur da alleyne/da sonst keyn hulff vñ mittel durch yhn
tzuvor geschaffen ist.

¶ Die Ander eynrede ist/das es ergerlich sey widđ
den gemeynen allten brauch vnd lere/vnd der schwa-
chen gewissen sey tzu schonen. Antwortt/Ergernis hyn
Ergernis her. Nott bricht eyßen/vnd hatt keyn erger-
nis. Jch soll der schwachen gewissen schonen/ßo fern
es on fahr meyner seelen geschehen mag. Wo nicht/ßo
soll ich meyner seelen radten/es erger sich dran die gan
tze odder halbe wellt/Nu ligt hie der seelen fahr ynn
allen stucken. darumb soll niemãt von vns begerẽ/das
wyr yhn nicht ergern. Sõdern wyr sollen begern/das
sie vnser ding billichen/vnd sich nicht ergern/das fod-
dert die liebe.

¶ Das will ich auff diß mall meyn gutter freũd kurtz-
lich tzur verantwortũg gegeben haben/fur euch/fur
mich/vnd fur diße iungfrawen/auch fur alle die dißem
exempel wollen nach folgẽ/byn auch gewiß/das wyr

Taylor Institution Library, ARCH.8°.G.1523(34), b1v

da mit fur Gott vnd der wellt vnuertaddelich beſte-
hen wollen. Aber den widderſachern vnnd verſteck-
ten kopffen/den Gott ſelber nicht kan gnug thun/wol-
len auch wyr vns nicht vermeſſen gnug tzu thun/ ßon-
dern ſie laſſen toben vnd leſtern/bis ſie es mude wer-
den. Wyr haben eynen richter vber vns der wirt recht
richten.

¶ Jch will aber auch die iūgfrawē hye nennē/auff
das alles ia frey am tage ſey/Vnd ſind nemlich dyße.
Magdalena Staupitzyn/Eliſabeth Canitzyn. Vroni-
ca Zeſſchaw/Margaretha Zeſſchaw yhr ſchweſter
Laneta von Golis/Aue Groſſyn/Katherina vō Bo-
re/Aue von Schonfelt/Margaretha von Schonfeldt
yhr ſchweſter. Der almechtig Gott wollt gnedigli-
chen erleuchten alle freunde der ihenygē/ßo mit far vñ
vnluſt ynn kloſtern ſind/das ſie yhn trewlich eraus
helffen/Wilche aber geyſt verſtendig ſind/vnd kloſte-
rey nutzlich wiſſen zu brauchē/vnd gerne drynnē ſind/
die laßz man bleyben ym̄ namen Gottis.

¶ Hie mit befelh ich euch Gott/vnd gruſt myr ewr
liebe Audi vnd alle freunde ynn Chriſto Gegeben tzu
Wittemberg am Freytag ynn der oſterwoche. Anno.
1523. B ij

www.ingramcontent.com/pod-product-compliance
Lightning Source LLC
Chambersburg PA
CBHW070342200726
48294CB00003B/756
* 9 7 8 1 8 3 8 4 6 4 1 6 5 *